UNDERSTANDING LAND LAW

Third Edition

Bryn Perrins MA, PhD, Solicitor
Senior Lecturer in Law
University of Birmingham

Cavendish
Publishing
Limited

London • Sydney

Third edition first published in Great Britain 2000 by Cavendish Publishing Limited, The Glass House, Wharton Street, London WC1X 9PX, United Kingdom

Telephone: +44 (0) 20 7278 8000   Facsimile: +44 (0) 20 7278 8080

E-mail: info@cavendishpublishing.com

Visit our Home Page on http://www.cavendishpublishing.com

Perrins, Bryn
Understanding land law – 3rd ed
1 Real property – England 2 Real property – Wales
I Title
346.4'2'043

ISBN 1 85941 538 5

Printed and bound in Great Britain

Preface

Albert Einstein claimed that his complex theory of relativity, reducing universal chaos to the elegant simplicity of $E=mc^2$, was in fact constructed from a series of elementary concepts, each of which was completely familiar to him before he reached the age of five. Believe it if you will, but, according to Lord Macnaghten, not even Albert Einstein could understand an English mortgage of real estate without a little help from his friends (*Samuel v Jarrah Timber and Wood Paving Corporation Ltd* [1904] AC 323, p 326).

Most students seem to find property law more difficult than other subjects. They find its concepts not only unfamiliar, but also abstruse and even arcane. They are, understandably, disconcerted to discover that the first principle of land law is that the landowner does not, in fact, own the land. The explanation of this apparent paradox leaves confusion worse confounded: the landowner actually owns a bundle of rights called a fee simple estate ... and a fee simple estate is apparently an inheritable estate which can never be inherited! No wonder they find difficulty in relating realty to reality.

A closely associated problem is that of language. Property lawyers, like all specialists, have their own jargon, designed to define and explain their ideas with absolute precision. It is struggle enough for the novice to try to cope with the curious concepts of property, without having them explained in a seemingly foreign language. Privity of estate has nothing to do with hedging; and socage, even less to do with football hooligans or lager louts. There is really nothing for it, except to learn the lingo. But property jargon is doubly deceitful, in that some expressions have ordinary, everyday meanings which differ significantly from their technical, property law meanings. Sometimes, the word has visibly grown from property roots; sometimes, it is simply an insidious homonym. So, the estate owner himself probably owns but one house on the estate, and if he allows his neighbour a right of eavesdrop, it may mean that he is wet behind the ears, but it does not necessarily follow that his neighbour is a 'nosy parker'. Moreover, even the most fervently evangelical preacher is unlikely to find real joy in perpetuity – although he may indeed experience cesser on redemption.

But perhaps the biggest problem of all is the relentless complexity of property law. Especially at the beginning, it seems that one needs to know everything before one can know anything, and yet the nature of the subject is such that it is necessary to proceed painfully, little by little; hence this book.

It is not, and does not pretend to be, yet another property textbook, not even a simplified text. It does not cover, and does not attempt to cover, everything. My intention is merely to take the main elements of property (or at least those elements most likely to be encountered by the novice student), to explain each in a general, but systematic way, and to sketch the whole scene, showing how the elements combine and interrelate. My main purpose is to provide something useful for the student to read at the very beginning of a property course, and preferably before it begins – a framework upon which the student can then begin to build. Some will, I hope, also find it a helpful refreshment during their course, when the terrain gets difficult and there is a danger of losing one's bearings. And for those unfortunates faced with examinations at the end of their course, the book may serve to provide a systematic set of revision headlines. The ultimate objective is to show that property is not as difficult as students sometimes think, to take some of the labour out of learning, and to give more space for thought, reflection and, yes, enjoyment of the subject!

This third edition brings the text up to date to 1 December 1999; several passages have been rewritten with the aim of making the exposition clearer, and the opportunity has been taken of introducing a glossary of technical and other words.

Bryn Perrins
University of Birmingham
December 1999

Contents

Table of Cases

Table of Statutes

Glossary

absolute	an absolute *estate* or *interest* is one which is not *modified*; that is, neither *conditional* nor *determinable*
administrator	a person appointed by the court to administer the estate of an *intestate* (cf *executor*)
adverse possession	squatter's rights
advowson	the right of presenting a clergyman to a vacant benefice
alienation	the act of transferring ownership to another
annexation	the act of attaching something to the land so as to make it part of the land, as in the case of a *fixture* or the benefit of a *restrictive covenant*
assent	a transfer of property from a *personal representative* to the person entitled, or the document effecting the transfer
assignment	transfer, especially of *leaseholds* or *choses in action* (cf *conveyance*)
assurance	a transfer or disposition, as in 'disentailing assurance'
barring an entail	converting an entail into a fee simple or other estate, thus defeating the claims of the heirs of the entail owner
base fee	a *determinable* fee simple produced by the partial *barring of the entail*
beneficiary	one who benefits, especially the equitable owner of property held in *trust* (cf *trustee*)
bequest	the leaving of personal property (including leaseholds) by will (cf *devise*)

BFP	an abbreviation for *'bona fide purchaser* of a legal estate for value and without *notice'*
bona fide	(literally, in good faith) honest
bona vacantia	(literally, empty goods) ownerless property; may be claimed by the Crown
caution	entering a caution on the register is one method of protecting an interest in registered land
charge	(as in 'legal charge', 'equitable charge') an *incumbrance* on land, usually given as security for a loan, or the document which creates it
chattel	(1) *personal property*; and especially (2) an item of tangible personal property (a chose in possession), such as a bell, book or candle
chattel real	old fashioned terminology for a *lease* or *term of years*
chose in action	intangible *personal property*, such as debts, shares in a company, or copyright
clog	(as in 'clog on the *equity* of redemption') a stipulation in a *mortgage* arrangement which prevents the borrower from redeeming his property entirely free and unfettered
co-parcenary	a kind of co-ownership all but abolished in 1925, applicable in the event of joint *heirs*
common law	(1) general law, as opposed to local (or manorial) law; (2) judge made law, as opposed to legislation; (3) Law, as opposed to Equity; (4) Anglo-American law, as opposed to Civil (or Roman) Law; (5) national law, as opposed to international law; (6) as an academic discipline: contract and tort, as opposed to public law, criminal law or property law
condition precedent	a condition which must be fulfilled before a disposition can take effect ('to A if she marries')
condition subsequent	a condition which will defeat a gift after it has taken effect ('to A, but if she fails to look after my tomcat Tiddles, then to B')

conditional	a conditional *interest* is one which is subject to a condition subsequent ('to X, unless the clock tower falls')
contingent	a contingent *interest* is one which is subject to a condition precedent ('to X if he passes his land law exam')
conveyance	transfer, especially of *freeholds* (cf *assignment*)
copyhold	a form of tenure originating in the Saxon manorial system; previously called *villeinage*; eventually abolished in 1925 (cf *freehold*)
corporation	a company which is a legal entity, an artificial person; a corporation aggregate has several members; a corporation sole, just one
covenant	a promise in a *deed*
deed	a formal written document, traditionally 'signed, sealed and delivered', but these days merely 'signed as a deed' and formally witnessed as such
demise	grant by way of *lease*
determinable	a determinable *interest* is one which is given for a period of time defined by the occurrence of some event which may or may not happen ('to X until the clock tower falls')
devise	the leaving of freehold property by will (cf *bequest*)
disclaimer	a formal refusal to accept, especially a refusal to accept the transfer of property
disentail	to *bar the entail*
distress, distraint	taking and selling chattels to satisfy arrears of rent, usually by sending in professional bailiffs
easement	a right over one piece of land (the servient *tenement*) for the benefit of another piece of land (the dominant *tenement*), for example, rights of way, water, light, drainage or support
enfranchisement	turning (*leasehold* or *copyhold*) into *freehold tenure*

entail	an *estate* or *interest* which is inheritable by the lineal heirs of the original grantee
equity	(1) in a general sense: fairness or justice; (2) by derivation ('Equity'): a set of principles which modifies the effect of the *common law*; (3) by derivation ('an equity'): an equitable right or interest
equity of redemption	the aggregate of a *mortgagor's* rights in mortgaged property
escheat	the reverting of land to the feudal lord in certain (now extremely unlikely) circumstances
estate	(1) the bundle of rights owned by the 'landowner' (cf *tenure*); (2) the property of a deceased person; (3) an area of land
estate contract	a contract for the purchase of an interest in land
executor	a person nominated in a will to administer the estate of a *testator* (cf *administrator*)
fealty	the duty of loyalty owed to a feudal lord
fee	literally, inheritable estate, but a fee simple is no longer inheritable in the strict sense after 1925 (cf *mere freehold*)
fee simple	(virtually) perpetual ownership
fine	(1) a capital payment or premium; (2) an obsolete method of *barring the entail*
fixture	an erstwhile *chattel* which has been annexed to the land and so become part of the land
foreclosure	a court order which extinguishes the *mortgagor's* rights in mortgaged property, thus vesting the title in the *mortgagee* absolutely
freehold	(1) free *tenure* (cf *leasehold, copyhold*); (2) an *estate* of uncertain duration (cf *leasehold*)
heir	the person(s) who, before 1926, automatically inherited the freeholds of an intestate (typically, the deceased's eldest son)

hereditament	(literally, inheritable property) *real* property; in effect: *freehold* 'land'; a corporeal hereditament is one which gives physical possession (eg, land, buildings, growing things); an incorporeal hereditament is intangible freehold property (eg, an *easement* or a *rentcharge*)
incumbrance	a liability which binds the land (eg, a *mortgage*, *easement* or *restrictive covenant*)
inhibition	an order preventing any dealing with registered land
injunction	an equitable remedy, ordering the defendant to desist from certain conduct (a 'prohibitory injunction') or (less commonly) ordering him to do certain things (a 'mandatory injunction')
inter vivos	(literally) between living persons
interest	(in a broad sense) any property right, including an *estate* in land; (in a narrow sense) an *incumbrance* as opposed to an estate in land
intestate	a person who dies without making a will (cf *testator*)
ius accrescendi	or right of survivorship (literally, right of accrual): the right of the surviving *joint tenant(s)* to the accrual of the interest of a deceased joint tenant
ius tertii	(literally) right of a third party
joint tenancy	a kind of co-ownership which is vested in a group of two or more persons; no individual has a separate share, and the last survivor of the group becomes sole owner (cf *tenancy in common*)
land charge	in relation to unregistered land: those classes of *incumbrance* which need to be registered in the Land Charges Registry
Land Charges Registry	records certain incumbrances (*land charges*) which affect unregistered land (eg, *restrictive covenants, estate contracts*)
Land Registry	deals with registered land (that is, where the whole title is registered)

lease	a *term of years*, or the document which creates it
leasehold	(1) a form of *tenure* which implies a duty to pay *rent* service (cf *freehold*); (2) an *estate* of which the maximum duration is certain (cf *freehold*)
letters of administration	a formal court order authorising an *administrator* to deal with the estate of a deceased person
licence	a permission, especially a permission to enter land
Local Land Charges Registry	a department of the district council or other local authority which records various (mostly local, public) charges on the land (tree preservation orders, planning permissions, etc)
mere freehold	a life estate (cf *fee*)
mesne	intermediate
minor interest	an interest in registered land which needs to be protected by an entry against the proprietor's title
modified	a modified *interest* is one which is made *conditional* or *determinable*
money	obviously cash, but note that the plural is 'moneys', not 'monies'
mortgage	the giving of ownership as security for a loan, or the document which creates such a security
mortgagee	a lender who takes a *mortgage* as security for the loan
mortgagor	a borrower who gives a *mortgage* as security for the loan
next of kin	the 'statutory next of kin' are those persons identified by the Intestate Estates Act 1952 as being entitled to the property of an *intestate*

notice	(1) in connection with registered land, entering a notice on the register is one method of protecting a minor interest in that land; (2) in relation to the *BFP*, notice means knowledge of some *incumbrance* which (a) was obtained ('actual notice'); or (b) would have been obtained had the purchaser exercised due care and diligence ('constructive notice'); or (c) was or ought to have been obtained by the purchaser's agent ('imputed notice')
overreaching	the process of transferring a *beneficiary's* right out of the land and into the purchase moneys; typically, a purchaser overreaches, and so takes free of, the beneficiary's right by paying his money to at least two trustees or a *trust corporation*
overriding interest	an interest which binds the purchaser of registered land notwithstanding that its existence is not indicated on the register; overriding interests are defined in s 70 of the Land Registration Act 1925
particular estate	an *estate* less than the *fee simple*
periodic tenancy	includes weekly, monthly, quarterly and yearly tenancies; the tenancy is automatically renewed unless due notice to quit is served
perpetuity	undue remoteness: gifts which may not vest until too far into the future are said to be 'void for perpetuity'
personal property	property which is not *freehold* property; personal property includes *leasehold* property, *chattels* and *choses in action*
personal representative	an *executor* or an *administrator*
personalty	another way of saying *personal property*
possession	(1) loosely, physical occupation; (2) the legal right to possession; (3) the right to receive a rent from a leasehold tenant
possibility of reverter	the grantor's right to the land in the event that a *determinable* fee comes to an end

prescription	the act of acquiring an *easement* or *profit* by long *user*
privity of contract	the relationship between contracting parties
privity of estate	the relationship of landlord and tenant
probate	(literally, proof) the process of 'proving the will' of a deceased person, resulting in a 'grant of probate' – a formal court order authorising an *executor* to deal with the deceased's estate (cf *letters of administration*)
profit à prendre	a right to enter another's land and take something from it, as in the case of sporting rights or grazing rights
puisne mortgage	a legal *mortgage* where the *mortgagee* does not have possession of the title deeds; in practice, a second or subsequent legal mortgage
pur autre vie	(literally, for another life) an estate *pur autre vie* is an estate for the life of another ('to A so long as B shall live')
purchaser	(1) in a broad, general sense: a buyer; (2) in a narrow, technical sense, one who takes by act of party (sale, gift, lease, mortgage) as opposed to one who takes by involuntary transfer (trustee in bankruptcy, administrator)
real property	*freehold* property (cf *personal property*)
realty	another way of saying *real property*
recovery	an obsolete method of *barring the entail*
registered charge	a *mortgage* of registered land
registrable interest	in connection with registered land: a fee simple or a lease with at least 21 years to run
remainder	an *interest* which is subject to a prior freehold interest or interests ('to A for life, remainder to B')
rent	(1) rent service is a money payment payable by a *leasehold* tenant to the landlord; (2) a *rentcharge*
rentcharge	a periodic payment secured on land (cf *rent*, *charge*); also known as a fee farm rent

restriction	entering a restriction on the powers of disposition of the registered proprietor is one method of protecting a minor interest in registered land
restrictive covenant	a negative *covenant*, a *covenant* which restricts the use of land; it constitutes an equitable *incumbrance* on the land
reversion	(1) the *interest* remaining in the grantor after the grant of a *particular estate* ('to A for life' impliedly leaves the grantor with a reversion in fee simple); (2) a freehold or leasehold estate which is subject to a lease (a leasehold tenant owns a term of years; his landlord owns the reversion on that term)
right *in personam*	(literally, a right against a person) a non-property right, a right which is not binding on third parties (cf *right in rem*)
right *in rem*	(literally, a right [which penetrates] into the thing) a property right, a right which is binding on third parties (cf *right in personam*)
right of (re-)entry	a right to repossess the land, as where a landlord forfeits a lease or a *mortgagee* (lender) evicts a borrower with a view to selling the property
right of survivorship	*ius accrescendi*: the right of the surviving *joint tenant(s)* to the accrual of the interest of a deceased joint tenant
second mortgage	a *mortgage* of property which is already subject to a mortgage
seisin	(broadly) possession of freehold land
settlement	a series of trusts in succession ('A for life, remainder to B') or the document establishing such a trust
settlor	one who creates a *settlement*
severance	the act of making separate, as where a *fixture* is severed and reconverted into a *chattel*, or where a *joint tenant* severs his interests and so converts it into a *tenancy in common*
socage	(the only surviving) freehold *tenure*

specific performance	an equitable remedy, ordering the defendant to perform his contract; available as a matter of course in relation to contracts for land, but not normally available in relation to a contract for chattels (where damages are typically an adequate remedy)
submortgage	a mortgage of a *mortgage*
tenancy in common	a kind of co-ownership where each owner has individual, but unpartitioned shares (as where A and B own a house in equal shares; cf *joint tenancy*)
tenement	(literally, property held by a tenant) in effect, a piece of land; a 'dominant tenement' enjoys the benefit of an *easement*; a 'servient tenement' is subject to the burden of an *easement*
tenure	the relationship between lord and tenant; the conditions upon which a tenant holds land (cf *estate*)
term of years	(in a broad sense, especially 'term of years absolute') any *leasehold* estate; (in a narrow sense) a fixed term as opposed to a *periodic tenancy*
testator	a person who makes a *will* (cf *intestate*)
time immemorial	before the year 1189
tithe	the right, now obsolete, of the church to take one-tenth of the produce of the land
title	a person's claim to property, or the evidence which supports that claim
trust	the relationship which arises where an owner of property (the *trustee*, typically the legal owner) is compelled by *Equity* to treat the property as if it belonged to another (the *beneficiary*, or equitable owner); Equity will also enforce a trust for charitable, and sometimes other, purposes
trust corporation	a large company such as a bank or insurance company which is authorised to conduct trust business or certain designated officials (such as the Public Trustee)

trustee	the nominal or apparent owner of trust property (cf *beneficiary*)
undivided shares	means unpartitioned shares (as where A and B own a house in equal shares); in most cases 'undivided shares' is synonymous with a *tenancy in common*
user	in relation to the acquisition of easements by prescription means the act of using ('user in fee simple')
value	money, money's worth, or (in Equity) marriage
vested	an *interest* is vested if it is either in possession or ready to take effect in possession, subject only to the dropping of life or lives
villeinage	an earlier version of *copyhold* tenure
voluntary covenant	a promise in a *deed* unsupported by any actual consideration; it is enforceable at Law (because of the formality of a deed), but unenforceable in Equity (because Equity looks to the substance, and sees that there is no real consideration)
volunteer	a donee; a person who gives no consideration
waiver	the abandonment of a legal right
waste	the doctrine of waste is a method of allocating the cost of property repairs as between the tenant for life and the owner of the fee
will	the declaration by a *testator* of his wishes regarding the disposition of his property after his death; normally a will must be in writing, signed by the testator in the presence of two witnesses, and signed by the witnesses in his presence
words of limitation	words which define an *estate* in land (cf *words of purchase*)
words of purchase	words which designate the person(s) entitled to an *estate* in land (cf *words of limitation*)
words of severance	words which indicate separateness and so indicate a *tenancy in common* rather that a *joint tenancy* (eg, 'in equal shares')

1 Property

(1) MEANING OF PROPERTY

'Property' means ownership. The word is derived from the Latin *proprius*, meaning one's own. My property is that which is my own, that which belongs to me. To say that I saw something with my proper eyes is an archaic way of saying that I saw it with my own eyes. So my 'property' is that which exhibits the quality of belonging to me, the quality of my 'own-ship' or ownership. The law of property is therefore the law of ownership and associated rights.

Lawyers still use the word 'property' in this abstract sense of ownership. For example, it is often said, in relation to a gift of chattels, that 'Property passes on delivery'. To the layman, that may appear a truism, but the lawyer understands it to mean that ownership passes at the moment when the item is physically handed over.

'Property' also means that which is owned. In days gone by, the owner of a goblet might say, 'This goblet is *the object of* my property,' meaning that it was the object of his ownership. But, later, the italicised words disappeared, and the modern usage is elliptical: 'This goblet ... is my property.' So 'property' comes to mean not only the ownership of a thing, but also the thing itself. The law of property may therefore be said to be the law of things, as opposed to the law of persons or the law of obligations.

It is, however, rather more accurate to say that property law is the law of *rights* to things. The vital and fundamental idea is that some rights are classed as property rights; and other rights, as mere personal rights. The concept of a property right is that I have a right to the thing itself. The thing is infected with my right, so that, wherever the thing is and in whosesoever possession it is found, I can point to it and say: 'That is mine.' So a property right is also called a right *in rem*. The Latin for 'thing' is *res*, and so a right *in rem* means a right against, a right which penetrates into, the thing itself.

However, rights need to be asserted against another person. The castaway on a desert island may lay claim of ownership to everything he sees, but it is an empty gesture unless and until there is someone who might dispute his claim. The statement, 'That is mine ...' implies the imperative: '... so hands off!' So, a property right or a right *in rem* is also described as a right which is 'good against the world'. No matter who has acquired possession of my thing, I can (in principle) go to him and demand it back. My watch is stolen; the thief sells it to an innocent purchaser. I can, as a general rule, go to the purchaser and demand the return of my watch. It is no defence for him to prove that he was unaware that the watch had been stolen, nor that he paid good money for it, nor that he had made all reasonable enquiries. It is his loss. He must render up my watch or pay me its value – and seek recompense from the thief, if he can find him.

The contrast is between property rights or rights *in rem*, on the one hand, and personal rights or rights *in personam* on the other. A personal right is a right which may be enforced against some particular person alone, and not against his successor or some other third party. The difference can be illustrated by a simple example.

Suppose Sam agrees to sell his book to Ben, on the basis that the book will become Ben's when he pays for it, but not before. There is a valid contract of sale. Ben goes off to find the cash. While he is away, Sam changes his mind and sells and transfers the book to Tilly. Sam's transfer to Tilly is a breach of his contract with Ben. But the contract gave Ben only rights *in personam* against Sam. It gave him no rights *in rem* in the book itself. Sam still owned the book, and could and did therefore transfer the ownership to Tilly, leaving Ben to sue Sam for money compensation for breach of contract.

Contrast the case where Sam gives his book to Ben as a birthday present. He physically hands it over with intent to transfer ownership. The book thereupon becomes Ben's. Ben temporarily leaves the book with Sam for safe custody, but while Ben is away, Sam, pretending the book is still his own, sells it to Tilly. In this case, Ben's ownership of the book was a right *in rem* in the book itself. Sam had no ownership and could transfer none to Tilly. Ben can therefore assert his ownership, his right *in rem*, against Tilly and demand that she return the book, leaving Tilly to sue Sam for damages for breach of contract.

There are two points to add. The first is that the question whether a right is a right *in rem* or merely a right *in personam* is not one which can necessarily be answered by the application of *a priori* reasoning. It is a policy decision. Some rights are admitted to the charmed circle; some are not. And the second point follows on from that: the list of property rights is not closed. From time to time new rights *in rem* are recognised.

(2) OWNERSHIP

To say that property means ownership merely invites the question: what is ownership? There is no easy answer. Ownership is a concept. It is a figment of the imagination. Ownership means what it is defined to mean, and different legal systems define ownership in different ways. It is not profitable at this stage to engage in a jurisprudential hunt for a final definition of an elusive concept. It is enough for present purposes to repeat that ownership is the right to assert that something is one's own, and that it is a right which, in principle, may be asserted against all comers.

It may, however, be useful to explore the *content*, or the typical characteristics, of ownership. Ownership is often regarded as a trinity of rights, described by the Latin tag, *ius utendi, fruendi, abutendi* – a right of using, of profiting from, of using up. First, *utendi*, using: 'use' here implies *exclusive* use. The owner of a thing may not only use it himself, but he may also prevent others from using it without his permission. Second, *fruendi*, enjoying the fruits: the nature of the 'fruits' or profits which may be taken by the owner depend on the nature of the thing owned. The owner of an apple tree takes the fruits of it in a literal sense, but the 'fruits' of property will more often be money profits: rent from the tenant of a house, interest on a bank or building society account, dividends on shares, and so on. Third, *abutendi*, using up: *abutendi* has a double meaning. The owner of a thing can 'abuse' it by damaging it or destroying it. But even more important is the right, not so much to use up the thing itself, but to use up one's *ownership* of the thing by the act of *transferring that ownership* to another person, by way of sale, gift or otherwise. In other words, the right to 'use up' implies the right to *alienate* the thing.

It may happen that a person enjoys some, but not all, of the component parts of ownership. That person may be described as a 'limited owner'. Suppose a donor gives £10,000 to trustees 'on trust for Laura for life, remainder to Richard absolutely'. The effect is that Laura can have the income from the fund during her lifetime, but she can never touch the capital; the capital is Richard's, but he cannot have any income from it during Laura's lifetime. She temporarily has the rights *utendi* and *fruendi*. This splitting up of the component parts of ownership is sometimes described as the *fragmentation* of ownership.

It may be a nice question whether a limited owner is properly described as an 'owner' at all. That depends upon how one defines 'ownership' in the first place, and that, as has been hinted, is a question which does not often trouble the English property lawyer.

(3) OTHER RIGHTS

There are other rights too, besides ownership itself, which are admitted to the class of property rights. Ownership of a thing can be regarded as a right in or to that thing. It is, however, possible also to own a right *over* or *against* a thing owned by another.

Property rights include, for example, *easements* and *profits*. An easement is right over one piece of land which attaches to and benefits another piece of land. A common example is a right of way. Suppose Sarah grants her neighbour, David, an easement of way across her land. David does not actually own any part of Sarah's land. He does not own the path on which he walks. But he owns the right to use the path. He has a right over or against Sarah's land, and his right is a right *in rem*. When David sells his land, the right to use the path will pass to his purchaser. When Sarah sells her land, her purchaser continues to be subject to the right of way. Other common easements are rights to run pipes and wires under or over a neighbour's land, or the right for the owner of a semi-detached or terraced house to have his buildings supported by adjoining buildings.

A profit, or, to give it its full title, a *profit à prendre*, is a sort of easement-plus. It is a right to go onto another's land and diminish it by taking something away. The right to graze cattle on another's land is an example of a profit, or the right to take gravel from beneath it. Sporting rights – hunting, shooting and fishing – are other common examples.

Another important category of property right is *restrictive covenants*. A covenant is a promise made in a deed. On the face of it, covenants create personal rights and are therefore part of the law of contract rather than the law of property. But, in certain conditions, a covenant given by one landowner to another may continue to be enforceable by and against their respective successors in title. Covenants thus creep into property law.

(4) TITLE

The reason one can generally avoid difficult questions about the true nature of ownership in English law is that English law is more interested in title than in ownership. The early English lawyers took a pragmatic approach rather than a principled approach. They never attempted to work out a systematic theory of ownership. They concentrated instead on the fact of possession. They developed remedies to protect the peaceful possession of property. A claimant who asserted that he had been dispossessed of his land or goods did not have to prove that he was the true owner. All he had to do was to prove that he had a better right to possession than the defendant. And an earlier right to possession was generally a better right to possession. Thus, ownership in English law came to mean, in effect, the best right to possession. Moreover, the law would assume that the present possessor had the best right to possession unless and until the contrary was proved – hence the old saws, 'Finders keepers; losers weepers' and 'Possession is nine points of the law'.

That is still the basis of the law today. English law does not have a theory of absolute ownership; it is more interested in the relative strength of competing titles. If I need to prove my ownership of anything, what in fact I prove is that I am in possession of the thing in circumstances such that it may be inferred that no one else is likely to come along with a better claim to possession. I do not really prove ownership at all. I prove an apparently undisputed claim to possession. I prove my *title*, my entitlement to possession. Whether my title is good, bad or indifferent depends upon how likely it is that someone will turn up with a better title. And the quality of my title will be reflected in the purchase price. A buyer will pay less for a doubtful title; and a really risky title may be unsaleable.

The degree of proof of 'ownership' required depends on the circumstances. With ordinary, everyday chattels, the fact of possession and the absence of suspicious circumstances is usually enough. You do not ask the shopkeeper to prove his ownership before you buy his wares. But you might think twice about buying a gold watch from a stranger in the street. If you were buying a second hand car, you would normally check the registration document (although in law it does not strictly prove ownership). And if you were spending a large amount of money on a racehorse or a work of art, you might well expect some documentary evidence of title. In the case of land, however, it is almost always the case that the purchaser insists on formal proof of 'ownership', and it is almost always the case that the vendor provides that proof by producing title deeds in the form of a certificate of title from the Land Registry or otherwise. But, in the end, his title deeds are just that: they demonstrate the strength or otherwise of the vendor's *title*, his right to possession of the land, and enable the purchaser to gauge whether there is any significant risk that someone else will turn up with a better claim to possession. A vendor with no paper title at all – he may have lost his title deeds, or he may never have had any – can nevertheless prove *a* title to the land by swearing a statutory declaration that he and (if relevant) his predecessors in title have been in undisputed possession of the land for so many years.

Two more important ideas need to be introduced at this point. The first is that, at least in the case of land, the competition is strictly between the claimant and the possessor: which of the two has the better right to possession? It is irrelevant that there may be some third party with a better claim than either. In general, it is said, English law knows no defence of *ius tertii* (third party's right). If you seek to reclaim land from me, it is no defence for me to say: 'Well, I know it is not really my property – but it's not yours either!' The same principle used to apply in a claim for goods, but statute now allows a defence of *ius tertii* to be set up in any action for 'wrongful interference with goods'. The purpose is to bring all interested parties before the court so that the issue of ownership can be adjudicated once and for all.

The other important idea which needs to be introduced at this point is that of *limitation of actions*. The law must have some mechanism for clearing out stale claims, and the Limitation Acts establish the principle that a right is lost if it is not asserted in due time. The time limit varies with the nature and circumstances of the claim but, as a general rule, a claim for possession of goods needs to be brought within six years; a claim for possession of land, within 12 years.

Add the idea of limitation of actions to the idea of the relativity of title, and it is possible to begin to see how 'ownership' works in English law. Suppose I own number 3 Rectory Gardens and I go away on an extended holiday. While I am away, Sally squats in my house. She moves in without my permission and behaves as if she owns the place. As against me, Sally is a trespasser and I can evict her upon my return. But she is entitled to retain possession against everyone else; for she can retain possession against all save one with a better right, and I am the only person with a better right to possession than hers. My neighbour, for instance, cannot evict her. My neighbour has no right at all to the possession of my house.

Suppose Sally in turn goes away on holiday, and while she is away, Tom squats in the house. His actual possession, no matter how short its duration, gives him *a* title to the land, and to that extent he is the 'owner' of it as against all save anyone with a better title. Sally can evict Tom on her return from holiday, because she has an earlier, and therefore better, right to possession than his. And, on my return, I can evict either of them, because my claim is earlier and better than either of theirs. But supposing my extended holiday is further extended, and I do not return until a full 12 years have elapsed. My claim to possession of the land is now statute-barred and extinguished. There are now only two live titles to the land:

Sally's and Tom's. Sally's is the earlier and therefore the better title, so Sally can evict Tom. If Sally does evict him, there will be no one in the whole world who can lawfully oust Sally, and Sally's squatter's rights will have matured into 'true ownership'. On the other hand, if Sally does not attempt to evict Tom until 12 years after he has taken possession, then Sally's right, too, has become statute-barred and Tom's title is now the only viable title.

There is rather more to squatter's rights – or adverse possession, as it is properly called – than that, but that is essentially how the system works.

(5)   THINGS CAPABLE OF OWNERSHIP

Not everything is capable of ownership. Fresh air is free for all. Nobody owns the rain, unless he first collects it in a water butt or some other receptacle. Similarly, nobody owns water percolating naturally beneath the surface of the land, but a landowner may sink a well and so claim the water as his. Wild creatures are owned by no one, unless and until they are killed or captured. People cannot be owned. In more brutish times and climes slaves were things capable of ownership, but English law does not now recognise slavery. It is not possible to draw up a definitive list of those things which are or are not capable of ownership, because the list is never closed. The law may and does admit new items to the list from time to time as the needs of society change and develop.

Land has always been regarded as capable of ownership. Besides land, the law in our early agricultural society generally needed to recognise only the ownership of physical items: clothes, food, utensils, the tools of a man's trade and so on, and, perhaps most important, his cattle. These physical things were, and are, compendiously called 'chattels'. Both 'chattel' and 'cattle' derive from the same Latin root, *capitale*, a person's capital possessions. But, as commercial activity grew, so the law had to recognise new items as capable of ownership. Intangibles, like debts, patents, copyright and business names became susceptible of ownership, and also, of course, shares in a limited company. In comparatively recent times, computer software became an important and merchantable item, and so computer programs were admitted to the category of things capable of ownership.

(6)   CLASSIFICATION OF THINGS

Things are divided into various categories, as follows. The table is introduced at this stage mainly for the purpose of explaining the terminology, but there is also the practical point that the legal rules applicable differ from category to category, and in particular the method of transferring ownership differs from category to category.

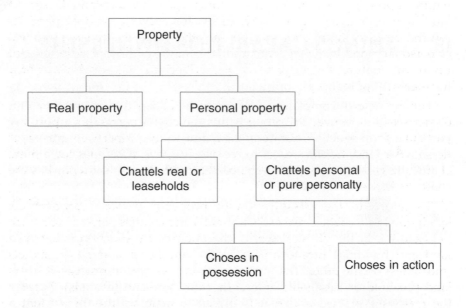

The first division of property is into real property and personal property, or realty and personalty. Real property means *freehold* land, and one or two oddments which are treated as freehold land. Everything else is personal property. Note in particular that leasehold land is personal property, not real property. The reason is purely historical. 'Real' is used here in the sense of being connected with the *res* or thing itself. Medieval law knew a kind of law suit called a real action. It was called 're-al' because success entitled the claimant to recover his property, the *res* itself, *in specie*. Other actions were personal actions, and they resulted in an order that the defendant pay money compensation to the claimant. Real actions were available for the recovery of freehold land, but not for the recovery of other property. In particular, real actions were never available for the recovery of leasehold land, although other means were found to restore leaseholders to possession. But, because in days gone by the leaseholder had to begin a personal action rather than a real action, leaseholds were, and still are, classified as personal property. So, real property still means that which in medieval law could be recovered by a real action, and that broadly means freehold land.

There is scope for confusion here. Beware the difference between real rights and real remedies. *All* property rights are 'real' *rights*, in the sense that property rights are rights *in rem*, rights to the thing itself. It is in the nature of property that the owner of a thing – be it freehold land, leasehold land or mere chattel – can always assert his authority and demand its return from a wrongful possessor. On the other hand, the division into real or personal property depends not upon the nature of the *right* asserted, but upon the nature of the *remedy* prescribed in medieval times for infringement of that right.

For the sake of completeness, it might be added that today, when an owner seeks to recover his property, his remedy depends, not upon any particular form of action, but upon the nature of the property concerned. If he sues for land, he can expect to recover *in specie*. If he sues for a mere chattel, he will probably have to be content with its cash value, unless the chattel is in some way unique.

To return to the classification of property: personal property is subdivided into chattels real (or leaseholds) and chattels personal (or 'pure personalty'). In the physical world, the important distinction is between land and buildings (immovables) on the one hand, and mere chattels (movables) on the other. The law recognises that, and in practice it treats land (freehold or leasehold) differently from non-land (chattels). But, for the reasons explained above, it is driven to maintain the theory that a leasehold is personal property, a kind of chattel. Leaseholds have, however, always been treated as a special kind of chattel, one which 'partakes of the realty' by being immovable.

Non-land is then 'pure personalty'. Pure personalty (or mere chattels, or choses) is then subdivided again into choses in possession and choses in action. (*Chose* was the Norman-French word for 'thing': the singular, chose, is pronounced '*shows*'; the plural, choses, is pronounced '*show-zez*'.) Choses in possession are those chattels which are capable of physical possession: in a word, tangibles. Choses in action are those items of personal property which have only a metaphysical existence – debts, shares, patents, copyright, and so on. They are called choses in action because, ultimately, the existence of the property is manifest only when the owner sues or threatens to sue for infringement of his rights.

As for the different modes of *transfer* of property: in the case of *land* (freehold or leasehold), a *deed* is normally necessary to transfer title, but there are some important exceptions. Ownership of a chose in action may be transferred by deed, but it may also be transferred by any *signed writing*. Ownership of a chose in possession may also be transferred by deed, but again a deed is not necessary: ownership may be transferred by simple delivery – physically handing over the item to the transferee.

Perhaps it should be said that a document is a *deed* if it says that it is a deed, and if it is signed, witnessed and delivered as a deed. 'Delivery' means some unilateral act or statement whereby the signatory demonstrates that he adopts the document as his own – formal 'delivery' usually takes place when the signatory (or his solicitor on his behalf) physically hands over the deed with intent that it shall thereupon become binding.

2 Law and Equity

When considering ownership in English law, it is necessary to apply two separate sets of rules: Law, then Equity.

(1)   CARICATURE OF THE COMMON LAW

At the time of the Norman Conquest in 1066, the basic social unit was the *manor*. Each manor was a community of agricultural labourers of servile status, governed and protected by the lord of the manor. The lord could not, however, rule in an arbitrary manner. Each manor had its own local law, the law and custom of the manor. The Norman invaders adopted and imposed their authority on this manorial system. As between the lord and his serfs, the local law and custom of the manor continued to apply. As between themselves, the Norman overlords were subject to the king's law. The king's law was, however, of general, as opposed to local, application and so became known as the *common law*. Gradually, the importance of the common law waxed, and that of the local or manorial law waned; but, at least in relation to the ownership of land, manorial law retained some importance right down to the 20th century.

The common law is thus older than Parliament. In origin, the king was the lawgiver, although common prudence dictated that he should generally govern with the advice of his council. And, of practical necessity, the dispensation of justice was soon delegated to the king's justices. In theory, the judges merely declared the law; in practice, they made it. Thus, the common law eventually became what it is today: a judge made law, unwritten and therefore capable of being developed and adapted to meet changing circumstances as the judges see fit.

Meanwhile, the king's council had become a larger parliament, and the issue was raised whether the king was bound to act on the advice of the parliament or whether he was free to do as he pleased. The Civil War resolved the issue against the king and in favour of the parliament. Thus, the common law may now be abrogated or amended by Act of Parliament.

It will be apparent that the expression 'common law' is a chameleon, taking its meaning from its context. Common law may mean, in the first place, the general law as opposed to the local or manorial law. Common law may mean, in the second place, judge made law as opposed to statute. In the context of property law, however, there is a third meaning of 'common law' which is of greatest importance: the contrast between the common law (or simply Law) and Equity – and in that context, 'the Law' means the common, judge made law as amended by statute from time to time.

(2)   CARICATURE OF EQUITY

By the end of the 13th century, the common law had become unduly ritualistic. A litigant's prospects of success might depend as much upon following the correct procedure as upon the substantial merits of his case. If he used the wrong incantation, he might fail altogether, without any investigation of the justice of his cause. Thus, it might happen that in dispensing law, the judges might also dispense injustice. What could an aggrieved litigant do in those circumstances? Well, since the law was in theory the king's law, he could go to its source and petition the king himself to remedy the injustice apparently perpetrated by his law. A typical opening was: 'Sire, for the Love of God and in the Way of Mercy, please ...' Note two features: this is a request, not a demand; and the appeal is based on grounds of moral justice and good conscience.

Initially, the king might deal personally with such petitions, but then he began to refer them to the Lord Chancellor, who in those days was a cleric and the 'keeper of the king's conscience', and soon it became the practice for a petitioner to send his petition directly to the Lord Chancellor.

Now the Lord Chancellor had no power or authority to alter the law. He was bound to accept that the law was what the common law judges said it was. But if he felt that the defendant had behaved *unconscionably*, then the Lord Chancellor might alter the *effect* of the law by directing the defendant, on pain of imprisonment, to behave in accordance with the dictates of good conscience, his strict legal rights notwithstanding. Note three more points: first, the Lord Chancellor does not actually alter the law, but assumes the continued existence and effectiveness of the law; second, he fixes his attention on the conscience of the defendant; and, third, his injunction is directed at the defendant *personally*.

This novel jurisdiction of the Lord Chancellor had a profound effect upon the administration of justice. Most significantly, it meant that a 'use' became enforceable. It sometimes happened – perhaps in Saxon times, but certainly in Norman times – that a landowner conveyed his land to another 'to the use of' some third party. A knight, riding off to the Crusades, might, for example, convey his land to his brother 'to the use of' the knight's family. In other words, the brother became the owner of the property, but he was supposed to hold it for the use and benefit of others. The common law, however, treated the added use as a moral obligation, but no more. The brother could hold the land for the benefit of the family if he wished, but the common law would not compel him to do so. The Lord Chancellor, however, would. He would say that it was contrary to good conscience for the brother to keep the property for himself. The brother was, and remained, the true owner of the land at common law, but the Lord Chancellor could direct him to use it for the benefit of the absent knight's family, with the threat of imprisonment in default.

From such beginnings, an entirely separate jurisdiction evolved, with its own entirely separate courts. The Lord Chancellor's court eventually became known as Chancellery or Chancery; the jurisdiction it dispensed, being based on true justice, was called Equity. In the early days, justice was dispensed according to the subjective impressions of each succeeding Chancellor, and the complaint was that Equity varied with the length of the Chancellor's foot. But Lord Chancellor Nottingham (1673–82, 'the Father of Equity') moulded its principles into a coherent scheme, and later Equity threatened to become as rigid and formal as the old common law.

Law and Equity continued as two separate jurisdictions with separate courts until the 19th century. The common law courts dispensed Law, the Court of Chancery dispensed Equity, and, if necessary, the litigant had to flit from one to the other and back again. The two *systems* continue as separate systems today. It is still necessary to consider first what is the position at Law, and then to consider whether Equity demands any modification. But the *administration* of the two systems was fused in 1875, so that today any court can dispense Law and any court can dispense Equity.

(3)   DOUBLE VISION

Property law can therefore be represented diagrammatically in this way:

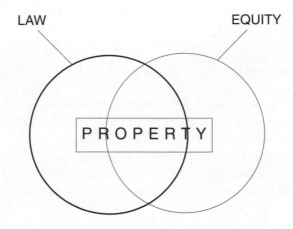

Some areas of property law are governed exclusively by the Law. For example, the Law will enforce a covenant (a promise in a deed) even where no consideration has been given in return for the covenant (a 'voluntary covenant'); Equity will not enforce a covenant unless valuable consideration has been given. Other areas of property law are governed exclusively by Equity. For example, the rights of a beneficiary against his trustee are exclusively Equity's concern; the Law 'sees' only the legal ownership of the trustee; it cannot even 'see' the beneficiary, let alone enforce his claims. But in most cases there is an overlap, and it is necessary to consider two questions: what is the position at Law? And then: does Equity take a different view?

The following points may be emphasised about the nature of Equity.

First, equity (in the non-technical sense) means fairness or justice; Equity (in the technical sense) is based on ideas of fairness or justice, but Equity does not and cannot right every wrong. Equity acts according to settled principles. Equity's principles are more flexible and more adaptable than the rules of the Law, but some order is necessary so that people can know how they stand.

Second, Equity is only a partial system. The Law claims to be comprehensive; it has an answer for everything. Equity intervenes in selected areas only; it has, for example, very little to do with the criminal law.

Third, Equity is a parasitic system, or, as it is usually put, 'Equity is a gloss on the Law' – gloss meaning a marginal note or comment on a text. Take away Equity, and the Law could continue to function; take away the Law, and Equity would collapse; it would have nothing upon which to bite.

Fourth, 'Equity acts *in personam*'. In theory at least, Equity does not alter the Law. Equity does not and cannot deny a person's legal rights. It merely fastens on the conscience of the legal claimant, and directs him how he should behave. Equity may thus alter the *effect* of the Law, but it does not alter the *rules* of the Law.

Finally, a court of Equity is a court of conscience, and, in particular, it will not assist a claimant if it would be unjust to do so: equitable remedies are discretionary.

(4)   THE CONTRIBUTIONS OF EQUITY

The contribution made by Equity to our jurisprudence was threefold.

First, Equity brought new *procedures*. In particular, because a court of Equity was a court of conscience, it could examine a defendant's conscience by putting him on oath to tell the truth – something unheard of in the early common law.

Second, Equity brought new *remedies*. The principal remedy at Law was, and is, damages: the claimant recovers money compensation for loss suffered by reason of the defendant's misconduct. But money does not always provide adequate compensation, and Equity can issue an *injunction* compelling the defendant, on pain of imprisonment, to desist from his misconduct, or to refrain from threatened misconduct, or to take corrective measures. It may also grant an order for *specific performance*, requiring the defendant actually to do that which he promised to do.

There are, however, continuing differences in the availability of legal and equitable remedies respectively, which may be traced back to medieval origins. In general, if the claimant proves infringement of a legal right, then he is *entitled* to a legal remedy. He can demand damages. If his claim is wholly without merit, he may be awarded nominal damages, and without costs. His victory may then be a Pyrrhic victory, but he wins his damages nonetheless. Equitable remedies are, however, *discretionary*. The claimant can never demand an injunction or specific performance. He can but ask for the remedy. And if the case falls within settled principles, he can expect his remedy as a matter of course. However, the court always has a discretion to refuse the remedy, if justice so demands.

Third, Equity gave birth to a new *institution*, the trust. A trust is defined as the relationship which exists when the apparent or legal owner of property is compelled by Equity to treat the property as belonging to another (or is compelled by Equity to use the property for specified, normally charitable, purposes). The person who creates the trust is called the settlor (or trustor). The person to whom he transfers the property and in whom he reposes his trust – the apparent or *legal* owner – is called the *trustee*. The person for whose benefit the trust is created is called the *beneficiary* or *equitable owner*.

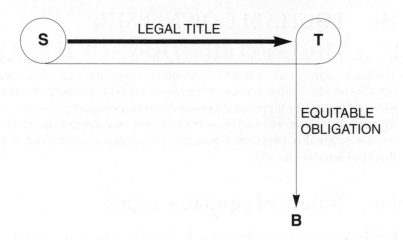

S is the settlor; T, the trustee;
and B, the beneficiary

It will be seen that the modern *trust* is, in principle, identical to the ancient *use*, described above. The history of how the one became the other does not matter for present purposes. What, however, is important is the idea that it is possible to have two 'owners' of the same property at the same time – one being the titular owner according to the rules of the Law; the other being the person entitled to be treated as the owner according to the principles of Equity.

The trust is an immensely flexible institution. It may be used to vest powers of management in one person or group of persons, and the benefit in another or others who cannot effectively manage for themselves (children, mental patients, clubs and associations). It can be used to provide for persons unborn and therefore as yet incapable of holding property. It can be used to dispose of property in such a way as to minimise taxation. It can be used to solve various technical problems in conveyancing. It can sometimes be used in a quasi-remedial fashion to prevent a fraudster benefiting from his unconscionable conduct. And the trust has many more functions besides.

(5)   EQUITABLE OWNERSHIP

It is necessary to say a little more about the nature of equitable ownership. The beneficiary under a trust is commonly called the equitable owner, and he is treated in Equity as though he were the owner of the property. He can sell, give away or otherwise dispose of his equitable property. If he does so, the trustee thenceforth holds on trust for the transferee instead of on trust for the original beneficiary. Equitable ownership is, however, less secure than full legal ownership.

(a)   Nature of equitable rights

Legal ownership is a right *in rem*. It is a right which, in principle, is good against the whole world. Equitable ownership falls short of that. Equitable rights are, in principle, good against the whole world except a *bona fide* purchaser of the legal estate for value and without notice – commonly known as 'the BFP' – but it is a principle which needs both explanation and modification.

Originally, the beneficiary's right in Equity was merely a right against the 'trustee' personally. The settlor had reposed a confidence in *him*. It was *his* conscience which was affected. It was *he* who was bound in Equity to treat the property as belonging to the beneficiary. If the trustee transferred the property to some third party, then, originally, that third party was not bound by the trust. However, from about the middle of the 15th century, Equity began to extend its notion of conscience, and began to enforce the beneficiary's rights not only against the original trustee, but also against various classes of successors in title. First, it held that the trust could be enforced against a *purchaser with notice* of the trust – one who took the property knowing of the beneficiary's claim. Then it began to enforce the trust against the trustee's *heir*, if the trustee himself died. Then it began to enforce the trust against any *donee* from the trustee – even one who took with a clear conscience and without notice of the beneficiary's claim. Then Equity asserted that the rights of the beneficiary should take priority even over the claims of the trustee's *creditors* in the event that he failed to pay his debts. The beneficiary's right, which had begun as a right *in personam*, had become, so to speak, a right *in personas* – enforceable against many people. In effect, although it was not finally confirmed until the start of the 20th century, the beneficiary's right had become *almost* a right *in rem*. It was a right which was good against the whole world except the BFP.

(b)   The BFP

If he is to claim the privileged status of BFP, the purchaser must satisfy five requirements. First, he must be *bona fide*, that is, honest. Second, he must be a *purchaser* in the technical sense. A 'purchaser' here means a person who takes by act of party, rather than by operation of law. A buyer is a 'purchaser': he acquires his title by the deliberate act of the vendor. But so is a mere donee of the property, or one who takes a lease or a mortgage on the property. They all take their title because someone transfers it to them. On the other hand, if a person is declared bankrupt, title to his assets vests *by operation of law* in an official called his trustee in bankruptcy. Or if a person dies intestate (without making a will), title to his assets vests *by operation of law* in an administrator appointed by the court to wind up his estate. These last two are therefore not 'purchasers' in the technical sense.

Third, the BFP must be a purchaser of a *legal estate* or legal ownership of the property. The BFP can say that he too has an equity (or moral claim) in his favour to counteract the equitable claims of the beneficiary. He acted in all innocence, his conscience is clear, and moreover he gave good value for the property. The moral arguments for the purchaser and for the beneficiary are equally balanced. The case for not interfering with the

Law's solution is as strong as the case for interfering with it. Equity therefore declines to interfere and allows the Law to take its course: 'Where the equities are equal, the Law prevails.' On the other hand, if the purchaser buys only an *equitable* interest in the property, then Equity must adjudicate between the purchaser and the beneficiary. Neither has the Law on his side to tip the balance. Equity then says, 'Where the equities are equal, the first in time prevails', and the beneficiary prevails over the purchaser.

Fourth, the BFP must be a purchaser *for value*. So a donee is a purchaser, but he is not a purchaser for value. 'Value' here means *money, money's worth* or *marriage*. Where the purchaser pays *money*, he need not pay the full market price, but a purely nominal payment is not value. *Money's worth* includes payment in kind – barter or exchange. *Marriage* may need explanation. Where a parent or some other person promises to settle property on the happy couple upon the occasion of their marriage, then the act of getting married constitutes consideration for that promise. The 'marriage consideration', as it is termed, is deemed given by both parties to the marriage and (a quaint rule!) by the children or remoter issue of that marriage ('because the parents have the seeds of future generations within them').

Finally, the BFP must be a purchaser *without notice* of the beneficiary's rights. A purchaser who actually knows of an equitable right or interest is said to have *actual notice* of it. But a purchaser who does not actually *know* of an equitable right or interest may nevertheless still have *notice* of it. Notice is wider than knowledge. Every purchaser is expected to behave in a sensible and reasonable manner. If he does not, then he is *deemed* to have notice of those rights which he would have discovered if he had behaved as a sensible and reasonable purchaser would have behaved. He is said to have *constructive notice* of those rights. Now a purchaser of *land* is expected to carry out a thorough investigation of his vendor's title. So, if a purchaser of land does not investigate title, he is nevertheless fixed with (constructive) notice of those rights which he would have discovered had he properly investigated. And if a purchaser of land investigates the title carelessly, he is nevertheless fixed with (constructive) notice of those rights which he would have discovered had he conducted his investigation in a reasonably careful manner. A purchaser of *goods*, on the other hand, does not normally ask for proof of title – the fact of possession and the absence of suspicious circumstances is usually accepted as sufficient proof of the seller's right to sell. The doctrine of constructive notice is therefore of limited application in the case of pure personalty. Lastly, in addition to actual notice and constructive notice, there is a third kind of notice: *imputed notice*. Where a purchaser employs a solicitor or other agent to conduct the purchase for him, then anything which was discovered or which ought to have been discovered by that agent is imputed to his principal, the purchaser.

(c) Effect of a *bona fide* purchase

The BFP as described above takes free of the beneficiary's rights. The defence of *bona fide* purchase acts as a brick wall, over which the beneficiary can never scramble. He can no longer claim that the property belongs to him in Equity. His equitable ownership is destroyed. His only claim is a claim for compensation for breach of trust against his trustee. It follows that anyone claiming through a BFP takes free of the trust, even if he himself had notice of the erstwhile equitable interest, because, *ex hypothesi*, the equitable interest ceased to exist when the BFP acquired the title.

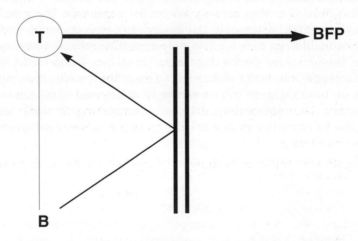

(d) Modern modifications of the doctrine

Although one continues to say that equitable rights are good against the whole world except the BFP, in practice the doctrine is much modified by statute. In the first place, some equitable rights are declared *registrable*. For that class of rights, registration generally supplants notice. If the item is duly registered, the purchaser is bound whether he checked the register or not; if the item is not registered, then a purchaser for value (or in some cases a purchaser for money or money's worth) will take free of the right *even if he actually knew of its existence*. In relation to such rights, one still refers to a 'BFP without notice', but one makes the mental translation that notice means registration.

In the second place, a purchaser *with* notice may nevertheless take free of certain other rights by the doctrine of *overreaching*. In order to overreach, the purchaser must comply with certain prescribed requirements. In the typical case, he must pay over his purchase money to at least two trustees. (He may pay his money to a *sole* trustee if that sole trustee is a trust corporation; a trust corporation is the Public Trustee or a company – say, a bank or an insurance company – which is authorised to act as a trustee.) If the purchaser does that, then the rights of the equitable owners are, so to speak, detached by statutory magic from the property itself and are attached instead to the money paid by the purchaser. The purchaser can then, so to speak, reach over the heads of the beneficiaries and take the property freed from their equitable interests. Overreaching is thus a device which attempts to reconcile commercial expediency and moral justice: the purchaser gets the clean title he wants, free of the beneficiaries' rights; their rights are not destroyed, they are merely transferred from one investment to another. The requirement that, for overreaching to work, there must normally be two trustees or a trust corporation, is some safeguard against collusion or fraud.

Registration and overreaching are considered in more detail later.

3 Land

It is necessary to distinguish *land* (freehold or leasehold) on the one hand from mere *chattels* on the other. The concept of ownership of chattels is comparatively straightforward; the concept of ownership of land, more complicated. The method of proving and transferring title differs as between land and chattels respectively; so do the formalities applicable both in relation to contract and in relation to conveyance.

In most cases, it is obvious into which category a particular item falls, but not always. In the first place, the legal definition of land includes several items which would not normally be thought of as land. In the second place, the borderline case may be difficult to classify. Is, for example, a greenhouse an integral part of the land which passes to a purchaser, or is it a personal chattel which the vendor can take away with him? And what of the apples ripening on the apple tree?

(1)   STATUTORY DEFINITION

The starting point is the definition of land set out in the Law of Property Act (LPA) 1925:

> '205–(1) *In this Act unless the context otherwise requires* ...
>
> (ix)   *"Land" includes land of any tenure, and mines and minerals, whether or not held apart from the surface, buildings or parts of buildings (whether the division is horizontal, vertical or made in any other way) and other corporeal hereditaments; and also a manor, an advowson, and a rent and other incorporeal hereditaments, and an easement, right, privilege or benefit in, over, or derived from land* ...'

The definition strictly applies for the purposes of the LPA only, but similar definitions are found in other relevant statutes. Notice that the definition is provisional only, in that it is expressly made subject to context. Notice, too, that the definition is inclusive, not exhaustive ('"land" *includes* land ...').

Other points to note about the definition are:

Land of any tenure: freeholds are realty; leaseholds are personalty; both are 'land'.

Mines and minerals: it is not uncommon to find that one person owns the surface and subsoil, and another person owns various strata of minerals beneath the surface '... together with all mines and powers of working and getting the same'. The mineral rights and any access tunnels are then a separate piece of 'land' and the owner of them can sell and transfer his 'underground land' independently of the surface. However, the state owns all coal, oil and natural gas (which it may license others to exploit), and the Crown has the right to all gold and silver mines.

Buildings and parts of buildings: it is sometimes difficult to decide whether an item is part of a building, or a chattel contained within a building but legally separate from it. That is discussed below. However, once something is part of a building, then it is part of the land. Observe that a part of a building can be a separate piece of 'land' even if it does not itself touch the ground. A penthouse atop a tower block can be a separate piece of 'land' – a 'flying' freehold or leasehold – although its owner obviously needs to secure rights of support and access.

Corporeal hereditaments: a hereditament literally means something inheritable. Inheritance strictly means the process whereby certain property passes automatically to the person designated by the law as the deceased's heir – usually the eldest son. Inheritance in that strict sense was (with minor savings) abolished in 1925, so that one must now understand 'hereditament' to mean property which *used to be* inheritable. It means roughly the same as real property, although technically it is a wider word.

Hereditaments were classified by the medieval lawyers as either incorporeal (see below) or corporeal. A corporeal hereditament is one which admits of physical possession. The expression therefore comprehends the land itself and the buildings and any other physical attachments – fences, poles, statues, trees, plants, turf and suchlike.

A manor: the manor is another relic of feudal times, but some still exist. The rights of the owner of a manor have been greatly attenuated, but not altogether abolished. Ownership of the manor carries with it the right to call oneself the Lord of the Manor. It may also carry mineral rights and the exclusive right to license fairs and markets within the manor, and maybe also the duty to clean the ditches. And the Lord of the Manor has the right to all the manorial records. In any event, ownership of the manor is ownership of land.

An advowson: this is the right to present an incumbent to a living in the Church of England – that is, the right to nominate the next vicar or rector or whoever. The right was often vested in the Lord of the Manor. It is technically a piece of land (but, to be pedantic, not land which is capable of registration under the Land Registration Act 1925).

A rent: rents are of two main kinds, rent service and rentcharge. The familiar rent payable by a tenant to his landlord is *rent service*. It is a periodic acknowledgment by the tenant of the landlord's superior right, and technically, it is an integral part of the landlord's ownership of the land. The rent referred to in the LPA's definition is a rent of the other kind: a *rentcharge* (sometimes known as a fee farm rent). A rentcharge is a periodic payment secured on land – almost in the nature of a mini-mortgage. For example, in a housing development, individual owners may grant a rentcharge of so much a year to an estate company to meet the cost of maintaining the common parts of the estate. If the rentcharge is not paid, the chargee may send in the bailiffs or take possession of the land in order to recover payment.

Incorporeal hereditaments: it will be inferred from what was said above about corporeal hereditaments that the expression 'incorporeal hereditament' means, broadly, intangible real property. These rights are treated as part of the land itself. The most important examples are rentcharges (see above) and easements and profits (see below). An advowson (above) is also an incorporeal hereditament. Other incorporeal hereditaments include titles of honour and various ancient offices.

Easement, right, privilege or benefit: an easement is, as noted earlier, a right over one piece of land for the benefit of another piece of land – such as a right of way to cross a neighbour's property, or a right to run pipes or wires under or over it. The right becomes part of the land benefited.

Profits à prendre are also 'land' within the LPA. These, too, have been mentioned earlier. They resemble easements in that they are rights in or over the land of another, but they differ from easements in that the owner of a profit may take something away from the land over which his right is exercised. Sporting rights (hunting, shooting, fishing) are profits. A profit, like an easement, may be attached to and become part of another piece of land, but, unlike an easement, it is not *necessary* that it should be attached to another piece of land. It can exist independently of any other land and be transferred or otherwise dealt with as a piece of land in its own right. It is an incorporeal hereditament.

The *benefit of a restrictive covenant* relating to land (say a covenant by a neighbour not to use his land otherwise than as a single private dwellinghouse) may be annexed to, and become part of, the land benefited thereby (see Chapter 16). It is not, however, classed as an incorporeal hereditament – because the concept of a hereditament is a legal concept, and the doctrine of restrictive covenants was a comparatively late (19th century) development in Equity.

(2) FIXTURES

A fixture is a chattel which has been annexed to, and so has become part of, the land. It can often be vital to know whether an item is land or chattel. In particular, on the sale of land, the vendor may take away with him any chattels, but, unless the contract itself otherwise provides, the purchaser is entitled to everything which was part of the land at the date of the contract of sale.

(a) Annexation

There is a two-stage test to be applied in order to determine whether a chattel has become part of the land. The first part of the test is a crude rule, but it determines the burden of proof. You look for the 'degree of annexation'. If an item is firmly attached to the land, then it is presumed to be part of the land unless the contrary is proved; if an item merely rests by its own weight or is only superficially attached, then it is presumed to be a chattel unless the contrary is shown. Nails, screws and cement make for firm attachment; drawing pins, sticky tape and electricity plugs provide superficial attachment.

The second part of the test is, however, the more important. You have to look to the 'purpose of annexation'. An actor's purpose is to be inferred by an objective examination of what he said and did. An item which is firmly fixed to the land may nevertheless still be a chattel, if it is shown that the purpose of the fixing was not to make the item a permanent feature, but was done simply for its better enjoyment as a chattel. A valuable painting, for example, might need to be very firmly fixed in place as a security precaution, but it is only to be expected that its owner will take it away with him when he moves house. On the other hand, an item which is completely unattached may be a fixture if the inference is that it was intended to be a (more or less) permanent feature. A dry stone wall is the classic example of that. Another example might be a statue placed as the centrepiece of an ornamental garden.

(b)   Severance

In some circumstances, it may be possible to take an item which has become part of the land and re-convert it into a chattel. The technical word for that is *severance*. The right to sever arises in certain situations where a limited owner, such as a leasehold tenant, attaches a chattel to the land so that it becomes a fixture. Upon expiry of his limited ownership, he may be entitled to sever the fixture, re-convert it into a chattel, and so take it away with him. Such removable fixtures are given the self-contradictory label 'tenant's fixtures'.

The leaseholder's right to sever is the most important example; but the right to sever arises in other cases too. The leaseholder may lawfully sever trade, ornamental or domestic fixtures, and there are special rules for tenant farmers.

(c)   Third parties

The point might be made that a chattel which is annexed to the land becomes part of the land, no matter to whom the chattel belonged before annexation. If a thief takes bricks and builds them into a house, the bricks belong to the owner of the land. The former owner of the bricks may sue the thief for the tort of conversion, but he is unlikely to have any remedy against the landowner in the absence of evidence of complicity.

(3)   GROWING THINGS

In principle, anything growing in the land is part of the land: trees, shrubs, plants, flowers, vegetables, grass. The *crops* to be harvested from the land are, however, sometimes treated as goods and sometimes treated as land. The distinction can be important. For example, an oral contract for goods is enforceable, an oral contract for land is not. The law is not altogether clear, but as a general rule, *annual* growing crops – those which are planted or sown and harvested all within 12 months – are treated as goods; other crops are generally treated as land, but they may be regarded as goods if they are to be harvested forthwith or if the seller contracts to harvest them for the buyer.

(4)   WILD CREATURES

Wild animals, birds and fish are owned by no one unless and until they are killed or captured. The landowner is, however, regarded as having a *qualified* right of ownership in wild creatures. He has the exclusive right to hunt, shoot or fish on or from his land and, if any such creature is killed or captured on his land, then ownership of it vests in the landowner.

(5)   AIRSPACE

The land includes the airspace above the land. The classic statement is that the land includes everything *usque ad coelum, usque ad inferos* (right up to the sky and down to the nether regions) but, these days, 'the sky' begins at a reasonable height above the ground. A landowner can complain that his airspace is infringed by an overhanging branch or an overswinging crane, but he cannot complain of an overflying aeroplane.

(6)   HIGHWAYS

Where land abuts a public highway, it is assumed in the absence of any contrary indication that the owner of the land owns the land beneath the highway up to its mid point, subject, of course, to the public right of way over it. In the typical case where a road or street has been adopted and is maintained at the public expense, then the relevant local or national authority owns the surface of the highway to a sufficient depth to enable it to discharge its duties.

(7) WATER

These days, the use of the nation's water resources is closely regulated by statute. In general, it may be said that water percolating through the soil belongs to no one. Captive water in a well or pond belongs to the landowner. Water flowing in a stream or river belongs to no one, but the riparian owner may have limited rights therein. In the absence of any contrary indication, the riparian owner owns the bed of any stream or river bordering his land up to its mid point (unless the river is tidal, when the bed and foreshore are owned by the Crown); he has the exclusive right to fish from his land and he has the right to abstract water from the stream or river for domestic or agricultural purposes.

(8) THINGS LOST AND FOUND

If a chattel is found lying in a *public* place then, as explained in Chapter 1, the rule is that the fact of possession gives the finder a title, so that he can claim to be the owner of it unless and until someone else can show a better title. Where a chattel is found lying on *private* land to which the public does not have access (for example, a private garden), then the chattel is generally to be taken to be in the possession of the landowner; the finder has a title by virtue of present possession, but the landowner has a better title by virtue of his earlier possession. Where an item is found *buried* in land, then, since the landowner owns everything in or attached to the land, the landowner has the better title. There is one exception: *treasure*. Upon discovery, treasure (as defined) belongs to the Crown subject to the rights (if any, and if provable) of the person who left or lost it. According to the old common law doctrine of *treasure trove* (treasure found), the Crown might claim unearthed items of gold or silver of unknown ownership which had been deliberately buried (as opposed to being abandoned or accidentally lost). But the common law could not thereby prevent treasure hunters armed with metal detectors from lawfully appropriating many artefacts of historical or cultural importance. Parliament therefore intervened to protect the national heritage. The Crown's right to treasure now depends on the Treasure Act 1996, and not on the common law. Broadly speaking, the modern notion of 'treasure' is a find of or including *either* any object which would have been treasure trove under the old law *or* any object which is 300 years old and which contains at least 10% gold or silver, provided that (1) a solitary coin is not treasure, but (2) 10 or more old coins are treasure, whatever their metallic composition. Any find should be reported to the local coroner. He determines whether the object is or is not treasure. If it is, then the likely outcome is that any item of historical or cultural importance will be transferred to a museum and the finder or landowner or both will be paid a reward.

4 Tenure

The doctrines of tenure and estate are the gravity and oxygen of English land law. Life as we know it would be impossible without them, but most people survive perfectly well knowing little, and thinking even less, about them.

The history of tenure and estate is of little practical consequence today, but it is necessary briefly to investigate what was, in order to understand what is. And, just occasionally, a point crops up which requires recourse to first principles.

(1)   TENURE AND ESTATE

Tenure is discussed in this chapter; estate, in the next. They are very different ideas, but experience shows that, for students taking their first steps in land law, it is very easy to confuse the two. Now the educationalists tell us that inventing a simple mnemonic is often a useful way of remembering unfamiliar information – and the sillier the notion, the more memorable it is likely to be.

So here is a simple and silly mnemonic for remembering the difference between tenure and estate. Contemplate their initial letters:

T is a downwards pointing letter, and Tenure tells us the *terms and conditions* upon which a tenant holds land of his lord.

E is a forwards facing letter, and Estate explains the *extent and duration* of the owner's interest.

(2)   THE CONCEPT OF TENURE

Concentrating for the time being on the doctrine of tenure, and pursuing the idea of making it memorable by silly mnemonics, it will be noticed that the letter T is made up of two lines, and Tenure teaches two things:

- no one *owns* land except the Crown;
- everyone else merely *holds* the land of some superior landlord.

The two lines also serve as a reminder that there are two tenures and two tenures only:

```
F R E E H O L D
        L
        E
        A
        S
        E
        H
        O
        L
        D
```

Most people would infer two things from the word *freehold*: first, that the freeholder has perpetual ownership; and, second, that he does not have to pay any rent to a landlord. Similarly, most people would infer two things from the word *leasehold*: first, that the leaseholder has an ownership of limited duration, be it long or short; and, second, that the leaseholder has to pay a regular rent to a landlord.

Those propositions are in fact broadly correct – but it takes a lengthy and circuitous exposition to explain why.

(3)   CARICATURE OF FREEHOLD TENURE

Tenure was a central feature of the feudal system which flourished in Norman times. The feudal system was a system of landholding which wove a social, political, economic and fiscal fabric.

(a)   The feudal system

In concept, all land was vested in the Crown alone. The king parcelled out land to his supporters and servants in return for an oath of allegiance and the payment of a form of tribute, called *services*. The services to be rendered depended on the circumstances. A powerful baron might promise to maintain so many armed horsemen at the king's disposal; a monastery might promise to say prayers for his soul; others might promise more humble tributes, the provision of food, drink or personal services. The king was their landlord; they were his tenants, and because they held directly of the king they were called tenants-in-chief. There were probably about 2,000 of them.

A tenant, instead of occupying his land personally, might grant away some or all of it to a subtenant. The process was called *subinfeudation*. The subtenant would swear an oath of fealty to his lord and would promise appropriate services. The subtenant in turn could subinfeudate. In theory, there was no limit to the number of rungs in the feudal latter. In practice, two or three was the norm, although there are recorded cases of six or seven.

The medieval lawyers classified these tenancies according to the type of services rendered. Each class of tenancy was a separate *tenure*, so that the tenant would be said to hold by *knight service*, or in *sergeanty*, or in *frankalmoign*, or as the case might be. The commonest tenure of all was *free and common socage*. Any kind of service might be reserved in socage, but socage was most frequently employed to secure some form of agricultural service – so many days ploughing, sowing, harvesting and so on.

Each tenure carried with it certain implied obligations on the part of the tenant. These obligations were automatically incidental to the relationship and so were called *incidents of tenure*. The nature of the incidents varied from tenure to tenure. For example, the tenant might be expected to contribute to the cost of knighting the lord's son or marrying off his daughter; perhaps a premium was payable to the lord when a tenant died and his son assumed the tenancy; or, if the tenant's heir were under age, the lord might claim the right to manage the land for his own profit during the heir's minority.

The principal features of tenure were thus, first, that the tenant *held* the land, he did not own it; second, that he owed a duty of *loyalty* (fealty) to his lord; third, that tenure involved other burdensome *incidents* for the tenant; and fourth, that the tenant had to render *services* to his lord.

One other vital point should be noted. All these tenures were *freehold* tenures. The tenant took up his tenancy as the result of his own choice and free will. The feudal system regulated the relationships of, so to speak, the ruling classes. It was superimposed on top of the existing Saxon manorial system. The feudal system descended from the king at the top down to the lord of the manor at the bottom. Beneath the lord of the manor, the Anglo-Saxon serfs continued to till the soil of their manor, and their relationship with the lord of the manor continued to be governed by the law and custom of their manor. The *manorial* system was appropriate for their servile status; the *feudal* system was reserved for free men – hence the label *freehold* tenure.

(b) Decay of the system

The feudal system decayed and eventually collapsed as a result of social and political change and economic pressures. From the lawyer's point of view, there are three salient dates.

(i) Prohibition of subinfeudation

The statute *Quia Emptores* 1290 decreed that there should be no further subinfeudation. Thereafter, if a tenant wished to dispose of his holding, he could transfer his existing tenancy to a purchaser, but he could not create a subtenancy. The maximum number of layers in the feudal system was thus fixed and, thereafter, the system could only shrink. Moreover, the rule was and still is that the current tenant is assumed to hold directly of the Crown, unless and until some *mesne lordship* is proved. (Mesne is pronounced *'mean'*; a mesne lordship is an intermediate lordship.) And, for the reasons explained below, as the years passed so it became less and less likely that any mesne lordship could be proved.

(ii) Reduction of tenures

The Tenures Abolition Act 1660 emasculated the system. By then, feudal *services* had lost much of their importance. The Act reduced the number freehold tenures to two, and limited the *incidents* applicable thereto.

As far as concerns *services*, from quite early days, it had become a common practice for the lord and tenant to agree to commute the payment of services in kind into a money payment. Over a period of time, many of these money payments had disappeared – either because inflation had rendered it uneconomic to collect them or for some other reason. With the disappearance of services, there disappeared also the evidence of many mesne lordships.

The *incidents* of tenure, however, remained important in 1660, but they were generally unpopular. The Crown had everything to gain and nothing to lose from feudal incidents; for the Crown was always the lord and never the tenant. And as mesne lordships disappeared, so the Crown's position became ever more dominant. Its coffers were filled by what was, in effect, unparliamentary taxation. The king's insistence that he had the right to levy tax without the consent of Parliament had been one of the major causes of the Civil War, and although the monarchy was restored in 1660, Parliament was determined to hobble the king. The Tenures Abolition Act was one of the instruments it used.

By the Act, all freehold tenures were converted into free and common socage, with the exception of land held in frankalmoign. Frankalmoign applied to ecclesiastical lands only, and depended upon the land being held continuously by the same ecclesiastical tenant since before 1290; alienation automatically converted the tenure to socage. Frankalmoign was comparatively rare, but it was expressly preserved by the Tenures Abolition Act. It was probably obsolete by 1925. The Administration of Estates Act (AEA) 1925 attempted formally to abolish it, but the Act was technically defective. So frankalmoign may or may not have been abolished; if not abolished, it is probably obsolete; if not obsolete, it is quite unimportant.

Aside, therefore, from the minor complication of frankalmoign, the Tenures Abolition Act 1660 reduced all freehold tenures to one: free and common socage. It also abolished most of the *incidents* of tenure. The one important exception was *escheat*. This was the right of the lord to retake the land in certain circumstances. It was of two main kinds. If the tenant was attainted of felony (in consequence of a sentence of death), then there was *escheat propter delictum tenentis* (escheat by reason of the tenant's wrongdoing) and the land reverted to the lord, subject to the Crown's right to take the profits of the land for a year and a day. (Contrast forfeiture for high treason, whereby all the property of a traitor was forfeit to the Crown absolutely.) That kind of escheat was abolished by the Forfeiture Act 1870 (and so was forfeiture for high treason).

The other kind of escheat was *escheat propter defectum sanguinis* (escheat by reason of failure of the bloodline). If the tenant died intestate and without an heir, then the land reverted to the lord. That kind of escheat survived until 1925.

(iii)   Abolition of escheat

By 1925, the only surviving manifestation of the feudal system of any great practical importance was escheat for want of heirs (escheat *propter defectum sanguinis*). That was abolished by the AEA 1925, which introduced the modern rule that the real property of a person who dies intestate passes (as does his personal property) to his statutory next of kin, or, if there are none such, then to the Crown as *bona vacantia* (ownerless goods).

Escheat was not, however, completely abolished by the AEA 1925. It is a necessary concomitant of the theory of tenure that if the tenancy ever ends for any reason, then the land escheats to the lord. There can, in rare cases, still be an escheat. One example is *disclaimer*. The trustee of a bankrupt individual or the liquidator of an insolvent company may disclaim (that is, in a real sense, dis-own) a freehold which is more of a liability than an asset. Should that happen, the tenancy ends and the land escheats to the lord (usually the Crown). It is an unlikely occurrence, but there are reported to be 200 or so cases a year. In practice, however, escheat may be less dramatic than it sounds. In the first place, escheat does not destroy any mortgage, lease or other incumbrance affecting the land (but the lord does not become personally liable for any debts or obligations of the former tenant). In the second place, if the lord takes no steps to enforce his rights (and he is unlikely to want an uneconomic property) then a squatter may take possession and establish a new title.

(c)   The modern law

The feudal system survives today in the *theory* that all land is owned by the Crown. All freeholders are merely tenants, holding of a landlord. In almost all cases the landlord is the Crown, but exceptionally there might be a mesne lordship interposed between the tenant and the Crown. In any event, the freeholder holds by socage tenure, all other freehold tenures having disappeared. But, since socage tenure is the only surviving freehold tenure, there is no point in distinguishing the species from the genus, and the tenure is simply referred to as freehold tenure.

The practical consequences of all this are, however, negligible. Feudal services have disappeared almost without trace. So have feudal incidents, save for the remote possibility of an escheat.

(4)   CARICATURE OF COPYHOLD TENURE

For hundreds of years, English law recognised another sort of tenure, called copyhold. It was eventually abolished in the 20th century.

The point has been noted above that, initially at least, the feudal system did not penetrate down into the life of the manor. The village serfs still held their land of the lord of the manor according to the custom of the manor. The serfs were mostly *villeins*, and they held their land by *villeinage* tenure. Villeinage, like other tenures, implied certain incidents, including fealty and escheat. And the villein was obliged to render agricultural services to his lord. But villeinage was an unfree tenure. The free socager was committed to rendering specific agricultural services; the unfree villein, when he went to bed at night, did not know to what work he would be put on the morrow.

Alienation of villeinage land was by surrender and admittance in the manorial court. The transferor and transferee went to the lord's court. The transferor surrendered his tenancy to the lord; the lord admitted the transferee to the tenancy; a fee was paid, and the steward of the manor recorded the transaction in the court rolls.

Economic and social pressures – especially after the Black Death of 1349 – caused significant changes in villeinage. In particular, there was a tendency to commute the obligation to render uncertain agricultural services into an obligation to pay a certain sum of money (a 'quit rent', because the tenant was thereby quit of his duty to perform the services). Thereafter, villeinage began to lose its servile status. And, as it lost its servile status, so it changed its name from villeinage, which sounded servile, to *copyhold*, which did not. The name copyhold was adopted because the vendor proved his title by asking the steward of the manor for a copy of the relevant manorial records.

Copyhold, therefore, became just another way of holding land. The principal practical difference between copyhold and freehold lay in the method of conveyancing: copyhold continued to be conveyed by surrender and admittance in the manorial court.

Copyhold was left untouched by the Tenures Abolition Act 1660. The country squires might be keen to deprive the king of the unparliamentary taxation he received in the form of feudal incidents of freehold tenure, but they saw no reason to deprive themselves of the benefits they, as lords of manors, received from copyhold incidents. In any case, copyholders were perhaps not as aggrieved as freeholders; copyhold carried incidental rights for the tenant as well as incidental obligations. In particular, the copyholder usually enjoyed rights of common pasture and other common rights.

During the 19th century, much copyhold land was *enfranchised*, that is, turned into freehold. In some cases, the lord willingly enfranchised; in others, the tenant was given a statutory right to compel enfranchisement. But large amounts of land remained copyhold until 1925. At the end of that year, all remaining copyhold was converted into freehold (socage) by the LPA 1922. Some of the incidents of copyhold tenure were, however, preserved – especially the lord's rights to mines and minerals and his sporting rights, and the tenant's rights of common.

Copyhold is thus no more, but traces of it remain in these surviving incidents, and the former lord in copyhold may now be found as a mesne lord in freehold.

(5)   CARICATURE OF LEASEHOLD TENURE

The point has already been made that leaseholds are personal property not real property. Essentially, leaseholds developed too late to be included in the scheme of realty. Indeed, initially, leaseholds were not property of any sort at all. In medieval days, a lease was nothing more than a personal *permission* to use land. The word *lease* is derived from the French verb *laisser*, to allow. A landowner (the allower or *lessor*) merely *let* another (the allowee or *lessee*) use his land. Any rights the user enjoyed were merely personal rights (for example, contractual rights) against the landowner, and not property rights in the land itself. That meant, in particular, that if the lessee was evicted, then he had no right to reclaim possession of the land.

However, by the end of the 15th century, the courts had begun to restore possession to a lessee who had been wrongfully ejected. It followed that the lessee had begun to acquire some sort of right *in rem*. He had more than a contractual right; he had a *status* in relation to the land. He was, in some sense, a land*holder*, not merely a land user. But if he was a landholder or *tenant*, then, according to the notions of the time, he must hold the land of some superior lord, and it followed that the lessor must be his *landlord*.

Thus, leasehold became recognised as yet another kind of land tenure. And leasehold tenure began to imitate the other tenures to some extent. The feudal idea of *fealty* was – and still is – reflected in the idea that the leasehold tenant must not deny his landlord's title to the land; if he does so, the lease is forfeit. Moreover, if the lease comes to a premature end for any reason, then the land necessarily reverts to the landlord in right of his lordship. The feudal idea of *services* was – and still is – reflected in the fact that the tenant must render service to his landlord by paying the agreed *rent* service. The rent is almost always a money rent, but a rent in kind is possible. Even if no rent is in fact reserved, that does not affect the proposition that the landlord could have insisted on a rent if he had wanted one – that was his tenurial right. The feudal idea of *incidents* of tenure is reflected in the fact that the parties may agree that the grant of the lease is *conditional* upon the tenant performing certain duties (typically, conditional upon his paying the agreed rent). If the tenant is in breach of condition, the landlord has a right to forfeit the lease.

These rights and obligations are clearly of continuing importance. Leasehold tenure is a living tenure. Therein lies the great irony. Freehold tenure, which was once so pervasive, is now but a theory of little, if any, practical importance. Copyhold tenure, which was once so widespread, has gone altogether. Leasehold tenure, which originally was not a tenure at all, is the only one which remains vital today.

5 Estate

If tenure teaches that no one save the Crown actually *owns* the land, then what exactly does a 'landowner' own? The answer is that he owns an *estate* in the land. He has a special *status* in relation to the land. He has a bundle of rights in the land. This bundle of rights – this status – is called his *estate*. The medieval lawyers thought of the estate as something separate from the land itself. The 'landowner' *held* the land; he *owned* an estate in the land. That comes close to saying that the landowner does not own the land, but he owns an ownership in the land.

There are several different kinds of estate – several, so to speak, prepackaged bundles of rights. The principal distinguishing feature is the extent or duration of the tenant's ownership – whether it is perpetual, or for life, or for a fixed period of time, or whatever.

One important consequence of the doctrine of estates is that one piece of land can be 'owned' by several people at once. In law, there is but one true owner of any piece of land, namely, the Crown. But any piece of land can have several apparent owners. These apparent owners are, in law, merely tenants of the land, but each can own his own separate estate, his own separate bundle of rights, in that same piece of land.

(1)   OVERVIEW OF ESTATES

The remark was made, at the beginning of the last chapter, that students often find the doctrine of estate baffling to begin with. It was suggested that a silly mnemonic for remembering what Estate is all about is to contemplate the initial letter, and to note that E is a forwards facing letter, indicating that Estate explains the *extent and duration* of a person's ownership.

Following are some more silly mnemonics which summarise the scheme of estates.

Estate begins with the letter E. The letter E is composed of four lines, and that serves as a reminder that there are *four* estates, and four estates only, known to English law:

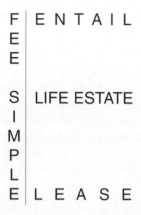

```
F | E N T A I L
E
E
S   LIFE ESTATE
I
M
P
L
E | L E A S E
```

Furthermore, the letter E also contains within itself a mnemonic for remembering the names of the four estates; for the letter E can be seen as four letters superimposed one on another:

⌐EE SIMPLE   Ɛ NTAIL   Ⅎ IFE ESTATE   L EASE

Each of the four estates will be described in more detail below, but, in terms of duration, the *fee simple* lasts virtually for ever, an *entail* lasts as long as there are descendants of the original grantee, a *life estate* lasts a lifetime, and a *lease* lasts for a set period of time – days, weeks, months or years.

There are variations on each of the four themes, but the fundamental proposition is that if a person wants an ownership of land, he must acquire one or other of those four estates. Parties can create whatever rights and obligations they wish within the realms of the law of *contract*, but contracts generate personal rights only. Ownership can be purchased only in the property supermarket, and the shelves in the property supermarket are stocked only with pre-packaged items.

Continuing with the silly mnemonics: the four estates are (for reasons which will be explained later) classified as either *freehold* or as *leasehold*. Freehold begins with F. F is composed of three lines. And there are three freehold estates:

Leasehold begins with L, and, obviously the only leasehold estate is the last of the four, the Lease – or what the LPA 1925 calls a term of years absolute. But the L of Leasehold is composed of two lines, and that serves as a reminder that there are two main varieties of lease: one is the term of years or fixed term (six months, seven years, 999 years); the other is the periodic tenancy (from week to week, or from month to month, and so on). The LPA 1925 defines 'term of years absolute' in such a way as to include both.

There is one more silly mnemonic. The point was made, in Chapter 2, that when dealing with ownership in English law, you should consider separately the position at Law and the position in Equity. It follows that, in considering the doctrine of estates, it is necessary to ask what estates are recognised at Law; and what estates in Equity. Now, Law begins with L, and L has two lines. The Law recognises two estates and two estates only. Equity begins with E, and E is made up of four lines. Equity recognises all four estates.

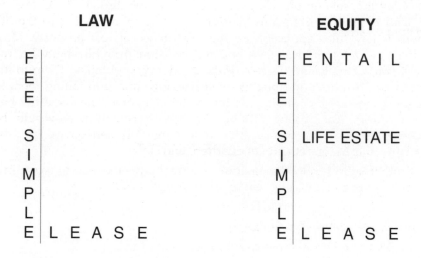

LAW

F |
E |
E |

S |
I |
M |
P |
L |
E | L E A S E

EQUITY

F | E N T A I L
E |
E |

S | LIFE ESTATE
I |
M |
P |
L |
E | L E A S E

In fact, the fee simple which the Law can see is a special kind of fee simple called the *fee simple absolute in possession*. It has already been mentioned that the LPA calls a legal lease a *term of years absolute*. These two are the only estates that can now be created or conveyed at Law. Their nature is briefly explained below.

Equity is more liberal and recognises all four estates. The point should, however, be stressed that ownership of an equitable estate is significantly different from ownership of a legal estate. Equitable ownership means the beneficial interest which arises under a trust (see Chapter 2). Someone, somewhere, must own a legal estate, and that legal owner is compelled by Equity to treat the property as if it belonged to the equitable owner. The legal owner holds the land in tenure of a lord. The equitable owner owns an interest under a trust imposed on the legal owner. The equitable relationship is trust, not tenure.

(2)   INHERITANCE

Before embarking upon a fuller explanation of the nature of the four estates, it will be as well, for reasons which will soon become apparent, to digress briefly into the idea of *inheritance*. The point was made earlier that inheritance in its strict sense is the process by which real property passed upon the death of the owner to the person or persons designated by the law as his heir. Inheritance in that sense is no longer a familiar concept in everyday life, save in one context: accession to the throne. The Crown of England is limited to descend, with one exception, according to the old common law rules applicable to the inheritance of real property. Most people have a rough idea of the line of succession: from Elizabeth II to the eldest son, Charles, and his line (William, Henry) and failing them to the second son, Andrew, and his line (Beatrice, Eugenie), and failing them to the third son, Edward, and failing him to the daughter, Anne, and her line (Peter, Zara). And failing all the Queen's descendants, it would be necessary to go back a generation (to George VI) and down the next available line: Margaret and her children, and so on.

That, broadly, is how the inheritance of real property used to work. In a simplified version, the rules can be summarised as follows:

• descendants are preferred to ascendants and collaterals;

• males are preferred to females;

• an elder male is preferred to a younger male; but

• females take equally as co-parceners; and

• in all cases, the issue of a deceased person represent the deceased.

The exception, where inheritance of the Crown differs from inheritance of real property, is the fourth point the list. If one were talking about inheritance of the Queen's real property, then, failing Charles, William, Henry and Andrew, it would have been the case that Beatrice and Eugenie would inherit as *joint* heirs in co-parcenary. (Co-parcenary was a special kind of co-ownership which was all but abolished in 1925.) It is obviously inconvenient to have joint queens, so, in relation to the descent of the Crown, the exception is made that an elder female is preferred to a younger female.

One more point needs to be made about inheritance. The terms *heirs general* and *heirs lineal* will soon be encountered. If property is available to the heirs general, then, in default of descendants, it is available for ascendants and collaterals. So, failing all the Queen's children and grandchildren, Margaret could take as the Queen's heir general. If, on the other hand, property is available only to the heirs lineal, then ascendants and collaterals and their respective lines are completely excluded; only descendants may take.

(3)   FEE SIMPLE

The fee simple is an estate which lasts virtually for ever. In effect, it is absolute ownership.

A fee simple may be a legal estate if it is a fee simple absolute in possession, as defined. A fee simple may exist in Equity whether it is absolute or not, and whether it is in possession or not.

The label 'fee simple' is, however, a misnomer. Parliament has retained an old label for a new concept. The word *fee* means an inheritable estate. The adjective *simple* imports that the inheritance is unrestricted, so that the estate is inheritable by the heirs general. In truth, however, the fee simple is *never* inheritable by anyone. It used to be an inheritable estate, but it is no longer an inheritable estate.

In medieval times, on the death of the estate owner in fee simple, the estate would automatically pass to his heir general. The estate could be transferred to another *inter vivos*, but it was not possible to devise land by will. Subsequently, wills of land were allowed. Thereafter, the heir took the fee simple only in the event that the estate owner died intestate. That remained the rule until 1925, when the AEA abolished inheritance of the fee simple altogether. The rule now is that, on the death of the estate owner in fee simple, the estate devolves according to his will; in default of a will, it passes to the persons designated by statute as his next of kin; in default of next of kin, it passes to the Crown as *bona vacantia*. The fee simple is not therefore strictly *inheritable* in any circumstances.

In effect, the fee simple has become a perpetual estate, but one conventionally adds the qualification, *virtually* perpetual, to cover the (extremely) remote possibility of an escheat, as explained earlier. If a *legal* fee simple should become ownerless by virtue of a disclaimer or otherwise, then the estate terminates and the land escheats to the lord. What happens in the event of an unexpected termination of an *equitable* fee simple is a question which does not admit of a simple answer – it depends upon the circumstances and upon the terms of the relevant trust.

(4) ENTAIL

The entail, or fee tail, is an estate which lasts as long as there are lineal heirs of the original grantee. It is an increasingly rare beast. No new entail may be created after 1996. Moreover, an entail may exist only in Equity under some form of trust.

The estate was invented by statute in 1285 to satisfy the dynastic aspirations of powerful landowners. Its nature is indicated by its name, fee tail. *Fee* means inheritable estate. *Tail* means that the inheritance is curtailed (French: *taillé*) by being restricted to the *lineal* heirs (that is, descendants) of the *original* grantee. The inheritance may be further restricted to *male* lineal heirs (tail male) or to *female* lineal heirs (tail female) or to the heirs descending from a particular marriage (tail special) or the male heirs of a particular marriage (tail male special) or the female heirs of a particular marriage (tail female special). There are ways and means of defeating the curtailment, if it is felt to be oppressive, as explained in Chapter 9.

Before 1925, the estate could exist at Law or in Equity. Since 1925, it can exist only in Equity. Strictly speaking, therefore, it is no longer an *estate* in land held in *tenure*, but an equitable *interest* arising under a *trust*, and it ought to be referred to as an entailed interest or entail, rather than a fee tail. *But all the old rules of inheritance still apply to the entail.* The entail is still inheritable in the strict sense, and it is still inheritable only by the next lineal heir of the original grantee in tail. Upon the death of his last lineal heir, the entail terminates, and the terms and circumstances of the trust will indicate who next becomes entitled to the land in Equity.

(5) LIFE INTEREST

A life estate or life interest means what it says. It is an estate which lasts for the lifetime of some person. Since 1925, a life estate can exist only in Equity under a trust, and so, strictly, it ought always to be referred to as a life interest, but the older terminology is often used in practice.

Typically, a life interest is granted for the lifetime of the grantee ('to Laura for life'), but it is possible to own an interest for the lifetime of some other person. The latter is called an estate *pur autre vie* (for another's life), and it can arise in two ways. It can be directly created as such: 'to Laura so long as Mary shall live.' Alternatively, it can arise where an ordinary life tenant sells his life interest. Suppose land is granted to Mary for life, and Mary then transfers her life interest to Laura. Mary cannot give away more than she has, and all she has is the land for her own lifetime. The effect of the transfer is therefore that Laura acquires the land for the remainder of Mary's life. (And, if Laura then dies *before* Mary, the remainder of Laura's life interest *pur autre vie* devolves with the rest of her property, according to her will or according to the rules of intestacy, as the case may be.)

A life estate was never a fee. It was never inheritable in the strict sense, not even when, in the case of an estate *pur autre vie*, the tenant for life died before the measuring life. The life estate is therefore sometimes called a *mere freehold*.

(6) LEASE OR TERM OF YEARS

A lease or term of years is an ownership which is limited in point of time, such that its maximum duration is fixed at or before the commencement of the term.

The maximum duration must be fixed in the sense that the ultimate *date* of expiry can be predicted right from the start. It is not possible to grant a lease 'for as long as the tenant wishes to reside in the property' or 'for the duration of the war'. Nor can a lease be granted 'forever'. But, if the maximum duration is fixed, then it matters not whether the term is short or long – a matter of days or thousands of years. And it is only the *maximum* duration which need be fixed. The lease can be made prematurely terminable, for example, by the giving notice or upon the happening of some event during the term.

There are some complications. One is the *periodic tenancy*. Weekly, monthly, yearly or other periodic tenancies are extremely common. On the face of it, the periodic tenancy does not appear to conform to the requirement that the maximum duration must be certain. It is impossible to say at the start of a monthly tenancy for how many months exactly the tenant will stay. In law, however, the maximum duration is deemed certain. The monthly tenant is treated as taking his tenancy initially for one month only. At the end of that month, his tenancy is automatically renewed for another month, and at the end of that month for another month, and then another, and then another. And so the arrangement continues until either side gives due notice to terminate it. In effect, notice to quit is, in this context, interpreted as notice that the next implied renewal will be the final renewal. Thus, in law, the maximum duration of a monthly tenancy is always predictable. Prospectively, the tenancy will terminate at the end of the next following month of the tenancy.

There are other minor complications in connection with leases for lives, leases until marriage, and perpetually renewable leases, but an explanation of those will be deferred until Chapter 11.

It is, however, true to say that if a lease is to be a legal estate, then it must be a *term of years absolute* as defined (see below, p 53), and that means that the maximum duration must be certain. A lease may also be created in Equity. One instance is the informal lease. It is a principle of Equity that 'Equity regards as done that which ought to be done'. In consequence, where two parties have entered (or are deemed to have entered) a *contract* for a lease, then Equity may treat them as if the lease had already been granted (see, further, Chapter 11). Equitable leases are also sometimes used for technical conveyancing purposes, especially within elaborate family settlements.

(7)   CLASSIFICATION OF ESTATES

Estates may be classified as either freehold or leasehold. Freehold estates are those which might, in feudal days, be held in freehold tenure: the fee simple, the entail and the life estate. The common characteristic is that the date of termination is unpredictable in advance. No one can say for sure when a life tenant will die, or when a fee might fail for want of heirs. In the case of leaseholds, on the other hand, the maximum duration is fixed in advance so that the date of termination is always predictable.

The leasehold is sometimes called an 'estate less than freehold' because it is of inferior *quality*. Quantity is irrelevant. A life estate granted to a centenarian is a freehold, and so of superior status to a 3,000 year lease.

(8) LEGAL ESTATES AND EQUITABLE INTERESTS

It is necessary now to return to the point that Law and Equity see things differently. In general terms, there are four estates: fee simple, entail, life estate, lease. But as far as the Law is concerned, there are only two estates: the *fee simple absolute in possession* and the *term of years absolute*. Any other estate is necessarily equitable, and so, to repeat a point made earlier, it is not, strictly speaking, an 'estate' in land held in tenure, but an equitable interest arising under a trust.

Similarly, in general terms, there are three *freehold* estates: fee simple, entail and life estate. But as far as the Law is concerned, there is really only one true freehold estate: the *fee simple absolute in possession*. Everything else is an equitable interest under a trust.

The proposition that, today, there are only two estates which are capable of being created or conveyed at Law, namely the fee simple absolute in possession and the term of years absolute, is a proposition of the most profound importance. These two estates are examined in more detail in Chapters 9 and 11 respectively, but their natures may be summarised here as follows.

(a) Fee simple absolute in possession

- *Fee* literally means 'inheritable estate' (as distinct from a 'mere freehold' or life interest), although a fee simple is in fact no longer inheritable in the strict sense of the word.

- *Simple* means inheritable by heirs general (as distinct from a fee tail or entail which is inheritable by heirs lineal), although the fee simple no longer in fact descends to the heirs general.

- *Absolute* means 'unmodified'. Any estate may be 'modified' in one of two ways: by making its existence dependent upon a continuing state of affairs ('until the clock tower falls down', 'until she marries' – a *determinable* interest), or by making its continuance dependent upon the non-occurrence of some event ('unless the clock tower falls down', 'unless she marries' – a *conditional* interest).

- *In possession* means *either* that the estate owner is in physical possession of the land (or has the immediate right to possession) *or* that he is receiving the rents or profits of the land (or has the right to any such).

The contrast is with an interest which is *in remainder* or *in reversion*, where the estate owner's right to possession is postponed by reason of the existence of some prior interest ('to Laura for life, *remainder* to Mary'). Note, however, that the definition of 'possession' includes the right to a rent, if any. That means, crucially, that *land let to a leasehold tenant remains in the 'possession' of the landlord*. Both landlord and tenant have possession. The tenant takes physical possession; the landlord retains legal possession, because he receives a rent. Even if he grants a rent-free lease, the landlord remains in legal possession because rent service is an incident of leasehold tenure, and the landlord thereby has the *right* to any rent which may be agreed – in this case a nil rent.

(b)   Term of years absolute

The statutory definition of 'term of years absolute' is a wonderful example of how the law can define something to mean exactly the opposite of what it appears to be. The LPA begins with the apparent meaning: '[a]"term of years absolute" means a term of years ...' That imports the basic idea that the maximum duration must be fixed in advance; there must be a finite *term*. The definition then proceeds to say, in effect, that:

* *term* includes periodic tenancies;
* *years* includes a period of one year or less;
* *absolute* includes determinable and conditional terms.

So a non-absolute non-term of non-years may nevertheless be a term of years absolute as defined!

(9)   DOUBLE MEANINGS

It follows from what has just been said that the words 'freehold' and 'leasehold' each have double meanings. They can be used to describe *either* the tenure *or* the estate – or *both at the same time*. As far as the Law is concerned, there is only one freehold estate (fee simple absolute in possession) and only one freehold tenure (socage). The two are necessarily interdependent. A person who owns the legal fee simple absolute in possession must necessarily hold in freehold tenure; a person who holds in freehold tenure must necessarily own the legal fee simple absolute in possession. Similarly, in the case of leaseholds: a person who owns a term of years absolute must necessarily hold in leasehold tenure, and a person who holds in leasehold tenure must necessarily own some sort of term of years absolute as defined.

For these reasons, it can now be seen that the common assumptions mentioned on p 34 are justified: the word 'freehold' implies perpetual ownership (estate in fee simple absolute in possession) without rent (in socage tenure, whereof the services are defunct); the word 'leasehold' implies limited ownership (estate for a term of years absolute) subject to a rent (in leasehold tenure, of which rent service is an automatic incident).

(10) FUNDAMENTAL IMPORTANCE OF THE LEGAL FEE

The consequence of all that has been said so far is that the legal fee simple absolute in possession is the centre of the conveyancing universe. The legal fee is indivisible, virtually indestructible and wholly indispensable. It is also exhaustive.

(a) Indivisibility

The legal fee is indivisible, in the sense that the owner cannot divest himself of only part of it. He can give it away whole, but not in part.

Consider, first, his position in the eyes of the Law. If he attempts to give away a life interest, then in Law he has done *nothing*, for the Law no longer recognises a life interest. If he attempts to give away an entail, then in Law he has done *nothing*; for the Law no longer recognises an entail. If he attempts to give away any freehold less than the entire legal fee simple absolute in possession, then in Law he has done *nothing*, for the Law no longer recognises any such lesser estate. On the other hand, he *can* still create a leasehold. The Law still recognises the term of years absolute as a legal estate. But if the owner of the legal fee does grant a lease, that does *not* deprive him of his legal fee; he still has a fee simple absolute *in possession* because possession includes the right to a rent (if any).

Turn to Equity. In Equity, the owner of the legal fee can create any recognised kind of estate. He can create a lease, a life estate or any kind of fee simple. (Before 1997, he could also create an entail.) He can even give away the entire fee simple absolute in possession in Equity. But all that alters his ownership of the *legal* fee not one jot. Equity can never alter the Law, although it may alter the effects of the Law. The owner of the legal fee therefore remains in the eyes of Equity just that: the owner of the legal fee. He is compelled to treat the property *as if* it belonged to the equitable owners. He holds his legal fee *on trust* to give effect to the equitable interests. But, even in the eyes of Equity, he still owns the legal fee.

Thus, neither at Law nor in Equity can the legal fee be dismembered.

(b)   Indestructibility

The legal owner cannot destroy his legal fee. He cannot break it up, as has just been demonstrated. He cannot destroy the entirety either. If he gives the whole estate away, that will destroy his *ownership* of the estate, but it will not destroy the estate itself. It will merely vest the estate in the transferee. Similarly, if he fails timeously to eject a trespasser who squats on his land, he may lose his *ownership* of the fee simple, because, it will be remembered, in English law, title is relative. The question is, who has the best claim to the fee simple? The earlier possessor of the land has the better claim, provided he asserts his rights within the limitation period. Otherwise, his claim is statute-barred, and the erstwhile trespasser has now become the only viable claimant to the fee simple.

If the owner of the fee simple dies still seised of the land (*seisin* is the technical word for possession of a legal freehold) then that does not destroy the legal fee. The fee passes immediately to the deceased's personal representatives, appointed to wind up his estate, and eventually to the appropriate beneficiary under the will, or (if there is no will) to his statutory next of kin, or (if there are no next of kin) to the Crown as *bona vacantia*.

In short, nothing the estate owner can do will destroy the legal fee. The only qualification is the point made several times earlier, that there remains the very remote possibility of an escheat. Should the legal fee simple become ownerless (for example, in the event that it is disclaimed by a trustee in bankruptcy or by the liquidator of a company) then the estate terminates and the land reverts to the lord.

Thus, the legal fee is virtually indestructible.

(c) Indispensability

The legal fee is indispensable in the sense that every other interest in land must eventually depend on it and descend from it.

A leaseholder may have a legal estate, a term of years absolute; but a legal leasehold is necessarily held in tenure of a lord. That lord may be the freeholder himself, the owner of the legal fee. Alternatively, a leaseholder may hold of a superior leaseholder, and he in turn may hold of a superior leaseholder, but ultimately, at the top of the leasehold ladder, there is bound to be a headlessee who holds of the freeholder, the owner of the legal fee.

Similarly, all equitable interests must ultimately depend on finding a legal owner who is compelled by Equity to hold his legal estate on trust to give effect to the equitable interests. That legal owner can only be the owner of the legal fee or the owner of a legal term of years, because those are the only two estates in land now recognised by the Law. And, if that legal owner is a leaseholder, then his rights in turn must depend, ultimately, on the legal fee. It follows that every equitable interest descends mediately or immediately from the legal fee.

(d) Exhaustiveness

The legal fee simple absolute is absolute ownership of the land in all but name, in the sense that nothing can exist after and beyond the fee simple absolute – apart from the safety net of the Crown's ultimate seigniorial rights. No *citizen* can enjoy a greater right in land than the legal fee simple absolute in possession.

Moreover, if the owner gives away his fee simple, whether at Law or in Equity, then he has nothing left. It is a general proposition that there can be no remainder after a fee simple.

(It might be mentioned in passing that to that proposition there is one exception: in Equity, there can be a remainder after a special kind of fee simple called a *base fee* which can arise when an entail is converted into a fee simple – see Chapter 9. There are also two minor qualifications which could be relevant either at Law or in Equity. The owner can sometimes give away his fee simple on the basis that in certain circumstances it will automatically return to him on a piece of legal elastic called a *possibility of reverter* – that is, the case of the *determinable* fee; or the owner can give away his fee simple on the basis that, in certain conditions, he can claim to repossess the land – that is, a *right of re-entry* which arises in connection with a *conditional* fee. Determinable and conditional fees are explained in Chapter 9.)

(11) EXAMPLES

It will have become apparent that the ownership of land in English law is as complicated as a game of chess. It is played on a standard board (tenure) with black and white chessmen (Law and Equity), some of which are pieces, and some, pawns (freehold and leasehold); different chessmen can make different types of move (estates), but, within those prescribed limits, the actual moves are variable in length and direction. Everything is structured; everything is ordered, and yet the whole is so flexible as to be capable of producing an almost infinite variety of patterns. To the outsider, it is baffling; to the insider, beauty.

Take the following as a comparatively simple example, of which a diagrammatic representation may be attempted. Adam is the legal estate owner in fee simple. On successive days in 1995: (1) Adam granted the land to Laura for life, remainder to Eric in tail; (2) Adam granted a 99 year lease to Terry; (3) Terry granted a seven-year sublease to Sam.

As far as the Law is concerned, the picture is this:

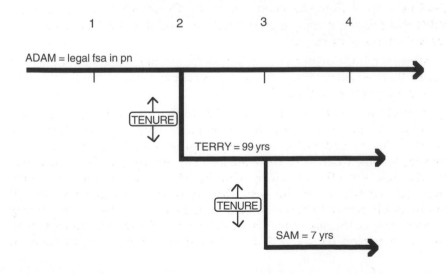

Note the following points. The events of Day 1 are of no significance at Law: the Law can see neither a life estate nor an entail. From Day 2, tenure exists between Adam and Terry (freeholder and headlessee). From Day 3, tenure exists between Terry and Sam (headlessee and underlessee). Tenure does *not*, however, exist between Adam and Sam (freeholder and underlessee). On Day 4, Sam owns one legal estate, a term of seven years absolute, and he is thereby entitled to physical possession of the land. On Day 4, Terry owns another legal estate, a term of 99 years absolute – subject, however, to Sam's seven year term. Terry is not entitled to physical possession while Sam's underlease subsists, but Terry is in legal possession by virtue of his right to a rent as landlord of that underlease. On Day 4 Adam still owns the legal fee simple absolute in possession – subject, however, to Terry's 99 year term. Adam is not entitled to physical possession while Terry's headlease subsists, but Adam is in legal possession by virtue of his right to a rent as landlord of that headlease.

The position in Equity on Day 1 is this:

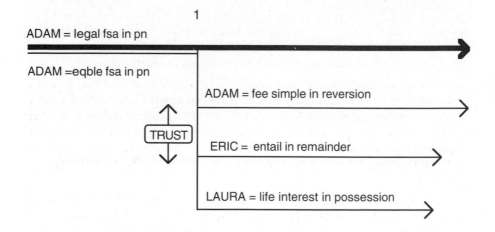

1

ADAM = legal fsa in pn

ADAM =eqble fsa in pn

ADAM = fee simple in reversion

TRUST

ERIC = entail in remainder

LAURA = life interest in possession

Note the following points. At the beginning of the sequence of events, Adam is the sole owner at Law. Equity has no cause to intervene. Therefore, 'Equity follows the Law', and Adam is sole *legal and beneficial* owner. Equity regards the events of Day 1 as a declaration of trust, and thereafter Adam, as legal owner, is compelled by Equity to treat the property as belonging to the equitable owners. There is no *tenure* involved. Equitable interests are held not in tenure, but under a trust. The first equitable owner is Laura, who is entitled to a life interest in possession. She is entitled, in Equity, either to take possession of the land or to take the income of the land for the rest of her life, depending on the circumstances. Eric has an entail, subject, however, to Laura's life interest. Note in particular that the entail is *already* vested in Eric. It is emphatically *not* the case that he will acquire the entail on Laura's death. True, he is not entitled to *possession* until Laura's death; but he *now owns* the entail (subject always to Laura's interest). Eric has an entail *in remainder* – in remainder subject to Laura's life interest. The equitable fee simple is still vested in Adam. He had the equitable fee simple to begin with. He has carved smaller estates (called 'particular estates') out of it, and with those estates he has granted away his right to *possession* in Equity, but he still *owns* the remainder of the rights contained in the equitable fee simple. He is ready to reclaim possession when Laura is dead and Eric is dead and all Eric's lineal heirs are dead. If Adam himself is dead, then his equitable fee simple will have devolved under his will or on his intestacy to some successor. Adam has the equitable fee simple absolute *in reversion* – in reversion expectant upon the demise of Laura and upon the determination of the entail.

(For the sake of completeness, it should be added that, in 1995, Adam's declaration of trust would have created a special kind of trust called a *strict settlement* under the Settled Land Act (SLA) 1925. Today, Adam's actions would instead create a *trust of land* under the Trusts of Land and Appointment of Trustees Act (ToLATA) 1996. The significance of that is explained in Chapter 12. For present purposes, the complication may be ignored.)

So, at the end of Day 1, Adam owns the legal fee simple absolute in possession, holding as trustee upon trust for the equitable owners. On Day 2, he grants a lease to Terry. The question then is whether Terry takes subject to the equitable interests arising under the trust or whether he takes free of them. Well, Terry is a purchaser of a legal estate – his term of 99 years. He is assumed to be *bona fide* in the absence of evidence to the contrary. The issue, therefore, is whether he had *notice* of the trust or not. If not, he takes his legal lease free of the equities; otherwise he takes subject to them. Assume Terry had no notice and takes free of the equities. The combined effect of Law and Equity may be demonstrated by superimposing the Law diagram (p 57) over the Equity diagram (p 58), thus:

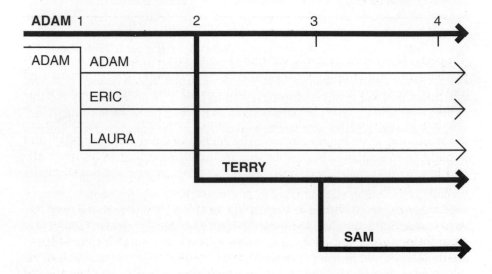

On Day 4, there are two claimants to possession, Sam at Law and Laura in Equity. Sam's right is stronger, because he claims through a BFP (Terry) and so he is not bound by the equities. So, Sam is entitled to physical possession. He is liable at Law to pay rent to his landlord, Terry. Terry is liable at Law to pay rent to his landlord, Adam. Adam receives his rent as owner of the legal fee, but in Equity he is bound by the trust. In Equity, therefore, he, as trustee, must pay over the rent income to the owner of the life interest in possession, Laura.

6 The Unregistered System

Property law today is built on foundations laid by a series of Acts of Parliament compendiously called 'the 1925 legislation'. Those Acts carried out a wholesale reform of the law, turning what was, in many ways, still a feudal system of land tenure into something more appropriate for a modern industrial society. On the other hand, the reform was effected more by evolution than by revolution. The legislators did not demolish and rebuild from scratch. They proceeded instead thoroughly to refurbish the old law, so that many parts are visibly the same as, and yet substantially different from, what went before.

One of the main aims was to simplify land law. The law of real property was excessively complex; the law of personal property was comparatively straightforward. The 1925 legislation therefore sought generally to assimilate the law of real property to that of personal property. The scheme of land law which resulted is hardly simple, but it is simpler than the old law.

Some attempt must now be made to draw together the various ideas and concepts discussed in earlier chapters and to sketch the outline and rationale of the modern system of land law as a whole. But the modern system is really two systems in one. The 1925 legislation attempted not only to bring the past up to date by instituting immediate reforms, it also sought to provide for the further simplification and modernisation of land law by providing for the extension of the scheme of *registered conveyancing*. This chapter will therefore look at the first stage, the modern system of *unregistered* landholding, produced in 1925 and still significant, but of diminishing importance – the 1925 System Part I, as it were. The next chapter will then go on to look at the further changes being brought about by the *registered* system which is now rapidly supplanting it – the 1925 System Part II.

The unregistered system is presented in the form of a table which is explained in the following text.

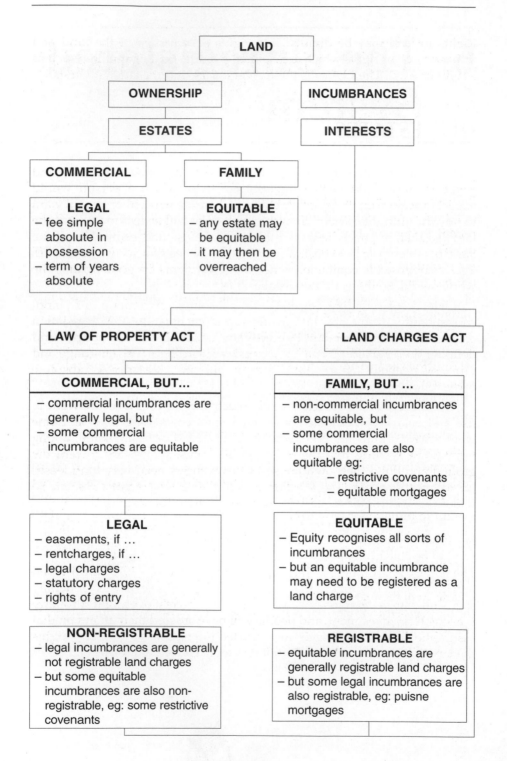

Rights to land may be divided into rights of *ownership* of the land and *incumbrances*, or rights which are claimed over the land of another (such as a right of way). The LPA calls the former *estates*; and the latter, *interests*.

(1)   ESTATES

Estates (ownership) may then be divided into *commercial* interests and *family* interests. Commercial interests are those which a person would expect to acquire on the property market. There are two: either he will want to buy the outright ownership of the land, or he will be looking to rent the land, so that, in effect, he pays merely for the use and enjoyment of the land. In either case, he expects a secure title. The need for security indicates *legal*, as opposed to equitable, ownership: legal rights are good against the whole world. So there are two legal estates.

Instead of creating directly an absolute ownership of land, corresponding to the absolute ownership of chattels, the 1925 legislation creates such an ownership indirectly by adapting the fee simple and defining the *fee simple absolute in possession* accordingly. The language and form of freehold tenure are retained, but the substance is absolute ownership – or very nearly.

The concept of a legal lease neatly meets the need for a secure right to use and enjoyment, but the commercial requirements are diverse. Some want to rent a home by the week. Some want a short term; some, a long term. Some want to rent the land and buildings; some want to rent the ground and build their own houses. Conveyancers need very long leases for technical reasons. The solution was to define *term of years absolute* so widely as to encompass every foreseeable commercial need.

All other rights of ownership were shunted into Equity. Property law has to serve social needs as well as commercial needs, and there is a family need to be able to create life interests or determinable interests or suchlike. The entail, too, fulfilled an important social function in 1925: it provided hereditary land to support an hereditary peerage. Moreover it is, generally speaking, inexpedient to abolish any property interest overnight. Property is a long term investment, and people will have ordered their affairs on that assumption. So the 1925 legislation tended to preserve all property rights then existing, but transmute them into a more convenient form.

The problem with these family (and other non-commercial) interests is that they tend to clutter the title and make it less marketable. The problem is solved by making them all *equitable*, so that they can exist only under a trust, and then by providing, broadly speaking, that the mechanism of *overreaching* shall operate in relation to any trust of land. Overreaching, it will be remembered, is a device for shifting equitable interests out of the land and into the purchase moneys. Provided he pays his money to at least two trustees (or a trust corporation), the purchaser takes a clean title to the land, free of any family interests; the family interests are preserved, but they are transferred into the purchase moneys instead. Overreaching is thus a means of reconciling family need (which prefers fair treatment to commercial efficiency) and commercial need (which demands an easily marketable title).

(The comment may be made in passing that overreaching occurs in other cases too: notably on a sale by a *mortgagee* (lender) in the event that the borrower defaults on his repayments, on a sale by a *personal representative* in the course of administering the estate of a deceased person, and on a sale by order of the *court*.)

(2) INTERESTS

It is less easy to explain the rationale of the 1925 legislation in relation to incumbrances. There are three relevant classifications: commercial or family; legal or equitable; non-registrable or registrable. The three classifications overlap to a considerable extent, but they do not coincide. The common ground across the three classifications is that most incumbrances which have a *commercial* use or value are *legal* rights. They are, therefore, of their very nature good against the whole world, irrespective of notice or registration – they are *non-registrable*.

Five classes of right conform to that thesis:

- *easements* (rights of way, etc) and *profits à prendre* (shooting rights, etc), *provided* they are of a commercial nature; that is to say, provided they are perpetual (equivalent to a fee simple absolute in possession) or for a fixed period (term of years absolute). Easements for life are equitable;

- *rentcharges*, subject to the same proviso, that they must be perpetual or for a fixed term. A rentcharge or fee farm rent, it will be recalled, is a periodic payment secured on land, and payable to someone other than a landlord;

- *legal charges* – the most common form of mortgage (see Chapter 14);
- miscellaneous *statutory charges* – the most common examples used to be land tax and tithe rentcharges, but both have been abolished;
- *rights of entry* attached to a legal lease or a legal rentcharge; that is to say, any right to *repossess* the land in the event that a leaseholder defaults on his obligations under a lease or in the event that a freeholder fails to pay his rentcharge.

Those five are commercial, legal and non-registrable. The other half of the common ground across the three classifications is that most incumbrances of a *family* or non-commercial nature are *equitable* and *registrable*. In principle, equitable incumbrances should bind the whole world except a BFP. But the doctrine of notice is unreliable and, therefore, commercially inefficient: it depends upon an *ex post facto* assessment of what a reasonable purchaser would or ought to have discovered – perhaps many years before. Therefore, once again, the 1925 legislation transmutes the old law into something more workable. The owner of a relevant incumbrance is expected to *register* it at the Land Charges Registry, and any purchaser is expected to search that register. As a general rule, if a registrable incumbrance was registered at the time of his purchase, then a purchaser is bound by it – whether he searched the register or not; whereas, if a registrable incumbrance is not registered, a purchaser for value takes free of it – even if he knew of its existence. Notice becomes registration. Instead of speculating about the assumed state of mind of the hypothetical reasonable purchaser, it is a simple matter to check the actual state of the register on any particular date.

The general thesis then has to be qualified. In the first place, there are some incumbrances which are commercial and legal but unexpectedly *registrable*. The prime example is a *puisne mortgage,* which is defined as a legal mortgage not protected by the deposit of title deeds. In effect, it means a second or subsequent mortgage. The perceived mischief is that, if he does not register them, the rights of a second mortgagee (lender) can easily be overlooked. He does not have the title deeds (the first mortgagee keeps them); he is not usually found in possession of the land; there is nothing to indicate to the world at large that there is a second mortgage outstanding. Requiring him to register cures the practical difficulty – but it creates a doctrinal oddity: here is a *legal* right which is *not* good against the world unless it is registered.

Then there are some rights which are commercially valuable, but which are *equitable* only. Prominent among these is the *restrictive covenant*. A restrictive covenant, it will be recalled, is a promise given in a deed which limits the use of one piece of land for the benefit of another (for example, a promise by a neighbour not to use his land otherwise than as a private dwellinghouse). It is, in substance, the equivalent of an easement, but it is an equitable creature, it emerged comparatively late in conveyancing history, and it has always been classified separately from easements. Being a valuable commercial right, it might have been converted into a legal interest in 1925, but it was not. The suggestion was considered too revolutionary at the time (although the Law Commission has subsequently revived it). *Ergo*, the restrictive covenant, despite being commercially valuable, is equitable and (usually) registrable.

There are other commercially valuable rights which, for various reasons, remain equitable and registrable; for example, equitable mortgages, or proprietary rights arising under a contract for an interest in land.

A third complication is that there are some *equitable* incumbrances which, contrary to the general scheme of things, remain *unregistrable*. The implication is that the untidy doctrine of notice still applies in these circumstances. Two important instances are restrictive covenants which were imposed *before the end of 1925*, and restrictive covenants in *leases*. It would have been unrealistic to expect all the owners of existing freehold restrictive covenants to rush off to register their covenants at the start of 1926, so the scheme of registration was not made retrospective in that respect. Leases were excluded because registration would, in most cases, be a waste of time. The purchaser of a term or of a reversion expectant on a term invariably inspects the lease itself. He therefore sees the actual covenants, and registration would be superfluous in those circumstances. But there are some awkward cases which do not conform to that theory. Suppose the *lessor* covenants with the lessee to restrict the user of the *lessor's* adjacent land. That is a covenant in a lease and so not registrable. But a purchaser of the adjacent land would not routinely see the lease, and might even be unaware of its existence. He might well be a BFP, and there is little the lessee can do to protect his covenant in those circumstances.

Other examples of equitable, non-registrable rights may be found which tend to undermine the 1925 scheme. The scheme suggests that, subject to carefully limited exceptions, all equitable interests in land should be either overreachable or registrable. However, since 1925, the courts have sometimes discovered or invented new equitable interests which fall into neither category. Therefore, the doctrine of notice applies to them. That might be commercially inconvenient, but justice is sometimes inconvenient – and, in any event, the inconvenience is mostly minor.

(3)   LAND CHARGES

Those incumbrances which require registration are called *land charges*, and they are registered by sending notice in the prescribed form to the Land Charges Registry. The Land Charges Registry keeps various registers as well as the land charges register. For example, there is a register of pending actions and a register of writs and orders affecting land. These are routinely searched by intending mortgagees (lenders) or their solicitors in order to check that an intending borrower is not the subject of bankruptcy proceedings.

As for the land charges register itself, there are six classes of entry (A–F), and some of the classes are subdivided. Those most commonly encountered include:

- C(i)   –   puisne mortgage
- C(iii)   –   general equitable charge
- C(iv)   –   estate contract
- D(ii)   –   restrictive covenant
- D(iii)   –   equitable easement
- F   –   spouse's statutory rights of occupation of the matrimonial home.

Registration operates as notice to the world, so any purchaser is bound by a registered right whether he searches the register or not. Conversely, if a registrable right is *not* registered, a purchaser for value (or, in some cases, a purchaser for money or money's worth) takes free of the right even if he actually knew of it. There is no formal time limit for registration, but, given that registration replaces notice, the right needs, from a practical point of view, to be registered before a BFP comes along.

If the land is *registered land* (see Chapter 7), then the land charges scheme is inapplicable. It is a completely different regime. What, in unregistered conveyancing, is a registrable *land charge* will often become, in registered conveyancing, a *minor interest* which needs to be protected by some entry on the land register, but that is by no means universally true.

7 The Registered System

As explained at the beginning of the last chapter, the 1925 legislation provided for the extension of a system of *registered conveyancing*. The registered system, whilst primarily directed at the *mechanics* of holding and dealing with land, incidentally made some important changes in the enforceability, and thereby in the nature, of various rights. In particular, under the registered system, the question whether a right is legal or equitable is usually less important than the question whether it is on the register or off the register.

The concept was brilliant in its simplicity; you have a national register of titles, in which you record every title to land and its corresponding incumbrances; an intending purchaser then inspects the register and takes the title as registered. If a right is on the register, the purchaser takes subject to it; if a right is off the register, he takes free of it. In practice, things are not quite as simple as that. In the first place, some rights which are on the register may be overreachable. The purchaser may take free of those rights – despite the fact that they are *on* the register – by paying his money to at least two trustees or a trust corporation. In the second place, some rights which are *off* the register may nevertheless bind the purchaser. It was found necessary to compromise the fundamental principle of registration by creating a limited class of *overriding interests* – so called because they override the title as officially recorded – which bind the purchaser, despite the fact that they are not recorded on the register.

One of the main reasons why compromise was necessary is that the registered system exists, and was intended to exist, alongside the old, unregistered system. Conversion from the old system to the new was intended to be a gradual affair, so that it was, and still is, quite possible that some houses in a street are covered by the registered system but other houses in that same street are still covered by the old unregistered system. The registered system was therefore designed in such a way as to achieve results which are similar to the results which would have been achieved under the old unregistered system, whilst simplifying and improving the mechanisms for achieving those results.

The process of conversion has taken longer than expected. The registered system has been common in the London area ever since 1925, but it did not begin to become widespread in the provinces until the mid 1960s. It was made universal in 1990, in the sense that thereafter, it became compulsory to register an unregistered title to land anywhere in England or Wales upon the occasion of the next sale. Then, in 1997, it was made compulsory to register an unregistered title not only on the occasion of the next sale, but also on the occasion of the next gift or mortgage. To be more precise, after 1997, the obligation to register an unregistered title arises upon completion of a relevant transfer of the legal fee simple absolute in possession, or upon the grant of a lease for more than 21 years, or upon completion of a relevant transfer of a leasehold when the lease still has more than 21 years to run, or upon the completion of a first legal mortgage of the fee simple or of a lease with more than 21 years to run.

In consequence, the registered system is now the norm. It is estimated that well over 80% of all titles have now been registered. But it follows that, even today, a significant amount of land is still held, and may for one last time be dealt with, under the old, unregistered system.

(1)   CONCEPTS

The system of registered conveyancing is based on the following concepts.

(a)   Registration of title

The registered system is based on the Land Registration Act (LRA) 1925. For that reason, the system is commonly referred to as registered *land*, but that might mislead. What is registered is not the *land* itself, but the various *titles* to the land. The point may be simply illustrated. Suppose there are three people interested in the same piece of land: a freeholder, a headlessee and an underlessee. To talk of 'registered land' might imply that, if any title to the land is registered, then all titles to that land must be registered. But that is not so. The conditional obligation to register applies to each title independently. Each title is the subject of a separate registration. Each estate owner gets a separate title number and a separate title certificate. If the headlease has changed hands recently, then the headleasehold title will probably be registered. If the freehold has not changed hands for many years, then it may still be unregistered. It can easily happen, therefore, that one title to a piece of land is registered whilst another title to the same piece of land remains unregistered for the time being.

(b)   The mirror principle

The land register provides an accurate and authoritative statement of the title. It reflects the information which would, under the old system, have been discovered from an examination of the title deeds.

It is commonly said that the land register 'reflects the title', but that can be misleading. The register reflects the *documentary* title only. There are many rights and obligations which never appeared in the title deeds under the old system and which are not, therefore, transcribed onto the register under the modern system. For examples, see *overriding interests*, below, p 78.

Some critics seize on the point that the land register does not reflect the totality of the title, and complain that the mirror is cracked. But, as explained above, it was a deliberate policy of the 1925 legislators that the modern system and the old system should operate side by side. Therefore, it was desirable that, despite their different forms and procedures, the substance of the two systems should, as far as possible, be the same. The title certificate in the registered system merely replaces the title deeds in the old unregistered system.

If the legislators had been able to begin with a completely clean sheet, they might have done things differently. Even then, the concept of an absolutely comprehensive register is probably unattainable. It is impossible to register some rights (for example, squatter's rights). It is impracticable to register others (for example, local land charges – see Chapter 8 – and short tenancies). And the corollary of insisting that all rights must be registered is that failure to register defeats the right. That is all very well for the commercially astute, but what of the deserving but blissfully ignorant?

(c)   Statutory magic

The estate owner owns the title as *registered*. The Land Registry has power to rectify the register, but it may not normally rectify so as to prejudice a registered proprietor in possession, in the absence of fraud, culpable negligence or some other special factor.

One consequence of the proposition that the estate owner owns the title as registered is that the Land Registry can cure defects of title. It is not uncommon – especially in unregistered conveyancing – to find a technical snag on the title; experience suggests that the title is actually a perfectly sound one, but there is some flaw in the documentary evidence of it – perhaps a missing signature, perhaps a long lost document. In registering a title, the Land Registry may, if they think the title offered is a good holding title, ignore any technical blemishes so that the title as registered is actually better than the title originally offered to the Land Registry.

Another consequence of the proposition is that a *registered* fee simple absolute is, in concept, even stronger than an *unregistered* fee simple absolute, for the registered proprietor may be deprived of his title only in accordance with the statutory scheme.

(d)   State guarantee

The title as registered is backed by a State guarantee. If a defect subsequently comes to light, the Land Registry must either rectify the register and compensate the registered proprietor for the degradation of his title, or else it must affirm the title as registered and compensate the adverse claimant.

(e)   Registered dealings

Once a title has been registered, then any subsequent disposition must be done through the Land Registry if it is to create a legal estate or interest. The registered proprietor is specifically empowered to transfer his title to the land or part of the land; he may grant out of it a lease, or an easement (perpetual or for a term of years), or a rentcharge (perpetual or for a term of years); he may also mortgage his title by creating a registered charge on it. Any such disposition must take place 'on the register' in the sense that the transferee does not acquire a legal estate or interest until the disposition is registered at the Land Registry. Pending registration, he acquires an equitable right only. The one exception is a short lease (21 years or less). Such leases are not registrable interests, and the lessee takes his legal estate at once.

The registered proprietor may also create any other right or interest in the land which he might have created had the land been unregistered. But these other dealings take place 'off the register', in the sense that their validity does not depend upon the intervention of the Land Registry. Any dealing off the register generates what the LRA calls a 'minor interest', which takes effect as an equitable interest and is vulnerable to a purchaser for value unless protected in some way, as explained below.

(2) GRADES OF TITLE

The land register reflects the *quality* of the title shown. There are four grades of title. The best is title absolute, which indicates that there are no significant defects at all.

The proprietor may be registered with title absolute whether he is the freeholder or a leaseholder, but to get an absolute *leasehold* title, the applicant must demonstrate not only that he has a good title to the term of years created by the lease, but also that the lease was validly granted in the first place. In other words, he has to prove the *freehold* title down to the granting of the lease in order to demonstrate that the grantor had power to grant it. If he cannot do that, then the leaseholder will be registered with the second grade of title: *good leasehold*. That means that, assuming that the lease was validly granted, then the proprietor's title is guaranteed; but the State guarantee does not cover the possibility that the lease was invalid. A good leasehold can be upgraded to title absolute if the validity of the lease is subsequently proved.

The third grade of title is a *qualified title*. This is accorded, as its name implies, where there is a significant doubt about or defect on the title. The title certificate will say something like: 'All estates rights and interests subsisting or capable of arising under the deed dated ... are excepted from the effect of this registration.' The qualification will be removed after a number of years if no adverse claims are in fact made.

The fourth grade of title is possessory title. That applies where the proprietor has an inadequate paper title or none at all. The Land Registry gives no guarantee against any rights prior to the registration but, as with a qualified title, a possessory title will be upgraded after a period of time if no adverse claimants in fact appear.

(3)   FORM OF TITLE

The authoritative version of the title is the one registered at the Land Registry. The Registry, however, issues a title certificate in respect of each registered title. Where there is no mortgage, the title certificate is called a Land Certificate and is issued to the registered proprietor. Where there is a mortgage, the Land Certificate is withdrawn and a Charge Certificate is issued to the mortgagee (lender) instead. A Charge Certificate is, in substance, the Land Certificate with a copy of the mortgage deed bound in. The title certificate is an authoritative statement of the title as it existed at the date of issue of the certificate, but there is always the possibility that the register has been amended since the date of issue.

In any event, up to date *office copies* of the title may be obtained at any time upon payment of the prescribed fee. ('Office copies' means official copies, made by the Land Registry and bearing the official stamp; photocopies made in a solicitor's own office are not authoritative.)

The title certificate itself contains copies of the *filed plan* and of the *register entries*. The filed plan is a plan of the registered land, based on a large scale Ordnance Survey map. The register entries consist of three sections. The first is the *property register*, which describes the land by reference to the filed plan, and states whether the land is held for a freehold or leasehold estate (and in the latter event it gives details of the lease). Secondly, the *proprietorship register* indicates the grade of the registered title (title absolute, good leasehold, or as the case may be) and gives the name and address of the registered proprietor. It also indicates any restrictions there may be upon the proprietor's powers of disposition. For example, if the registered proprietors are trustees, there is likely to be a restriction that no disposition is to be registered unless the capital money is paid to at least two trustees or a trust corporation. The third part of the register entries is the *charges register*, which lists the incumbrances to which the land is subject. Into this part of the register go details of any mortgages, leases, restrictive covenants and so forth.

(4) CLASSIFICATION OF INTERESTS

For Land Registry purposes, property rights are classified as one of four kinds.

(a) Registered interests

The LRA distinguishes between those interests which may be 'registered' and those interests which may be 'protected by an entry on the register'. The terminology is potentially confusing, but the distinction is fundamental. It is the difference between, on the one hand, an interest in respect of which a person may be registered as proprietor with *his own* title and title number, and, on the other, an interest which the owner needs to protect by an entry on somebody else's title. The former are usually referred to as 'registrable interests'; the latter are 'minor interests'.

Registrable interests, in that sense, are *legal* interests. The principal interests which may be registered interests are the two legal estates in land, namely:

- the legal fee simple absolute in possession;

- a term of years absolute, *provided* the lease has more than 21 years unexpired. (It is not worth the effort and expense of registering shorter leases.)

The other legal interests identified by the LPA are also registrable interests. A person may be separately registered as proprietor of a legal rentcharge. A person may be registered as proprietor of a legal easement, but, since an easement is part of ('appurtenant to') the land which it benefits, it follows that the title to an easement cannot be registered independently, but must be bundled with the title to the land which it benefits. Similarly, a legal right of entry is necessarily attached to the reversion on a legal lease or to a legal rentcharge, and so the title to a legal right of entry must be bundled with the title to the reversion or rentcharge to which it relates. A person may be registered as proprietor of a legal charge, but that, for reasons explained below, is a special case.

(b)   Minor interests

A *minor interest* is a complex notion. It is any interest which is neither a registered interest (see above, p 75) nor an overriding interest (see below, p 78).

Thus, minor interests comprise two main classes of right:

- beneficial interests under a trust;

- incumbrances, such as restrictive covenants and rights under an estate contract.

However, the point was made earlier that a scheme of registration of title necessarily involves the proposition that dealings with the title must be 'on the register' and recorded at the Land Registry. So, if a registered proprietor transfers the land to another, the transferee acquires the legal title, not at the moment of transfer, but at the moment when the transfer is perfected by registration at the Land Registry. It follows that, during the interval between transfer and registration, the transferee has only an equitable title. Thus, minor interests include a third kind of right:

- registrable interests which are not yet registered.

A minor interest, as such, is vulnerable and needs to be protected by some entry on the title to which it relates. A purchaser for value from the registered proprietor takes the title as registered. He takes free of any minor interest the existence of which is not indicated on the face of the register. The severity of that rule is tempered by the existence of a class of overriding interests (see below, p 78), but that does not detract from the principle that a minor interest, as such, needs to be protected by some entry against the title which it encumbers.

There are four ways of protecting a minor interest. Which is the appropriate method depends on the nature of the right and the circumstances in which it is asserted.

A *restriction* on the registered proprietors' powers of disposition may be entered on the proprietorship register when, for example, they are trustees of some sort. That has the effect of protecting the beneficial interests which arise under the trust. If there is no restriction, a transferee for value takes free of the equities as the equivalent of a BFP. If there is a restriction, the transferee cannot be a BFP, but, being warned of the equities, he can take steps to *overreach* them instead, by paying his money to at least two trustees, or as the case may be.

Other incumbrances may be protected by getting the Land Registry to put a *notice* in the charges register of the title. A notice is the appropriate way of protecting, for example, restrictive covenants, equitable charges, and short leases where the lessee is not in actual occupation. The entry of a notice is a 'friendly' act, in the sense that it requires the co-operation of the registered proprietor. He has to lodge his title certificate at the Land Registry before a notice can be entered.

By way of contrast, entering a *caution* is a 'hostile' or unilateral act. A caution may be entered by someone who has a legitimate claim to the land which he fears may be cheated by a disposition made by the registered proprietor. For example, the lender on an informal mortgage might enter a caution to prevent the registered proprietor from dealing with the land without first repaying his loan, or a purchaser who has contracted to buy the land might enter a caution to prevent himself from being 'gazumped', or one spouse might enter a caution to prevent the other from secretly selling the matrimonial home. A caution is entered on the proprietorship register and entitles the cautioner to be given due warning of an impending disposition, so that he can take appropriate steps to assert his claim.

The final method of protecting a minor interest is by *inhibition*. An inhibition puts a total freeze on the title, temporarily preventing any dealings at all. It is used mainly to protect creditors in the event of bankruptcy or fraud.

(c) Registered charges

A registered charge is the name given to a mortgage of registered land. As explained in Chapter 14, in English law a legal mortgage, depending on the form it takes, either gives the lender a 3,000 year lease, or else entitles him to the same rights as a 3,000 year lessee. In terms of Land Registry classification, therefore, a mortgage is something of a hybrid, midway between registrable interests and minor interests. To the extent that it is equivalent to a 3,000 year lease, it is a registrable interest. To the extent that it is, in truth, an incumbrance on the borrower's title and is not intended to be an independent title in its own right, it is akin to a minor interest.

A registered charge is therefore treated differently from other rights. It is incapable of *independent* registration, but it is capable of a sort of parasitic registration. The borrower's title certificate is withdrawn, and a title certificate (Charge Certificate) is issued to the lender instead. But the Charge Certificate is a certificate that the *borrower* is the registered proprietor of the land and it gives particulars of the *borrower's* title to the land (including the mortgage on it) and it carries the *borrower's* title number. It then further certifies that the lender is the proprietor of the registered charge on the land.

In this way, the process of mortgaging registered land is made to correspond as far as possible to the process of mortgaging unregistered land. In unregistered conveyancing, the lender retains the title deeds until the loan is repaid. In registered conveyancing, there are no title deeds as such, but the issue of a Charge Certificate to the lender serves a similar function.

(d)   Overriding interests

The LRA appears to destroy the integrity of the very concept of registered land by enacting that there shall be a class of interests in land which shall remain effective and binding notwithstanding that they do not appear on the register. They override the registered title. The result may be represented diagrammatically as follows.

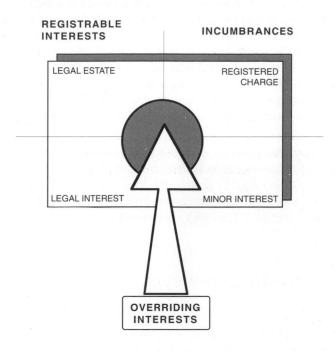

REGISTRABLE INTERESTS

INCUMBRANCES

LEGAL ESTATE

REGISTERED CHARGE

LEGAL INTEREST

MINOR INTEREST

OVERRIDING INTERESTS

The reason for the existence of this class of *overriding interests* has been explained above: the Land Certificate in registered conveyancing is supposed to reflect the title deeds in unregistered conveyancing. There are rights which are not revealed by examination of the title deeds; the same kinds of right are exempt from the need to be registered or protected by entry on the register.

Some of the more important examples of overriding interest are these:

- legal easements (although it has been held that even an equitable easement may override if it is openly used and enjoyed at the relevant time);

- squatter's rights;

- the rights (*in the land*) of any person in actual occupation of the land;

- local land charges (see Chapter 8);

- leases not exceeding 21 years.

Note especially that occupation may protect a person's rights. If the land is occupied, a purchaser is expected to inquire of any occupier whether the occupier claims any interest in the property. Should he fail to do so, then the purchaser takes subject to any such rights – not only (and not necessarily) any rights of occupation, but any proprietary rights vested in the occupier, including, for example, an option to purchase the land in question.

In practice, an overriding interest often finds its way onto the register, either as a registered interest or as a minor interest. Any right which does so thereupon ceases to be an overriding interest. It becomes part of the registered title, instead of overriding the registered title.

8 Conveyancing

Land law is the theory; conveyancing is the practice. For most people, the theory becomes far more intelligible when it is put into practice. Below is a brief, and very simplified, account of a typical house purchase transaction – first under the old, unregistered system of conveyancing, then under the modern, registered system. It is no substitute for real practical experience, but it may assist the imagination of those who lack that advantage. The information is presented in tabular form, followed by an explanation.

A house purchase proceeds in two stages: a *contract*, by which the parties formally bind themselves to buy and sell; and *completion*, when the vendor formally transfers his title to the purchaser in fulfilment of the contract. It will be seen that, superficially, there is a close resemblance between a registered transaction and an unregistered transaction. That is only to be expected. The policy of the LRA was to keep differences between the two systems to a minimum But a registered transaction involves far less effort. There are also important differences in the final (pre-completion) searches made by the purchaser's solicitor and in his post-completion activity.

At the end of 1999, proposals were made which would have the effect of shortening the pre-contract stage of the transaction (when the purchaser is vulnerable to 'gazumping'). In particular, it was suggested that a *vendor* be obliged to make a local search and obtain a surveyor's report *before* putting his property on the market. These documents would then be immediately available to a prospective purchaser.

In any event, further changes in practice are imminent as the profession moves towards a system of *computerised* conveyancing.

	CONTRACT		COMPLETION

UNREGISTERED

Vendor:	**Vendor:**	**Vendor:**
– obtain deeds	– deduce title	– hand over deeds
– draw contract	– reply to requisitions	– pay off mortgage
		– account

Purchaser:	**Purchaser:**	**Purchaser:**
– local search	– raise requisitions – Land Charges	– pay moneys
– prelim enquiries	search	– [complete mortgage]
– check finance	– draw conveyance	
		– stamp documents
	– [prepare mortgage]	– register title

REGISTERED

Vendor:	**Vendor:**	**Vendor:**
– office copies	– reply to requisitions	– hand over deeds
– draw contract		– pay off mortgage
		– account

Purchaser:	**Purchaser:**	**Purchaser:**
– local search	– raise requisitions – Land Registry	– pay moneys
– prelim enquiries	search	– [complete mortgage]
– check finance	– draw transfer	
		– stamp documents
	– [prepare mortgage]	– register dealing

(1)   UNREGISTERED CONVEYANCING

(a)   Pre-contract

A contract for the sale of land has to be made by signed writing, so neither side is committed until there is an exchange of contracts. The contract is prepared in duplicate. Each side signs one copy, and, when both are ready, they physically exchange parts.

The vendor's solicitor begins the process by obtaining the title deeds. If the property is in mortgage, he probably borrows them from his client's bank or building society against his own undertaking (his personal promise as a professional lawyer) to pay off the mortgage out of the proceeds of sale. He peruses the deeds to determine what exactly his client has to sell, and draws the contract accordingly. He probably uses a standard form contract or otherwise incorporates a set of standard clauses ('general conditions') tailoring them to the needs of the particular transaction ('special conditions'). He sends the contract to the purchaser's solicitor for approval.

The general principle is *caveat emptor* (let the buyer beware), and so the purchaser's solicitor will try to discover whether there are any skeletons in the vendor's cupboard before he commits his client. First, he will make a *local search*. The local authority (district council or London borough) maintains a *register of local land charges*, containing details of various incumbrances affecting properties in its district. They are mostly public charges: items like charges for street works or sewers, the conditions attached to planning permissions, smoke control zones, tree preservation orders, compulsory purchase orders. The purchaser needs to check the local land charges register. He does that by sending the prescribed form to the local authority and paying a fee. At the same time, he sends another standard form containing additional inquiries, hoping to elicit any further information the local authority may have about the property: Are the roads adopted? Is the property connected to a public sewer? Does the council know of any other actual or potential events which may adversely affect the purchaser? The expression 'local search' implies both the official search and the additional inquiries.

Some councils can take weeks to reply and, in order to save time, it may happen that the *vendor's* solicitor will make a local search even before a purchaser is found, so that the result of the search is available to be sent out with the draft contract.

The second step which the purchaser's solicitor will take is to obtain from the vendor's solicitor replies to certain *preliminary enquiries*. The vendor is not under a general duty to disclose any information to the purchaser unasked, but the purchaser's solicitor will invariably seek at least the answers to a standard set of questions: Are there any boundary disputes? Has the vendor duly observed any restrictions affecting the property? What fixtures and fittings will be left in the property, and what taken? And so on. These days, in order to save time, the vendor's solicitor often sends out with the draft contract his replies to the standard form enquiries – without waiting to be asked.

The third thing a purchaser's solicitor will do is to ensure that his client has sufficient financial resources to see the purchase through. That usually means waiting for a formal, written offer of a mortgage loan by a bank or building society.

Assuming he is satisfied on all three scores, the purchaser's solicitor is ready to proceed – or almost. The bugbear of conveyancing is the chain transaction. When people move house, they generally expect to use the sale price from the old house to finance the purchase of the new. Therefore, the typical buyer is unwilling to exchange contracts to buy on the one hand unless and until he is ready to exchange contracts to sell on the other; by the same token, the typical seller is unwilling to exchange contracts to sell on the one hand unless and until he is ready to exchange contracts to buy on the other. This phenomenon is called 'tie in', and results in a, sometimes lengthy, chain of transactions. At one end is a first time buyer or someone who is not dependent on a sale. At the other is someone who is not waiting to buy another house. In between, everybody is waiting for those above or below them in the ladder. Eventually, when all are ready, all exchange – all (usually) on the same day.

At that point, the contract becomes binding. It is customary for the purchaser to pay over a deposit of 10% of the purchase price upon exchange of contracts.

(b)   Post-contract

Contracts exchanged, the vendor's solicitor deduces title. The contract has stipulated the nature of the title on offer, and it is for the vendor now to prove that he can convey a good title to the land. In days gone by, title was deduced by sending an Abstract of Title – a typewritten summary of the essence of the title deeds, set out in a traditional pattern. Today, the vendor probably sends photocopies of the relevant deeds (perhaps listed in an Epitome of Title). The purchaser's solicitor examines the title and *raises requisitions* – he sends a list of any objections he may have to the title offered, perhaps asking the vendor's solicitor for evidence of this event, or seeking further information about that. He also draws the draft conveyance and sends it to the vendor's solicitor for approval.

Meanwhile, if the purchaser is borrowing some of the purchase price, work will be proceeding on drawing up the mortgage deed, formally reporting to the lender that the title is a good and marketable one, and requisitioning the money in time for completion. Many banks and building societies instruct the purchaser's solicitor to act for them too, so as to save costs, but some lenders insist on instructing their own lawyers.

Shortly before the day fixed for completion, the purchaser's solicitor will send a search form to the Land Charges Registry designed to check that there are no unexpected land charges registered in respect of the property. The purchaser will take the legal title on completion, and so the issue whether he is a BFP (remembering that notice, in this context, means registration) is to be judged as at the date of completion.

If the purchaser is borrowing some of the purchase price, a search will also be made at the Land Charges Registry against his name to check that no bankruptcy proceedings have been commenced against him.

The reply from the Land Charges Registry is in the form of an official certificate which gives details of any relevant entries. It carries a priority period of up to 15 working days. That means that the purchaser is not affected by anything registered between the date of search and the date of completion, provided he completes within (approximately) three calendar weeks of the date of the search.

If all is in order, completion takes place. The purchaser's solicitor pays over the purchase moneys (usually 'down the wire' by electronic transfer of funds from his bank to the vendor's solicitor's bank), collects the deeds (probably by post) and completes the mortgage, if any. The purchaser is now the legal owner of the house, and may move in.

(c)   Post-completion

After completion, the vendor's solicitor has only to tidy up the loose ends. He must redeem the vendor's mortgage out of the proceeds of sale if he gave an undertaking to that effect. In any event, he reports completion and settles his account with the vendor.

The purchaser's solicitor, on the other hand, still has much work to do. He must have the conveyance duly stamped and pay any stamp duty levied on it. Then he must convert the title from unregistered to registered by sending in the appropriate application form to the Land Registry. The application should be submitted within two months of completion.

(2)   REGISTERED CONVEYANCING

(a)   Pre-contract

The comparative simplicity of registered conveyancing becomes apparent at the very beginning of the conveyancing process. The vendor's solicitor finds it much easier to draw the draft contract. He will doubtless requisition the Land or Charge Certificate from the vendor or his mortgagee, as he would requisition the title deeds for unregistered land, but he also applies to the Land Registry for *office copy entries* of the vendor's title. These give him a clear and authoritative report on the current state of the title; he does not have to ferret through several deeds to find out. The actual drafting of the contract is easier too. The vendor's solicitor simply describes the property by reference to the office copies, and sends the office copies out with the contract.

For the purchaser's solicitor, the pre-contract stage is not very different. He still obtains his local search; he still makes his preliminary inquiries of the vendor, and he still awaits a mortgage offer. And the problem of tying in sale or purchase or both may still arise.

(b)   Post-contract

After contract, the vendor's solicitor theoretically deduces title to the purchaser's solicitor, but it is an empty obligation: the title consists of the office copy entries, and they were supplied with the contract. The purchaser's solicitor raises his requisitions, but they are of a formal nature. There cannot be anything of great moment, for the title is guaranteed by the State. Moreover, the purchaser's solicitor saw the title before contract, and if there had been anything untoward he would have delayed exchange of contracts until he was satisfied.

Drawing the transfer document is scarcely an onerous task. It is just a question of taking the appropriate Land Registry form and filling in the blanks. Mortgage arrangements (if any) do not differ very much from unregistered to registered conveyancing – save that the examination of title on behalf of the lender is simplified.

The final searches, however, are different. The purchaser's solicitor sends his search to the Land Registry. The application states the date of issue of the office copies supplied by the vendor's solicitor and asks whether there has been any entry on the register since that date. Armed with the office copies and an official certificate setting out the result of his search, the purchaser's solicitor knows exactly what is the current state of the title. The official search carries a priority period of 30 working days. But – and this is the major difference – the purchaser needs not only to complete his purchase within the 30 days, he also needs within those 30 days to lodge at the Land Registry *an application to register* his purchase. The reason is that, whereas in the case of unregistered conveyancing the purchaser acquires the legal title on completion of the deed of conveyance, nevertheless in registered conveyancing he does not acquire the legal title until his name is entered on the land register. His registration as the new proprietor will be backdated to the date upon which his application was received at the Land Registry, but until he lodges his application, his interest in the registered land ranks only as a minor interest and is, therefore, vulnerable.

If the purchaser is borrowing money, a search will be made against his name at the Land Charges Registry to check for possible bankruptcy, but there is no point in doing a bankruptcy search against the vendor there. The purchaser of registered land takes the title *as registered*, and if there is no inhibition or other relevant entry at the Land Registry, then that is an end of the matter.

Otherwise, completion will follow the same procedure as in an unregistered transaction.

(c)   Post-completion

After completion, the vendor's solicitor tidies up the loose ends, as in the case of an unregistered transaction, and the purchaser's solicitor also has the same sort of chores to perform. There are, however, two significant differences for him. First, an application to register dealings is more straightforward than an application for first registration. Second, he must be sure to get his application to the Land Registry before the expiry of the priority period of his search.

9 Freeholds

It is now necessary to say a little more about the estates of freehold. It will be recalled (see Chapter 5) that only one freehold estate can now exist at Law, namely the *fee simple absolute in possession*. Equity still recognises all three freehold estates, the fee simple, the entail and the life estate. These three are commonly referred to as equitable estates, but it is strictly more accurate to describe them as equitable interests, arising as they do under a trust.

It is proposed first to say something about the *absolute* or ordinary form of the three estates; then to consider *modified* or non-absolute estates; then to consider *future interests*, or estates which are not in possession.

(1)   NATURE OF THE THREE ESTATES

The essential nature of the three estates was explained in Chapter 5:

*   the *legal fee simple* absolute in possession is a virtually perpetual estate and is in practice equivalent to absolute ownership;
*   the *equitable fee simple* is the equivalent interest held under a trust; it is, in the eyes of Equity, the absolute or ultimate interest, but it may be temporarily subject to one or more particular estates;
*   the *entail* is an interest under a trust which is inheritable (in the strict sense) by the lineal heirs of the original grantee;
*   a *life interest* is an interest under a trust which lasts for the lifetime of the grantee or for the lifetime of another (*pur autre vie*).

(2)   CREATING AND CONVEYING THE ESTATES

(a)   Words of limitation

The different estates and interests may be created or conveyed by using appropriate words to describe and define what is intended. The technical expression for such words is 'words of limitation', and the contrast is between *words of limitation* on the one hand, and *words of purchase* on the other. Words of limitation are words of *definition*; words of purchase are words of *gift*.

So, for example, if there is a grant of land 'to Adam in fee simple', then, obviously, 'to Adam' are words of purchase, identifying the taker of the interest, and 'in fee simple' are words of limitation, defining what it is that he is given. Less obvious, but equally definite, is the case of a grant 'to Adam and his heirs'. It has been settled since medieval times that the words 'and his heirs' are always to be construed as words of limitation. 'To Adam' are words of purchase, identifying Adam as the taker; 'and his heirs' are words of limitation, defining the nature of the interest Adam takes – in this case, the fee simple, for reasons explained below. Other cases are less clear. In a grant 'to Adam and his children forever', the words 'to Adam' are clearly words of purchase, and the words 'forever' are clearly words of limitation importing a fee simple. But 'and his children' could be either. The grantor might intend that Adam and his children take the fee simple *jointly* (using 'and his children' as words of purchase), or he might have been using 'children' in a loose sense as meaning 'future generations' so that 'and his children forever' are words of limitation indicating that Adam is to have the fee simple *exclusively*. It is a question of construing objectively the words used in the context in which they are used.

When the words of limitation have been segregated, they are to be interpreted according to the following principles.

First, the law now leans in favour of generosity. If a grantor conveys land, or if a testator devises land, without any words of limitation at all, then the inference is that he gives away the largest estate he can, and that usually means the fee simple. The inference is displaced if the document discloses a contrary intention.

(b)   Fee simple

It follows, therefore, that, in order to transfer a fee simple, it is not strictly *necessary* to use any words of limitation, and, indeed, on the transfer of a *registered* freehold, none are used. The relevant form says simply that the transferor transfers to the transferee 'the land comprised in the title above mentioned' – but the title itself will identify the land as freehold (fee simple) or leasehold (term of years) so that there is no ambiguity.

In the case of an *unregistered* freehold, again it is not strictly *necessary* to use words of limitation, but they are desirable if only to make the intention plain and unambiguous. Any expression may be used which implies perpetual ownership ('forever', 'absolutely' and so on), but there are three traditional phrases which leave no room for doubt:

- to Adam *in fee simple* is the expression almost invariably used today;
- to Adam *and his heirs* used to be the standard expression in days when the fee simple was an estate inheritable by the heirs general; it is still effective today to convey the fee simple, but it should be shunned as an anachronism;
- to the Archbishop of Canterbury *and his successors* is the correct expression to use in the case of a *corporation sole*, a concept which needs brief explanation.

A corporation is an artificial person, a legal entity separate and distinct from the human beings it represents. A corporation may exist at common law (for example, the Crown), be created by charter under the Crown prerogative (for example, the University of Birmingham), or be created by or under statute (for example, limited companies under the Companies Acts). A corporation which represents several human beings, such as the ordinary limited company, is called a *corporation aggregate*. A corporation which represents just one human being, such as a bishopric, is called a *corporation sole*.

A grant of freehold land to a *corporation aggregate* cannot but be in fee simple. It is not alive, and so cannot take a life interest (save, to be pedantic, *pur autre vie*). It has no heirs, and so could never take an entail. The choice is fee simple or lease. In principle, the same is true of a *corporation sole*; but there is a potential ambiguity in this case. Take a grant 'to the Archbishop of Canterbury, George Carey'. Does that give a fee simple to the See of Canterbury, or to His Grace in his personal capacity? The correct words of limitation to ensure that a gift goes to the office and not the man are 'to the Archbishop of Canterbury *and his successors*'.

(c)   Entail

No entail may be created after 1996. Any attempt to create an entail today takes effect as a declaration of trust for the grantee *in fee simple*. But entails created before 1997 may continue to exist, and it is necessary to be able to recognise an entail in the event that you encounter one.

In order to create an entail, it was vital to use words of limitation – and special words at that. One of two formulae had to be used. Nothing else would do. Other wording might create a fee simple or a life estate, but not an entail. The two magic formulae were:

- *in tail*; and

- the word *heirs*, followed by *words of procreation*.

The first formula needs no explanation, except to say that words could be added to make it a restricted entail: in tail male, in tail female.

As for the second formula, the word *heirs* was indispensable. 'Words of procreation' are words which indicate that the grant was limited to the *lineal* heirs of the grantee. '*Of his body*' was the usual expression, but any suitable words of procreation might be used. Thus these are entails: 'to Adam and the heirs by him begotten', 'to Beth and the heirs female by her born', 'to Colin and the heirs of his body to him born by Dilys'. But 'to Frank and the issue of his body' did not create an entail (because *heirs* was not used), and created a fee simple instead.

(d)   Life interest

In order to create a life interest *some* words of limitation must be used, otherwise the gift will be assumed to be in fee simple; but no *special* words of limitation are necessary as long as the meaning is plain: 'to Adam for life,' 'to Beth as long as she may live.'

(3)   POWERS OF THE ESTATE OWNER

The powers of the owner of the *legal* fee simple absolute in possession are the powers of an absolute owner. He effectively owns the land (as defined – see Chapter 3), with full powers of use, enjoyment and disposition.

His rights are, however, 'absolute' only within the constraints imposed by the law and by society. He may own subject to *incumbrances*, and be bound to acknowledge the rights of the incumbrancer. He is subject to the law of tort, and if he uses his land in an unreasonable way, he may incur liability in *nuisance*. If he wishes to carry out any substantial building or engineering works on his land, or if he wishes materially to alter the use to which it is currently put, then he will probably need *planning permission* from the local authority.

If he holds his legal estate as *trustee*, then he is of course further constrained by Equity to manage the property in the best interests of all the beneficiaries.

The rights of the owner of an equitable estate are principally the rights of any beneficiary under a trust: the right to have the property properly managed by the trustee, to restrain proposed mismanagement by seeking an injunction, and to remedy actual management by suing for compensation for breach of trust. The position may be complicated by the fact that a trustee may also be a beneficiary.

As for the rights and liabilities of the beneficiaries *inter se*, they are adjusted according to the rules which used to be applicable to the old common law estates. In particular, the owner in fee (whether simple or entailed) is the ultimate owner of the capital interest; the owner of a mere freehold (life interest) is entitled to the use or income interest only. The tenant for life therefore has the right temporarily to occupy the land, but, given the nature of his interest, it follows that he must enjoy the land without diminishing it in any way. He should leave the remainderman's land more or less as he found it. That in turn means that he is under some liability to the remainderman to maintain the property and repair any damage caused. The liability for repairs is expressed in this context as the doctrine of *waste*.

(4) WASTE

If there is a life interest, then there must be a trust. If there is a trust, then there must be trustees. It is the trustees who are primarily responsible for managing the property and for actually carrying out any repairs which may be necessary, but they may lawfully delegate those functions to a tenant for life in possession. However, although any repairs will actually be carried out by or on behalf of the trustees, the question remains: who should bear the *cost* for those repairs? The doctrine of waste determines whether liability should fall on the tenant for life (so that the repairs are paid for out of the income of the land) or on the remainderman (so that they are paid for out of capital).

The tenant for life is liable for waste; the owner of the fee is not. Note especially that a tenant in tail is *not* liable for waste; for he owns a fee (albeit now only in Equity). His fee tail is less than a fee simple only in that his powers of alienation are limited; in all other respects, his status is equivalent to that of the fee simple owner. Depending on the terms of the settlement, the tenant for life may be liable either for positively wasting the property, or for negatively allowing it to go to waste, or both.

There are four categories of waste:

* Permissive waste

  This is passively allowing the property to deteriorate – fair wear and tear. The tenant for life is *not* liable for permissive waste unless the settlement expressly imposes the duty upon him (which would be unusual).

* Voluntary waste

  This is positively damaging the property. A tenant for life *is* liable for voluntary waste, unless the settlement excuses him (as it frequently does). A tenant who is thus excused is said to be *unimpeachable of waste*.

* Ameliorating waste

  This apparent contradiction in terms means *improvements*. If the tenant for life carries out improvements, then he deliberately alters the property and so, technically speaking, he commits an act of voluntary waste. Unless he is made unimpeachable by the settlement, he is theoretically liable to the remainderman for 'damaging' the property. However, since the improvement increases the value of the remainderman's interest, the court will not look favourably on a claim for waste in these circumstances.

- Equitable waste

  This is an act of wanton destruction. Where the settlement makes the tenant for life unimpeachable of waste, Equity is reluctant to construe the exemption clause so widely as to excuse sheer vandalism. Unless, therefore, the clause plainly does excuse such conduct, Equity will hold the tenant liable for it, the exemption clause notwithstanding.

(5) BARRING THE ENTAIL

The entail *as such* is inalienable – but, if he so wishes, the entail owner can always convey away a fee simple! He can even convey a fee simple to himself.

The story of the entail is quaint, not to say absurd. It is of little relevance today, except to explain why the entail is now apparently a prison with open doors. Briefly, the fee tail was created by statute at the behest of landowners who wanted to ensure that their land stayed in the family. The entail achieved that end, because a tenant in tail could not effectively dispose of the land for an interest greater than his own life. On his death, the next lineal heir could always reclaim the land. The common law judges, however, preferred to promote free market policies. They were therefore hostile to the entail – so hostile that they were prepared to countenance collusion in order to free the land from the fetters of the entail. They allowed two common law actions to be adapted as a means of converting a fee tail into a fee simple. One of the actions was called *levying a fine*; the other, *suffering a recovery*. The details are now unimportant, because the common law has now been superseded by statute, but it may be noted in passing that the judges' hostility to the entail was taken to absurd lengths. For instance, the action for a recovery was based on the fiction that the land belonged to the court usher! Everybody concerned in the case knew that it was untrue; everybody concerned was prepared to pretend that it was true in order to destroy the entail. The common law has, however, now been supplanted by the Fines and Recoveries Act 1833. It achieves the same results as the common law, but by a direct route instead of hiding behind fictions. The Act remains relevant and operative, despite the fact that entails have now been transported into Equity, and despite the fact that no more entails can be created after 1996.

By virtue of the Fines and Recoveries Act 1833, the tenant in tail may deal with the land as if it were not entailed. He may create a fee simple or any lesser interest by executing a *disentailing assurance*, that is, a deed which defeats the entail. The act of disentailing is called *barring the entail*, because it bars the claims of those who would have succeeded to the land, had there been no disentailment. The deed simply says that the tenant in tail thereby conveys the fee simple (or whatever other estate is desired) to himself or to some other person. The tenant in tail can even (since the LPA) disentail posthumously, by his will – despite the fact that, strictly, the rights of the heir arise at the moment of death and the will does not operate until the moment after death.

There is still some detailed learning about the *effects* of a disentailment in different sets of circumstances. Entails are so rarely encountered that it is hardly worth mentioning the rules, but, for those who are interested, they are summarised below.

There is a further complication in that, where an entail does exist, it almost invariably exists under a special kind of trust called a *strict settlement* under the SLA. The details are explained in Chapter 12, but, for present purposes, the important point is that in a strict settlement the *legal* title to the land is vested in the *tenant for life or other person entitled in possession* under the trust. The tenant for life (or other person) therefore wears two hats. He holds the legal estate as trustee upon the trusts declared in the settlement; he is also a beneficiary with an equitable interest under the trust.

That said, the rules for barring the entail work as follows. Suppose, for the sake of simplicity, that in every case the tenant disentails in favour of himself.

The first and easiest case is where there is a tenant in tail *in possession*. Land is held for Eric in tail, remainder to Fiona in fee simple. Under the SLA, the legal estate will be vested in Eric upon trust to give effect to the settlement. Eric disentails. That destroys the claims of his heirs and produces a *fee simple absolute*. Because the fee simple is the ultimate estate in the land, there is nothing beyond it. Therefore, the disentailment also destroys Fiona's fee simple. So, Eric is now sole legal owner and sole equitable owner. Therefore, the trust has come to an end and the land is Eric's, legally and beneficially:

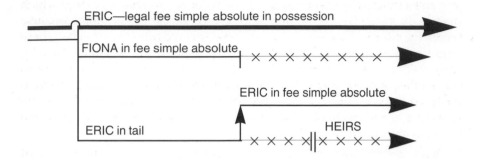

The second case is where an interest or interests exist prior to the entail, so that the entail is *in remainder*: to Laura for life, remainder to Eric in tail, remainder to Fiona in fee simple. In this situation, the owner of the first subsisting interest under the settlement (here, Laura) is called the *protector of the settlement*. The owner of the entail can still procure a fee simple absolute, but:

- the protector of the settlement must consent by deed to the disentailment;

- the fee simple produced by the disentailment destroys the entail and all subsequent interests, but it leaves untouched any prior interests (here, Laura's own life estate); and consequently

- the settlement does not come to an end.

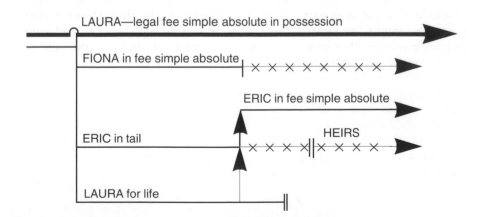

The third case is the case where a tenant in tail in remainder purports to disentail *without the consent* of the protector of the settlement. Here, the tenant in tail cannot create a fee simple *absolute*, but he can still bar the entail and create a kind of fee simple, called a *base fee*. A base fee is a fee simple *determinable* (see below, p 99) – *a fee simple which will last as long as the entail would have lasted*; that is, a fee simple which will subsist until the death of the last lineal heir of the original tenant in tail. Disentailing in these circumstances bars the claims of those claiming *under* the entail, but it leaves untouched the claims of those *subsequent* to the entail. If ever there comes a time when the entail would have ended then, at that point, Fiona or her successors can assert their claim to the land. This is the one exceptional case where a remainder can exist after a fee simple. (As in case 2, so in case 3, interests *prior* to the entail are unaffected by a disentailment.)

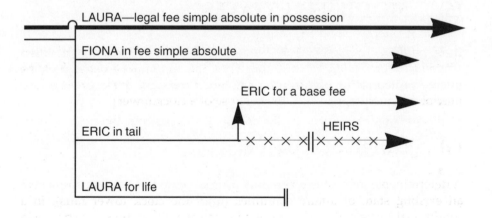

The base fee is as freely alienable (in Equity) as any other fee simple, subject always to the possibility that it will determine by virtue of the failure of the heirs of the original tenant in tail. The owner of the base fee may, however, *enlarge* it into a full fee simple absolute in various ways. Illogical though it is, the erstwhile tenant in tail can execute a *fresh disentailing assurance*. He can belatedly get the consent of the protector of the settlement (case 2), or wait until the time when the entail would have fallen into possession (case 1), and disentail a second time. Even more illogically, if the tenant in tail is dead, the next lineal heir – who by definition never acquired any interest at all in the property – can execute a fresh disentailing assurance and turn the base fee into a fee simple absolute. Otherwise, if the owner of the base fee *remains in possession* for 12 years from the time when the entail would have fallen into possession, then, by statute, the base fee becomes a fee simple absolute. Otherwise, if the owner of the base fee *buys in* the ultimate remainder (Eric buys Fiona's interest) that has the effect of destroying the ultimate remainder and enlarging the base fee into a fee simple absolute.

If the question is, 'why all these apparently silly rules?', the answer is because the current law simply preserves the consequences of the ancient collusive actions at common law. If the question is, 'why do tenants in tail not always bar their entails at the first opportunity?', the answer, in short, is *noblesse oblige*. Entails exist in the settlements of aristocratic families, and are often associated with hereditary titles of honour. Social and family pressures preserve them.

(6)   MODIFIED ESTATES

It is possible to modify any estate or interest by making it either *determinable* or *conditional*. In either case, the continued existence of the interest is tied to the occurrence or non-occurrence of some event which may or may not happen (say, the collapse of a clock tower).

(a)   Different concepts

A determinable interest is given only for that period of time during which an existing state of affairs continues (until the clock tower falls); in a conditional interest, the gift is recalled in the event that there is a change in an existing state of affairs (unless the clock tower shall fall).

It may reasonably be objected that there is no difference in substance between the two gifts. They are merely saying the same thing in two different ways. A chessboard may be manufactured by painting black squares on a white board, or white squares on a black board. Similarly, the conceptual difference between determinable and conditional limitations is no more than the difference between *until* and *unless*. Nevertheless, significantly different consequences flow from the choice of words used. If words of duration are used (until, while, for as long as), then the interest will be determinable and one set of consequences will follow. If the same gift is expressed in the form of a condition subsequent (but if, unless, provided), then different consequences follow.

In particular, a determinable limitation is conceived as one entire, indivisible limitation, which is therefore either wholly valid or wholly void. A conditional limitation, on the other hand, is conceived as divisible into gift and severable condition; in some circumstances, the condition may be struck out, leaving the underlying gift still valid.

Determinable life interests are quite common. It is not unusual to find a will leaving a life interest to a widow 'until she remarries'. A determinable interest may also be used as the foundation of a 'protective' or 'spendthrift' trust, where property is given to a beneficiary until he attempts to dispose of it. Conditional interests are less common, for reasons which will soon become apparent. But a grant of land subject to a rentcharge is usually made conditional upon payment of the rentcharge, and leasehold terms are invariably granted on condition that the tenant pays the rent reserved by the lease.

(b)   Initial validity

A *condition* which is considered to be contrary to public policy will be struck down. Thus, a condition subsequent must not operate as an undue restraint on alienation or marriage. It must not attempt to cheat creditors by altering the course of devolution of property which is prescribed by the law in the event of insolvency or bankruptcy. Whether or not a particular condition contravenes public policy has to be decided in the light of the facts of the case. A total restraint on alienation is void; a partial restraint may be allowed, provided it is not too onerous. A gift to a daughter, conditional upon her not marrying, may be seen as a restraint on marriage and void; a similar gift to a maiden aunt may be seen as an act of generosity in providing for a poor spinster.

If the condition is void, then, because a conditional limitation is conceived as two parts, gift plus condition, the condition alone can be struck out, leaving the underlying gift as an *absolute* gift. The beneficiary is not thereby prejudiced, and the court is therefore less hesitant about interfering with a conditional gift than with a determinable gift.

In theory, a *determinable* limitation is subject to the same rules about public policy, but in practice the courts are far more relaxed in their attitude towards determinable limitations. Gifts *until* attempted alienation, *until* marriage or remarriage, *until* bankruptcy, are all common and accepted, whereas conditions subsequent designed to achieve the same ends would be void. The excuse for such leniency is that a determinable limitation stands or falls as a whole. If the determinable limitation is struck down, the beneficiary gets nothing, and it is thought better to give him a restricted benefit than nothing at all. That is not to say that a determinable limitation will *never* be struck down on grounds of public policy, but the case would have to be extreme ('until you stop beating your wife'?).

Limitations, both conditional and determinable, may of course fail on other grounds – for example, uncertainty – with consequences similar to those described above.

(c)   Termination

A *determinable* gift terminates automatically upon the happening of the relevant event – as soon as the clock tower falls. With a determinable life estate or entail, the right to possession immediately passes to the person next entitled under the settlement.

In the case of a determinable fee simple, the estate reverts to the original grantor or his successors. This is a conceptual oddity. The fee simple is the largest estate known to the law, so, on the face of it, if the grantor has given away the fee simple, he himself has nothing left. There can be no remainder after a fee simple. Nevertheless, determinable fees simple are allowed and will revert immediately upon the happening of the determining event. To the objection that this is allowing a remainder after a fee simple, the common lawyers said no, it was not. During the subsistence of the determinable fee, the grantor retained no estate and no interest in the land but a mere *possibility of reverter* – a vague hope of recovering his former estate. The right of reverter was regarded as too nebulous to count as any sort of property interest. Nevertheless, this non-interest has sufficient substance (probably) to be capable of transmission by the grantor.

In the case of a *conditional* limitation, termination is *not* automatic. The grantor retains a *right of re-entry*, that is, a right to repossess. A right of re-entry is recognised as a proprietary interest. If and when the specified event occurs (the clock tower falls), the grant becomes *voidable*, but it is not actually avoided unless and until the grantor (or his successor) exercises the right of re-entry, and the grantee may lawfully continue in possession until that time.

(d)   Perpetuities

A right of reverter may not operate, and a right of re-entry may not be exercised, at too remote a time in the future. Both are subject to the *rule against perpetuities*, which is briefly described in the next chapter. The right of re-entry has always been subject to the rule; the possibility of reverter, only since 1964. If either is void for perpetuity, the grantee's interest becomes absolute.

(e)   Law and Equity

It might be expected that every modified interest must be equitable. The only freehold estate capable of existing at Law is the fee simple *absolute* in possession; and determinable and conditional interests are, by definition, less than absolute. There are, however, some exceptions.

A *determinable* fee simple is almost always equitable. However, in the case of land donated for public purposes (land for schools, hospitals, libraries and so forth), then various *statutes* may provide for reverter in the event that the land is no longer required for the specified purposes. A fee thus made determinable *by statute* remains a legal estate, by way of exception to the general rule.

A *conditional* fee may be either legal or equitable, depending on the circumstances. A little history has to be noted here. Rentcharges used to be common in some areas of the country (especially in and around Manchester and in Somerset). A landowner might grant away a fee simple, but reserve thereout an annual rentcharge, and reserve also a right of re-entry in the event of non-payment. But the existence of the right of re-entry made the fee simple a fee simple *conditional*. The LPA then declared that only a fee simple *absolute* could be a legal estate. The effect was unwittingly to turn most fees simple subject to a rentcharge into equitable interests only. Therefore an amendment was immediately enacted to the effect that a fee simple subject to a right of re-entry shall be *deemed* a fee simple absolute and so capable of being a legal estate.

The deeming is not restricted to the case of land subject to a rentcharge but is of general application. On the other hand, apart from rentcharges, conditional gifts are most likely to occur in family settlements and be expressly limited as equitable interests under a trust.

(7)   FUTURE INTERESTS

(a)   Present possession or future interest

Estates or interests may be *in possession*, *in remainder* or *in reversion*.

An interest is *in possession* if *either* it gives the right to immediate physical possession *or* it gives the right to receive the rent or profits or other income of the property.

So if George grants land to Tessa for 99 years, both Tessa and George have interests in possession; she, because she is entitled to physical possession under the lease; he, because he is entitled to her rent. If, on the other hand, George grants land to Laura for life then, at Law, George retains his fee simple absolute in possession because his purported grant is incompetent at Law; but, in Equity, the grant is effective, giving Laura a life estate in possession, and leaving George with a fee simple which is no longer in possession.

An interest is *in remainder* if it is granted subject to a prior interest: to Laura for life, remainder to Mary for life, remainder to Richard in fee simple. In Equity, Laura has a life interest in possession; Mary, a life interest in remainder; Richard, a fee simple in remainder. Remainders are so called because, upon termination of the prior interest, possession remains away from the grantor.

An interest is *in reversion* when the grantor grants away less than he owns, so that possession will revert to him (or his successors) upon termination of the lesser interest. So if George grants land to Laura for life, then, in Equity, she has a life interest in possession and his fee simple has now become a fee simple in reversion.

Freehold remainders and reversions are necessarily *equitable*, because only a fee simple absolute in *possession* can exist at Law. Freehold remainders and reversions give neither the right to immediate physical possession, nor the right to any rent or income.

Freehold remainders and reversions are together called *future interests*. The label is misleading. What is future about them is the right to *possession*. The interests themselves may exist *now* and be capable of conveyance *now*. If land is granted to Laura for life, remainder to Mary for life, remainder to Richard in fee simple, Mary *now owns* a life interest (subject to Laura's life interest) and can now deal with it accordingly. Similarly, Richard *now owns* the equitable fee simple (subject to the two life interests) and can now deal with it.

(b)   Vested or contingent

Mary's and Richard's interest are described as *vested* interests. An interest is vested if two conditions are satisfied:

- the taker is ascertained; and
- the interest is *either* in possession *or* ready to take effect in possession, subject only to the dropping of a life or lives.

Mary's and Richard's interests satisfy both conditions.

An interest which fails either test is called a *contingent interest*, that is, an interest subject to a condition precedent. A gift to 'the widow' of a living man, or 'the eldest son' of a childless couple, is necessarily contingent because the taker is not yet ascertainable. In a grant 'to Laura for life contingently on her attaining the age of 18 years, remainder to Richard if he qualifies as a solicitor', both gifts are contingent because they fail the second test.

Laura is not entitled to possession until her 18th birthday, whereupon her life interest becomes vested – she will then be *vested in possession*.

Richard's gift is contingent because it is not ready to take effect in possession subject *only* to the dropping of Laura's life; he must *also* first qualify as a solicitor. As soon as Richard qualifies, his interest vests. If Laura has died in the meantime, then Richard's interest will vest in possession. If Laura is still alive, then Richard's remainder will still become vested (because it is then ready to take effect in possession subject *only* to the dropping of her life) but clearly he is not vested in possession, because he is not entitled to possession until her death. In these circumstances, Richard's remainder is described as being *vested in interest*.

(The question might be asked, by way of interjection, what happens if Laura dies *before* Richard qualifies as a solicitor? Where is the equitable ownership between Laura's death and Richard's qualification? The answer is: in the grantor or his successors. It is a general principle of Equity that whenever there is a gap in a disposition, the beneficial interests *results* (jumps back) to the grantor.)

As one would expect, a *vested* interest is fully alienable and may be dealt with by its owner, subject, of course, to any prior interests affecting it. But confusingly a *contingent* interest is also treated as an item of disposable property, even though the contingency may never be satisfied and the gift may never vest. Buying a contingent interest is, therefore, in the nature of a gamble that the contingency will be satisfied, but it can be done.

Contingent interests give rise to problems of perpetuity, which are discussed in the next chapter.

(c)   Mere expectancy

More remote than a contingent interest is a mere expectancy or *spes successionis* (hope of succeeding). A gift under the will of a living person is a mere expectancy, because a will is always revocable until death and so the prospective beneficiary can never be sure of the gift. So is the entitlement on intestacy of the statutory next of kin of any living person, because that person may always make a will defeating those claims. It is held as a matter of policy that an expectancy cannot be assigned as such. It is not considered sufficiently substantial. The most that can be done is to *contract* to assign it, if and when the expectation is fulfilled. And a purported assignment *for value* will be treated as a contract to assign.

(d)   Leasehold reversions

Note the ambivalent position of the landlord of a lease. Because he has granted away physical possession to a tenant, he is said to own the *reversion* on the lease (the 'freehold reversion', where there is a headlease; a 'leasehold reversion', where there is an underlease). Nevertheless, despite the confusing terminology, his 'reversion' is actually an interest *in possession*, because possession includes the right to a rent (if any), and leasehold tenure implies the right to a rent.

10 Perpetuities

The rule against perpetuities used to be the conveyancer's tightrope over Niagara: one slip might prove fatal. Statute now provides a safety net, and perpetuities are no longer so prominent in land law courses. For those, however, who need it, the following is offered as a basic introduction to the topic.

(1)   INTRODUCTORY

The law is generally in favour of the free alienability of property. One aspect of that policy is the *rule against perpetuities*. Future interests tend to tie up property. Even though specific items of property, including land, can usually be released from the settlement by the mechanism of overreaching, nevertheless the wealth, the corpus, remains tied up, and that may be economically unhealthy.

If a gift is limited to take effect at too remote a time in the future, then it is said to tend towards a perpetuity and so is declared 'void for perpetuity'. Some jurisdictions deal with the problem by generally disallowing any gift to an unborn person. English law developed a more complicated rule. First, it was prepared to admit the validity of a gift to an unborn child of a *living* person (a 'life in being'). Then it was prepared to accept that the gift to the unborn child could be made contingent upon that child's attaining its majority (21 years of age in those days). Then it conceded that the measuring life did not need to be directly connected with the benefit of the gift, and that the 21 years did not need to be an actual minority. Thus, the 'perpetuity period' became simply a measuring period of any lifetime plus 21 years (plus, if necessary, to cover the case of a child conceived but not born, any period of gestation before or after the 21 years, or both – and that should be taken for granted hereinafter).

Hence the modern rule against perpetuities:

A contingent interest is void for perpetuity, unless, at the date of the gift, it is certain that, if the interest is ever to vest, it must inevitably vest within the perpetuity period of a life or lives in being plus 21 years.

A gift which fails that test may yet be saved by statute, but statute saves only those gifts which are void at common law, so that it is still necessary to begin with the common law rule.

(2) PRELIMINARY CONSIDERATIONS

There are several preliminary points to be made:

- The validity of the gift is, initially at least, to be judged as at the date of the gift. For a gift *inter vivos*, that means the date of the deed or other date upon which the gift was actually made; for a testamentary gift, it is the date of the death of the testator.

- Where there is a series of gifts ('Adam for life, remainder to Beth'), the perpetuity rule should be applied to each component separately.

- Instead of using the common law period of a life in being plus 21 years, the settlor may, if he wishes, stipulate any fixed period of years, up to a maximum of 80 years, as the perpetuity period applicable to any gift. Many modern settlements choose to do so. But the fixed term alternative must be expressly invoked, otherwise the common law period will apply.

- There are certain presumptions about the age of potential parenthood. Subject to the evidence in any particular case, it may be assumed that a male cannot father a child until he is 14, and that a woman is capable of bearing a child from 12 to 55 inclusive.

- Where there is a gift to a group or class of persons (for example, 'all my grandchildren'), then there are special rules of construction, called the *class closing rules*, which will be applied, in the absence of some contrary indication in the gift, to 'interpret' the meaning of the class gift – whether the class consists of grandchildren alive at the date of the gift, or those born before some event (such as the death of a prior life tenant), or whether the class means literally *all* the grandchildren whenever born.

(3)   A WORKED EXAMPLE

The nature and operation of the perpetuity rule is best explained by working through an example. Assume the following settlement was made before 1997:

- to Adam (a bachelor) for life;
- remainder to his widow for life;
- remainder in tail to his first child to attain the age of 25;
- remainder to Beth in fee simple.

A perpetuity problem is approached by asking three questions in the following order.

(a)   Is the gift vested or contingent?

The rule against perpetuities attacks contingent gifts only. If the gift has already vested, whether it is vested in possession or vested in interest, the rule has no application.

The meaning of 'vested' was noted in the last chapter. Generally, a gift is vested if it satisfies two tests:

- the taker is ascertained; and
- the gift takes effect in possession, or else is ready to take effect in possession subject only to the dropping of life or lives.

For the purposes of the perpetuity rule, however, a gift does not count as a vested gift unless it also satisfies a third test:

- the size of the share is known.

This third test is relevant where there is a class gift of some sort. For non-perpetuity purposes, a class gift vests when the *first* member of the class is ready to take, subject to incremental divesting as further members of the class qualify. For example, suppose there is a gift to the children of a childless couple. On the birth of their first child, the whole gift vests in him provisionally. On the birth of their second child, the first is divested as to half. On the birth of a third child, the other two are each divested as to one sixth, and so on progressively.

For perpetuity purposes, however, it is the final division, not the provisional vesting which is important, and the destination of a class gift is not finally settled until the *last* member qualifies. (But remember that there are special class closing rules which may artificially restrict, and so save, an over-large class.)

Applying that first question, 'vested or contingent?', to the four gifts set out above:

- the gift to Adam for life is clearly vested in possession, and there is no perpetuity issue;

- the second gift, to his widow, is contingent because the taker is not yet ascertainable, and will not be ascertainable until Adam's death;

- the third gift, to Adam's first child, is also contingent, assuming he has not fathered an illegitimate child;

  (These days, in a disposition of property, unless a contrary intention appears, no distinction is to be made between legitimate and illegitimate children save in relation to titles of honour and land devolving therewith. So, for the sake of completeness, perhaps it should be said that if Adam already has a 25 year old child, the gift has vested; otherwise the gift is contingent.)

- the fourth gift, to Beth, is *vested*. She is not entitled to possession of the land until all prior interests are exhausted, but she is nevertheless vested in interest. Her gift satisfies all three tests. Even if the prior entail lasts for generations and generations, it is still true to say that Beth is *ready* to take effect in possession subject only to the dropping of lives. She has a vested fee simple which will devolve under her will or on her intestacy, and Beth or her successors can take possession when all the prior lives have dropped. No further perpetuity issue arises in relation to Beth.

In relation to the gifts to the widow and the child, it is necessary to proceed to the second question.

(b)   Is the gift valid or void at common law?

The question is: Assuming the gift does vest, *must* it vest within the perpetuity period, or is there a *possibility*, no matter how far-fetched, that it might vest outside the perpetuity period? If there is such a possibility, the gift is void at common law.

(i)   General approach

Note two features in particular. First, the question is not, *will* the gift vest? but, *if* the gift vests, *when* will that be? In relation to the widow's gift, for example, it is irrelevant, for perpetuity purposes, that Adam might never marry, or that he might outlive his (last) wife. It is irrelevant that he might never leave a widow. The question is, *if* the gift to the widow ever vests, *when* will that be? Similarly, in relation to the gift to Adam's child, it is irrelevant, for present purposes, that Adam may never have a child, or that, if he does, the child may die young. The question is, *if* he has a child, and *if* that child attains 25, will it be within, or could it be without, the perpetuity period?

The second feature to note is that the common law rule deals with *possibilities*, not probabilities. It is not permissible to wait to see what in fact happens. The validity must be judged at the date of the gift. It is necessary at every turn to assume that the *worst* will happen, whilst still leaving open the possibility that the gift will eventually vest. You have to see if it is possible to invent a sequence of events – no matter how unlikely – which would force the gift to vest outside the perpetuity period. To put it luridly, it is necessary to assume that disaster lurks round every corner, that women are likely to die in childbirth, that fathers will die of shock the moment they hear of their prospective parenthood, that only the last and youngest of all possible takers actually survives.

(ii)   Common law lives in being

In order to determine what is the relevant perpetuity period, it is first necessary to identify who are the *lives in being*. A life in being means nothing more than any person in the whole wide world who is *alive at the date of the gift*. In that sense, there are always millions and millions of lives in being. But, given the need to adopt a morbidly pessimistic outlook, most of the people in the world could die tomorrow without that having any impact on whether or not the particular gift vests within the perpetuity period. In other words, the only lives in being worth considering are those whose lives are somehow *relevant* to the eventual vesting of the gift.

As a rule of thumb, it can be said that the relevant lives in being are those expressly or impliedly identified in the gift itself. Sometimes a life in being is *expressly* identified: 'all my issue alive at the death of the present monarch.' More usually, the identity of the lives in being is *impliedly* indicated in the gift, and, again as a rule of thumb, they will usually consist

111

of all those people alive at the date of the gift who: (1) could be an eventual winner; or (2) could produce an eventual winner.

So in a gift to 'all Colin's grandchildren contingently on attaining the age of 21', Colin (if he is still alive) is a relevant life in being because he can produce possible beneficiaries. Colin's existing children (if any) are relevant lives in being for the same reason. Any existing grandchildren of Colin are relevant lives in being because they may become beneficiaries. If Colin is married, his wife is a life in being, in the sense that she is a person alive at the date of the gift; but she is *not* a *relevant* life in being. She could die tomorrow, and it would have no effect on the vesting of the gift. Colin could always marry again and produce children by his new wife, whereas, if Colin died tomorrow, his widow's continued existence becomes irrelevant to the vesting of the gift – *she* cannot produce Colin's children without him. For the same reason, if Colin has existing sons-in-law or daughters-in-law, they may in a general sense be lives in being, but they are not *relevant* lives in being, because their lives do not *necessarily* affect the vesting of the gift. They could all die tomorrow and Colin's children could all remarry and still produce grandchildren to Colin, whereas if any of Colin's children die, the continued existence of his or her spouse is irrelevant.

(iii)   Application

So, applying these rules to the gift to Adam's widow: Adam is the only relevant life in being. The gift is a gift to the wife (if any) who is alive at Adam's death, so that the gift itself effectively nominates Adam as the life in being. The perpetuity period is therefore Adam's lifetime plus 21 years. *If* the gift to the widow ever vests, what is the latest possible moment of vesting? The answer, obviously, is immediately upon Adam's death, and that is well within the perpetuity period. There is no possibility whatsoever that the gift could vest outside the perpetuity period, therefore the gift is valid at common law.

Applying the rules next to the gift to Adam's first child to attain 25 (and assuming, as before, that the gift has not already vested): Who are the lives in being? Adam is a relevant life, because he can father the eventual taker. Any existing (illegitimate) child of Adam is a relevant life, because that child could become the eventual taker. So the perpetuity period expires 21 years after the death of the last to die of Adam and Adam's existing children. Is there any possibility that the first child of Adam to attain 25 will attain that age outside the perpetuity period? What is the worst that could happen? Well, suppose all Adam's existing children die tomorrow. Adam would then be the only surviving (relevant) life in being. It has to be supposed that he would subsequently father another child (otherwise the gift would *never* take effect), but, to take the most pessimistic view possible, Adam dies the moment the child is conceived. Now (in this imaginary scenario), all the lives in being have gone. The new child is not a life in being, because it had not been conceived at the date of the gift. Therefore, only 21 years are now left on the perpetuity clock. But the new child would not attain a vested interest in those circumstances for another 25 years – four years too late.

Because it is *possible* that that might happen, the contingent gift to Adam's child is *void* at common law. In relation to that gift, therefore, it is necessary to ask the third question.

(c)   Does the Act save the gift?

The relevant Act is the Perpetuities and Accumulations Act 1964. Its attitude is the opposite of the common law's approach. It prefers to deal in actualities rather than possibilities. It applies, however, only where a gift fails the common law test.

(i)   General approach

The general approach of the Act is: *first wait and see*. You wait to see what *actually* happens, whether the gift *does* in fact vest within the perpetuity period. The maximum period for which you may wait is the statutory perpetuity period, and the statutory perpetuity period is the *statutory* lives in being (see below, p 114) plus 21 years (unless the disposition itself expressly specifies a fixed term alternative). If, during that waiting period, the gift does in fact vest, then 'wait and see' has saved it.

If, however, during the statutory period it becomes apparent that 'wait and see' is not going to save the gift, or if you wait to see for the whole of the statutory period and it becomes apparent that 'wait and see' has not in fact saved it, then the Act may offer a more drastic solution. For example, if the problem is that the contingency specified in the gift is the attainment of an age greater than 21, and the beneficiaries are too young, then the Act may allow you to substitute some lower age in order to save the gift. If the problem is that there is a class gift, and it is possible that some members will qualify too late, then the Act may allow you to shut out the stragglers and pretend that the class consists exclusively of those who have already qualified. And there are other provisions along the same lines.

In these cases, the Act is, in a sense, defeating the donor's intention by not allowing the property to vest in those whom he actually intended. The Act does, however, salvage part of what would otherwise have been a total wreck, and, offered the choice between total failure and partial success, most donors would choose the latter.

(ii)   Statutory lives in being

The statutory perpetuity period may be stated in the same terms as that of the common law: a life or lives in being plus 21 years. But the lives are *statutory* lives in being, and they may or may not be the same as the common law lives. Statutory lives must satisfy two conditions. They must be persons who:

- are *ascertainable* at the date of the gift; and
- are within one of the four classes specified in the Act.

Generally, the statutory lives are more numerous than the common law lives, but it is not always so. The classes of person listed are similar to the common law lives in that they include (to paraphrase) potential winners, and grandparents and parents in the case of gifts to grandchildren, and parents in the case of gifts to children, but they go beyond the common law by allowing the *donor* as a life in being and also the owner of any *prior interest*. Neither of these would, as such, be relevant lives at common law.

On the other hand, the Act is narrower than the common law in so far that it insists that a life in being must be a person who is *ascertainable* and not merely alive at the date of the gift. Suppose there is a gift to Dawn (a spinster) for life, remainder to her husband for life provided she marries someone older than herself, remainder to such of their children as survive them both. The potential husband is a common law life in being, because, if he is older than Dawn, it can be guaranteed that he is alive at the date of the gift. But he is not a statutory life in being, because he is not ascertainable at the date of the gift.

(iii)   Application

In applying the Act to the gift to Adam's child: Adam is a statutory life in being. So are any existing children of Adam. Adam's future wife is unascertainable, and so cannot be a statutory life. But, if the settlement is an *inter vivos* settlement, then the settlor is also a statutory life.

You then wait for a maximum of the longest of those lives plus 21 years. In all probability, Adam's first child to attain 25 will do so during his father's lifetime. If not, it is highly likely that he will do so within 21 years of his father's death. But if it should turn out that Adam is the last statutory life to drop, and if it should turn out that his only child or children are posthumous, or are younger than four at his death, then it has become apparent that 'wait and see' will not save the gift. At that point, you may turn to the more drastic remedies in the Act, and in this case you are allowed to substitute a different age in the gift to Adam's child. Instead of a qualifying age of 25, you may substitute the nearest age which would save the gift – in this case, the age of the child at Adam's death plus 21 years. So if the child is posthumous, you substitute 21; if the child is three, you substitute 24. (If there are several children, you probably substitute the age of the youngest child plus 21.)

11 Leaseholds

Leases were introduced in Chapter 5. It is now necessary to say a little more about leaseholds, but the law of landlord and tenant, as it is usually called, is an immense topic in its own right and the following is no more than a brief introduction.

A lease is an estate in land which endures for a fixed period of time, such that its maximum duration is known before the term begins, but a periodic tenancy is deemed to satisfy that requirement. A lease is capable of being a legal estate if it is a *term of years absolute* as defined by the LPA.

There are three essentials for a legal lease: the tenant must have exclusive possession, the duration of the term must be certain, and the statutory formalities must be satisfied. Equitable leases are sometimes used as conveyancing devices in elaborate family settlements, but they are more commonly encountered as *informal* leases which fail to satisfy the statutory requirements.

(1)   TERMINOLOGY

The word 'lease', depending on the context in which it is used, means either a leasehold interest – a term of years – or the document which creates that interest. Similarly, the word 'tenancy' changes its meaning with its context. Sometimes, it means that which is held by a tenant – an estate in land, and, typically, a leasehold estate – and in that sense 'lease' and 'tenancy' may be used interchangeably. Sometimes, however, 'lease' is used to point a contrast with 'tenancy'. In that context, 'lease' implies a fixed term, whereas 'tenancy' implies a periodic tenancy. The word 'demise' (noun or verb) is a formal conveyancing word which means 'grant by lease'.

(2)   EXCLUSIVE POSSESSION

The first requirement of a lease or tenancy is that the tenant be granted the right to *exclusive possession*. That means that the tenant, as estate owner, has not only the legal right to occupy the land, but also the right to exclude all others from the land. In particular, he has the right to exclude the landlord and the landlord's agents. (In practice, the tenant frequently agrees, as a term of the tenancy, to allow the landlord to enter from time to time to view the state of decoration and repair; but that does not affect the proposition that the tenant has the initial *right* to exclude – the landlord enters by the tenant's *permission*.)

However, a distinction has to be made between *possession* and *occupation*. In a non-technical sense, they describe a physical state of affairs and can be used interchangeably. In a technical sense, possession is stronger than occupation. Occupation is the physical aspect; possession has the metaphysical connotation of the legal *right* of possession. The two do not necessarily coincide. A hotel guest, for example, occupies a room; but the legal right of possession remains in the hotelier.

A person who occupies another's property exclusively in return for a regular payment is usually a lessee or tenant. But the conclusion is not inevitable. It is possible that the occupier has a *personal* right to occupy the land, as contrasted with a tenant's *proprietary* right *in* the land. A personal right to occupy is called a *licence* to occupy.

(3)   LEASE OR LICENCE?

(a)   Licence

'Licence' means nothing more than 'permission'. If you have no right to be on another's land, you are a trespasser. If that other has given you permission to be there, then you are not a trespasser, but a licensee. Licences may arise in various situations and may be used for a variety of purposes. For example, a right of way is often created by licence. A right of way granted by one landowner to another landowner will usually be an easement; a right of way given to another *personally* cannot be an easement (because it is not for the benefit of land) and so it is called a licence.

Licences may be classified. One significant feature of the classification is the *revocability* of that kind of licence.

A *bare licence* is a simple permission or invitation, gratuitously allowing another to use your land – as when you allow a schoolboy to retrieve his football from your garden or invite visitors into your home. A bare licence implies no commitment to continuing the arrangement. It may be revoked at any time, and a licensee who refuses to leave thereupon becomes a trespasser.

A *contractual licence* may exist where the user pays for the right to be there (a spectator at a sporting event) or where he is paid to be there (a building contractor). A contractual licence may be revoked in accordance with the terms of the contract, express or implied. Revocation otherwise than in accordance with the contract is breach of contract giving rise to contractual remedies. Typically, the remedy is damages. Exceptionally, the contractor may obtain an injunction to prevent a breach.

A *licence coupled with a grant* is said to exist where a landowner grants a property right to another which necessarily implies a right to come onto the grantor's land. So granting a right to fish in a river (*profit à prendre*) necessarily implies a right to walk along the river bank.

There is also said to be a *licence coupled with an equity*, although this is a controversial area of the law. The 'equity' referred to is an equity to prevent revocation. It has already been said that, exceptionally, Equity will intervene to prevent premature revocation of a contractual licence. But Equity has occasionally also intervened to prevent revocation of what appears to be a bare licence in circumstances where it would be unconscionable for the licensor to revoke. The most controversial feature, however, is that this equity against revocation has sometimes been held binding on a third party who buys the licensor's land. At that point, the licence begins to look like a novel equitable interest in the land.

(b)   Licence to occupy

A contractual licence to occupy land closely resembles a tenancy – indeed, in outward appearance they may be identical. And yet the law ascribes very different consequences, depending on the proper categorisation. The licence generates personal rights (contract); the tenancy, proprietary rights (estate). Therefore, in principle, a licence should not be binding on a third party, whereas a tenancy does bind a third party. That principle holds good as a general rule but, as noted above, there are cases where even a licensee has been held to have rights which bind a third party (although it is strictly the possessory right generated by, or in consequence of, his contract, rather than the contract itself, which binds).

The question of lease or licence, has, however, been debated more in the context of the relationship of the original parties. At first sight, that might seem surprising. As between the original parties to a transaction, it does not usually matter whether the transaction generates rights *in rem* or rights *in personam*. Each can sue the other in either event. In this particular case, however, even the rights of the parties *inter se* depend upon the classification. That is because Parliament has sought over the years to regulate the private housing market in order to prevent landlords exploiting tenants. With minor exceptions, this legislation has sought to regulate the relationship of *landlord and tenant*, but not that of licensor and licensee. When regulation has been tight, landlords have preferred to parade as licensors, and that has resulted in much litigation to determine whether an apparent licence was truly a lease.

(c)   Statutory regulation

Of course, different governments have different views of what amounts to improper exploitation, and how and to what extent they should interfere with market forces. But two issues have attracted particular attention. One is the *regulation of rent* – limiting the amount by which, and the circumstances in which, the landlord can increase the rent. The other is *security of tenure* – limiting the circumstances in which, and the procedure by which, the landlord can evict the tenant. There has been a whole series of Rent Acts and Housing Acts dealing with these issues.

Broadly, rent control has now gone. Tenancies concluded under earlier laws continue to be governed transitionally by those earlier laws, but for tenancies concluded today, the landlord is free to stipulate a market rent, although there may be procedures to be observed if he wishes to increase the rent.

Security of tenure, too, has become greatly attenuated. Today a periodic tenancy will typically take effect as an *assured shorthold tenancy*, which the landlord may terminate by giving two months' notice to quit, provided that the tenant is normally entitled to a minimum of six months' occupation under the tenancy. (Note, however, that these days a landlord may not physically evict *any* residential occupier without a court order.)

The landlord may choose to confer greater security of tenure upon the tenant by offering him an *assured tenancy* (often referred to as a 'fully assured' tenancy) instead. In order to do that, the landlord must give the tenant formal notice (in prescribed form) before the tenancy begins. The landlord cannot terminate a fully assured tenancy without first showing (to the county court) good cause, as specified in the Act, for evicting the tenant, and in some cases he must offer the tenant suitable alternative accommodation.

As statutory regulations have been relaxed, so landlords have found it less and less necessary to try to hide behind licences. Indeed, the very purpose of deregulation was to stimulate the private housing market. Nevertheless, the years of regulation have left a legacy of litigation.

(d)   Distinguishing lease and licence

Given that exclusive possession is a necessary characteristic of a lease or tenancy, it follows that if an occupier does not have the right to *exclusive* occupation, then he cannot be a tenant. The lodger is a typical example of this sort of licensee. He is a (paying) guest in the house of another. 'His' room is his only in the sense that he has the use of it, as a child may have 'his own' bedroom. He cannot keep the householder out, and he does not keep the householder out when it comes to matters of cleaning and redecoration. Similarly, students in a university hall of residence, or residents in an old people's home, typically have non-exclusive occupation and are accordingly licensees.

However, although exclusive occupation provides a negative test, in that *non-exclusive* occupation predicates a licence, nevertheless, it does not always provide a positive test, in that *exclusive* occupation is consistent either with a lease (estate) or with a licence (contract). The courts have found it difficult to formulate a test for distinguishing the two. After much contradictory case law, the House of Lords eventually restated the law (at least as respects residential accommodation). In short: *exclusive possession* for a *term* (including a periodic arrangement) at a *rent* gives a lease, save in exceptional circumstances (*Street v Mountford* [1985] AC 809; [1985] 2 All ER 289, HL). The difficulty is to determine whether the occupier (in the physical sense) strictly has possession (in the metaphysical, legal sense). It seems that the right of exclusive possession is generally to be inferred from the fact of exclusive occupation, and in order to determine whether the occupation was exclusive, you look at the reality of the situation and not, or not only, at the terms of the agreement.

So it is to be inferred that the sole occupier of a small bedsit who pays rent through an agent to a landlord whom he has never seen is a tenant, even if he apparently holds under a 'licence' whereby he nominally agrees to share his cramped flat with anyone else the landlord may send along.

The exceptional cases, where exclusive occupation at a 'rent' does not give rise to a tenancy, fall broadly into two categories: those where the parties do not intend to enter any sort of *legally* enforceable relationship (family and domestic arrangements, or where the arrangement is an act of charity or generosity on the part of the landowner), or where they do intend to create a legal relationship, but their relationship is clearly something other than that of landlord and tenant (purchaser under a contract for sale, mortgagee in possession, and so on). One important example of the latter category is the service occupancy.

(e) Service occupancy

A service occupancy arises where an employee is required to live 'on the job' – he is *required* to occupy the employer's property *for the better performance of his duties*. A caretaker is the obvious example. The employee's right to occupy is personal to him and cannot be assigned. He is a licensee and not a tenant. His right and duty of occupation is a term of his contract of employment (contract of service), so that when he leaves the job, he must leave the accommodation.

Where, however, an employer provides his employee with living accommodation in circumstances other than those mentioned, then there is no service occupancy, and the arrangement is probably a tenancy.

(4) CERTAINTY OF DURATION

At Law, the maximum duration of a lease must be certain in the sense that, at or before the commencement of the term, the ultimate date of expiry must be predictable, whether or not the term is liable to premature determination by notice, forfeiture or otherwise. A periodic tenancy, weekly, monthly, yearly, or as the case may be, is deemed to satisfy the requirements of certainty of duration for the reasons explained above, p 50.

The duration of the term of a lease may be as long or as short as the parties wish – from a matter of days to thousands of years. And the period need not be continuous ('three successive Saturdays', 'the first week in August every year for 80 years'). Moreover, the term does not have to begin at once. It can begin at some time in the future, but not more than 21 years hence (save for equitable leases under a settlement).

There are one or two oddities to be noticed. The first is a *lease for life*. A lease granted for the lifetime of a person, or a lease determinable on someone's life ('to Tessa for 50 years, if she shall so long live') is *not* a term of years absolute as now defined. Such leases are unheard of in a commercial context today. Nevertheless, they were apparently quite common in the early part of the 19th century, and so some might have been subsisting in 1925 at the time of the great reforms. The LPA therefore provides that a *commercial* lease for life ('at a rent or in consideration of a *fine*' – that is, a capital payment, a premium or 'key money') is to take effect as if it were a grant of a 90 year term, terminable by notice served after the relevant death. And a 90 year term terminable by notice *is* a term of years absolute as defined. The other use of a lease for life was in a family settlement – where there would be no rent or fine. Such leases are untouched. They are not within the definition of term of years absolute, and they are not turned into 90 year terms. They remain equitable leases and take effect under a settlement.

A lease until the *marriage* of the lessee is treated in the same way as a lease for life: if it is commercial, it becomes a 90 year term, determinable by notice given after the marriage; if non-commercial, it takes effect under a settlement.

Less esoteric than a lease for life or marriage, but nevertheless uncommon, is a *perpetually renewable lease*. This is a lease which contains an option for the tenant to renew the term upon all the same conditions including the option to renew. It is therefore, in effect, a lease for as long as the tenant wants to keep renewing it. The LPA turns it into a 2,000 year lease, terminable by the tenant (only) by notice expiring on what would otherwise have been a renewal date. The practical effect of the change is that the tenant has to remember to cancel the lease instead of having to remember to renew it.

A *tenancy at will* is said to arise when one person is in possession of another's property in a continuing relationship of landlord and tenant, but where no term is agreed upon. Either party can terminate the arrangement at a moment's notice. Conceptually, it is bare tenure without any estate. In practice, what begins as a tenancy at will may become a periodic tenancy.

If the tenant at will begins to pay a periodic rent then it is a possible, but not a necessary, inference that he has become a periodic tenant – a weekly rent may result in an implied weekly tenancy; a monthly rent, a monthly tenancy; a quarterly rent, a quarterly tenancy; a six monthly or yearly rent, a yearly tenancy.

By way of contrast, a *tenancy at sufferance* is not a true tenancy at all. It is the name given to the relationship where a tenant *holds over* (stays in occupation) after the expiry of an agreed term against the landlord's wishes. The lack of the landlord's consent to a continued tenancy means that the tenant is not a tenant at will. The 'tenant' is liable to pay for his continuing 'use and enjoyment' of the property, but the landlord will be careful not to accept *rent* as such from him, lest that impliedly create a new tenancy.

A *tenancy by estoppel* arises where a person who has no legal title purports to grant a lease and the tenant goes into possession. Each having by his conduct represented to the other that the lease is valid, neither may deny it as against the other. They and their successors are bound as if the lease were validly created. If the landlord subsequently acquires the legal title, that 'feeds the estoppel' and the tenant is thereupon invested with his full legal term of years.

(5)   FORMALITIES

(a)   Statutory formalities

The general rule is that a lease must be made by *deed* if it is to create a legal estate. The exception is a three year lease: a written or oral grant of a new lease or tenancy for a term not exceeding three years creates a legal lease if the tenant takes immediate possession and the rent is the market rent.

(b)   The rule in *Walsh v Lonsdale*

A lease which for want of formality fails to create a legal estate may nevertheless have some effect at Law, and it may even be treated as a valid lease in Equity.

At Law the failed lease, if made for value, will at least be treated as a *contract* to execute a lease in due form. Moreover, if the tenant takes possession under the failed lease then, although he gets no estate under the document, his possession may first make him a tenant at will and then, if he pays a periodic rent, he may become a periodic tenant, as explained above.

Equity may go further. The failed lease, if made for value, will first be treated in Equity, as at Law, as a contract to grant a formal lease. And then, according to the doctrine of *Walsh v Lonsdale* (1882) 21 Ch D 9, 'a contract for a lease is as good as a lease' in Equity. The doctrine proceeds by four steps:

(1) Is there a contract to grant a lease? – Yes, the failed lease itself is deemed to be a contract.

(2) Is it an enforceable contract? – Yes, at least if the failed lease is in writing. (By statute, a contract for the sale of land or any interest in land must be in writing.)

(3) Is it a specifically enforceable contract? – Yes, at least in a routine case. Equity will normally grant the remedy of specific performance in the case of a contract for land as opposed to chattels, but it must be remembered that equitable remedies are always discretionary.

(4) If so, then 'Equity regards as done that which ought to be done' and Equity treats the parties as if the contract had already been carried out. *Ergo*, there is in Equity a lease for the agreed period and upon the agreed conditions.

The argument works equally well if there is an *express* contract in writing to create a lease. Indeed, tenants regularly take possession on the basis of a tenancy *agreement* (whereby 'the landlord *agrees* to let and the tenant *agrees* to take ...') rather than on the basis of a formal grant of a term.

The doctrine may not work, however, if the contract (express or deemed) is oral. In that event, the argument breaks down at point (2). But sometimes the gap can be bridged. There is another principle that 'Equity will not allow a statute designed to prevent fraud to be used as a cloak for fraud'. Now, the purpose of the statutory requirement that contracts for land must be in writing is to prevent fraud. If, therefore, it would be unconscionable to allow a party to rely on the absence of writing, then Equity will 'give the go-by' to the statute and enforce the contract notwithstanding the absence of writing. That argument might be used, for example, if the tenant has actually moved into possession in reliance on the landlord's oral promise.

An agreement for a lease is not, however, really as good as a lease. The proposition may be true as between the original parties – although even there, the equitable doctrine depends upon the continued availability of specific performance – and certainly there are drawbacks when a third party appears. From the tenant's point of view, the position is not very satisfactory if he wants to assign his equitable lease. And having only an equitable interest, he may be at a disadvantage if the landlord sells the land. Where the land is registered land, then the tenant's equitable lease is a minor interest which should be protected by a notice or caution on the register, although if the tenant is in actual occupation, his rights may override the register. Where the title to the land is unregistered, the tenant should register his contract as an estate contract, Class C(iv), in order to give notice to any prospective purchaser.

(6) RENT

Rent is strictly a consequence of a lease rather than a prerequisite. The tenant has a duty to pay rent service to his lord, the amount of the rent being what is agreed between the parties (almost invariably cash, but possibly kind). However, as mentioned above, precisely because rent is a characteristic of the landlord and tenant relationship, the court may infer from the payment of rent that there must be a lease or tenancy in existence.

(7) RIGHTS AND OBLIGATIONS

The rights and duties of the parties under a lease are determined by an amalgam of agreement, common law and statute. Some of the more important features are as follows.

(a) Quiet enjoyment

The landlord impliedly covenants that the tenant shall have quiet enjoyment. This quaint expression means, not that the tenant shall be free from noise, but that he shall be secure in his enjoyment of the property. The landlord gives a guarantee that the tenant's possession shall be free from physical disturbance. The landlord promises that he himself will not disturb the tenant, and he guarantees that no one claiming under him has a right to disturb the tenant. (If others disturb him by a *wrongful* act, then the tenant must sue the wrongdoer directly in tort.)

(b) Non-derogation from grant

The landlord impliedly promises that he will not derogate from his grant. This is a general principle applying not only to leases, but to other grants as well. It is based on the commonsense notion that a grantor should not be allowed to give with one hand and take back with the other. So the landlord may not grant a lease for a particular purpose and then use his adjacent land in such a way as to render that purpose impossible.

(c) Covenant not to assign or sublet

Leases often contain a covenant on the part of the tenant not to assign, sublet or part with the possession of the whole or any part or parts of the demised property. The covenant does not actually prevent an assignment or subletting. The tenant has a legal estate which he can transfer, or out of which he can carve an underlease. But his act of assigning or subletting may put him into breach of his covenant, and his breach of covenant may entitle the landlord to forfeit the lease. And forfeiture of the lease will, subject to what is said later, destroy the term of years of any sub-term granted out of it.

Covenants against assignment may be absolute or qualified. An absolute covenant is a covenant not to assign or sublet in any circumstances at all; a qualified covenant is a covenant not to assign or sublet without the landlord's consent. In the latter case, statute implies a proviso that such consent shall not be unreasonably withheld. The tenant can serve a notice on the landlord, requiring him to consent. The landlord then has a duty to reply within a reasonable time, and also a duty to consent unless he has reasonable grounds for withholding his consent.

But in a *business* letting (as opposed to a *residential* letting) it is not unreasonable for a landlord to insist upon any condition specifically agreed in advance by the tenant (whether in the lease or otherwise).

(d)   Repairing obligations

A formal lease will usually make provision for repairs. In the absence of express agreement (or in some cases despite it), the following principles apply.

(i)   Tenant

A tenant *for years* is subject to the doctrine of *waste* (see above, p 94). He is impliedly liable for both voluntary and permissive waste unless the contrary is agreed. In other words, he must keep the property in the condition in which he took it. A *yearly* tenant must not commit voluntary waste, but his liability for permissive waste is less extensive. He must keep the property 'wind- and water-tight', fair wear and tear excepted. The duty of a weekly or monthly tenant is, it seems, simply to behave in a reasonable, tenant-like manner, unstopping sinks and mending fuses and so forth. If any significant repair is needed, the periodic tenant is not required to see to it himself. Instead, he should warn the landlord of the need for repair, because notification may put the landlord under a statutory duty to repair (see below).

(ii)   Landlord

At common law, the landlord is under no implied duty to repair, save in one respect: in the case of a *furnished* letting, the landlord impliedly undertakes that the property shall be fit for human habitation at the commencement of the tenancy – but there is no liability thereafter. Fitness for human habitation broadly means that neither the tenant nor his family should be endangered in respect of life, limb or health in the ordinary course of their occupation of the dwelling.

Statute, however, imposes certain obligations on the landlord of residential property. In the first place, if a house is let on a *low rent*, there is an obligation to keep the property fit for human habitation. The obligation is of limited importance, because a 'low' rent here means £1 per week outside London (or £80 per year within London). In any event, it extends only to defects of which the landlord has notice.

More significant is the landlord's obligation in relation to a dwellinghouse let on a *short lease* – less than seven years. Here, the landlord is under a statutory obligation to maintain the structure, exterior and mains services. Again, the obligation extends only to defects of which the landlord is aware.

The landlord (of any premises) may be indirectly obliged to carry out repairs as a result of his potential liability in tort. Where he has a duty *or right* to carry out repairs, then he owes a duty of care towards those who might reasonably be expected to be affected by any defect in the premises. It applies to a defect of which he knew or ought to have known.

(8)   ASSIGNMENT

The next question is how far the lease is binding on successors. The lease constitutes a contract between the original lessor and the original lessee. It also creates a legal estate, a term of years. Clearly, the lessee can assign his leasehold estate to another; and the lessor can assign his reversionary estate to another, subject to the lease. There is no difficulty with those propositions. But more difficult questions arise in connection with the continued enforceability of the *covenants* contained in the lease. By whom may they be enforced? Against whom may they be enforced? The theory of covenants is explained more fully in Chapter 16. It is a complicated topic, and there is some tricky detail, but as far as concerns landlord and tenant, the main principles are as follows.

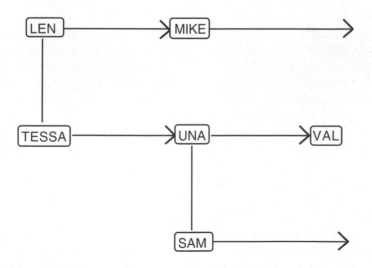

Suppose Len grants a lease to Tessa. As explained above, a lease has a dual operation. It is a contract between the original lessor and the original lessee. But it also creates a new leasehold estate in the land. Where two people make a contract, there is said to be *privity of contract* between them. And, when two people are currently in the relationship of landlord and tenant, there is said to be *privity of estate* between them.

It will be apparent that, initially, as between the original lessor (Len) and the original lessee (Tessa), there is both privity of contract and privity of estate.

Should Len assign his reversion to Mike, then Mike becomes the landlord and there is privity of estate between the new landlord (Mike) and the current tenant (Tessa); but there is no direct contractual relationship between Mike and Tessa, and so there is no privity of contract between them. Alternatively, if Len retains the reversion, but Tessa assigns her lease to Una, then Una becomes the tenant and there is privity of estate between the current landlord (Len) and the new tenant (Una); but there is no privity of contract between Len and Una. If both events occur – Len assigns his reversion to Mike, and Tessa assigns her lease to Una – then there is privity of estate between the new landlord (Mike) and the new tenant (Una), but there is no privity of contract between Mike and Una.

If Una grants a sublease to Sam, then, initially, there is both privity of contract and privity of estate (the underleasehold estate) between Una and Sam; there is privity of estate only (the headleasehold estate) between Una and Mike; there is no privity at all between Mike and Sam – Sam is not *Mike's* tenant, and there is no direct contractual relationship between Mike and Sam.

Finally, if Una assigns her interest to Val, then Una thereby assigns both her tenancy under the headlease (as against Mike) and her reversion on the underlease (as against Sam). Val becomes Mike's tenant and Sam's landlord. There is privity of estate between Mike and Val (the headleasehold estate); there is privity of estate between Val and Sam (the underleasehold estate); there is no privity of any sort between Sam and Mike.

Now the point of all that is that covenants may be enforced *either* on the basis of privity of contract, *or* on the basis of privity of estate – or both. As a general principle, where there is privity of *contract*, then *all* covenants bind: either party may insist that the other perform the contract in full, and may sue for breach in the event of default. If, however, there is privity of *estate* without privity of contract, then those covenants only will bind which are regarded as being *typically* part and parcel of the relationship of landlord and tenant – covenants such as the landlord's covenant for quiet enjoyment and the tenant's covenants to pay the rent, to repair, to insure and so forth. Those covenants will continue to be enforceable as between the current landlord and the current tenant. Where there is no privity of either kind, then the question becomes more complicated still – but further discussion of that last case must be postponed until Chapter 16.

Those, then, are the basic principles, but they are not always easy to apply. In all cases, there are two main questions to be answered. One main question is: When and to what extent does an *assignee acquire* rights and liabilities? In that connection, a particularly tricky sub-point is whether an assignee may sue for breaches of covenant committed before the date of the assignment. The other main question is: When and to what extent does an *assignor cease* to have rights and liabilities? And in that connection, a particularly tricky sub-point is whether the assignor may be made liable for breaches of covenant committed *after* the date of assignment.

The law was simplified by the Landlord and Tenant (Covenants) Act 1995 (LT(C)A). Accordingly, the answers to the questions posed will differ, depending on: (1) whether the lease was granted before 1996 or after 1995; and (2) whether it is an assignment of a lease (by a tenant) or an assignment of a reversion (by a landlord).

(a)   New tenancies

For leases granted since 1995 ('new tenancies'), the rules are contained in the LT(C)A. The prime purpose of the Act was to provide an *original lessor* and an *original lessee* with the means of escaping liability after assignment. At common law, it is generally possible to assign the *benefit* of a contractual obligation (the right to have it performed); it is, however, impossible to assign the *burden* of a contractual obligation (the duty to perform it). The common law was therefore driven to hold that, in so far as a lease was a contract between the original parties, the original parties must remain liable *throughout the term of the lease* to perform their respective obligations under the lease. The LT(C)A changed that rule. It also changed the rules which determine what covenants may be enforced on the basis of privity of estate. Accordingly, the principles which apply to new tenancies are as follows.

(i)   Lease

Suppose the lease is assigned (Tessa to Una). Consider first the position of the assignee (Una). After the assignment, Una may enforce *all* the landlord's covenants, express or implied, except for any covenants which were *expressed* to be personal to Len. She cannot, however, sue for any breach of a landlord's covenant committed before the date of assignment (unless the right is expressly assigned to her by Tessa). Likewise, after the assignment, Una is bound by *all* the tenant's covenants, express or implied, except for any covenants *expressed* to be personal to Tessa. Una incurs no direct liability for any breach of a tenant's covenant committed *before* the date of assignment, but, from a practical point of view, she may need to remedy a prior breach if the landlord has a subsisting right to forfeit the lease.

Consider next the position of the assignor of the lease (Tessa). Tessa can sue for a breach of a landlord's covenant committed *before* the date of the assignment. She cannot sue for any breach committed *after* that date. She remains liable for any breach of covenant that she herself has already committed, but, subject to what is said below, she incurs no liability for the breach of a tenant's covenant committed after the date of the assignment.

There are some exceptions to the proposition that Tessa incurs no liability for subsequent breaches. One important exception is that if the lease contains a *covenant against assignment*, then, as a condition of giving his consent to the assignment, the landlord may insist that the outgoing tenant (Tessa) enter an 'authorised guarantee arrangement', whereby Tessa gives a guarantee that the incoming tenant (Una) will duly perform the tenant's covenants. Tessa can, however, be required to stand surety for the performance of her *immediate* assignee (Una) only, and not the performance of any future assignee (Val). The purpose of insisting upon such a guarantee arrangement is, of course, to encourage an assignor to ensure that the assignee is a responsible person. In the event that Una defaults, the landlord may enforce the guarantee against Tessa, but if he wants Tessa to pay Una's rent or some other fixed sum of money, then he must give Tessa notice (in prescribed form) of his intent within six months of Una's default. In the event that Tessa has to pay out, then, under the LT(C)A 1995, she can ask the landlord (Len) for an 'overriding lease', sandwiched between Una's lease and the reversion on Una's lease: Tessa thereby becomes the tenant of Len and the landlord of Una. Tessa can then claim landlord's remedies against Una and so seek to recoup what she has lost under the guarantee.

(ii)   Reversion

Suppose next the case where a landlord assigns his reversion on a new (post-1995) tenancy (Len to Mike). Consider first the case of the assignee (Mike). After the assignment, Mike may enforce *all* the tenant's covenants, save for any covenants *expressed* to be personal to Tessa. He may not sue for any breach of a tenant's covenant committed *before* the date of assignment (unless the right is expressly assigned to him by Len), but he may in some circumstances be entitled to forfeit the lease for such an earlier breach. As from the date of the assignment, Mike becomes bound by all the landlord's covenants, save for any covenants expressed to be personal to Len.

Consider finally the case of the assignor of the reversion (Len). Len is naturally liable for any breach of covenant committed *before* the date of assignment. He may or may not be liable for a breach of a landlord's covenant committed *after* the assignment. As explained earlier, at common law, Len's contractual obligations last throughout the length of the lease. Moreover, in the absence of any contrary indication, the covenants given by Len are deemed to be covenants by him 'for himself and his successors in title'. In other words, he promises to observe and perform the various obligations himself *and he promises that his successors will also observe and perform those obligations*. The effect is that, at common law, the original lessor guarantees the performance of the landlord's covenants for the lifetime of the lease. The LT(C)A allows him to escape that continuing liability, but release is not automatic. If he wishes to be released from future liability, Len must serve a notice (in prescribed form) on the current tenant, asking to be released. If the tenant does not object, Len is released from his landlord's obligations as from the date of the assignment; if the tenant does object, then the county court adjudicates.

Should Len forget or fail to obtain his release when he assigns the reversion to Mike, he can try again whenever the reversion is assigned in the future – when Mike sells, or when any successor to Mike sells.

The LT(C)A adds that, if and when Len ceases to be bound by the landlord's covenants, he thereupon ceases to have the benefit of the tenant's obligations, but it is not clear on what basis Len could possibly sue for breach of a tenant's covenant committed *after* he has assigned the reversion.

(b)   Old tenancies

The rules about assignment are even more complicated in the case of a lease granted before 1996 (an 'old' tenancy).

(i)   Lease

Suppose, once again, that the lease is assigned (Tessa to Una). Where an 'old' tenancy is assigned, then the position is governed mainly by the common law.

Consider first the position of the assignee (Una). She has privity of estate with the current landlord, but no privity of contract. And the rule is that where there is privity of estate, then those covenants bind which are regarded as typical of the relationship of landlord and tenant. In the case of old tenancies, the traditional test is whether the covenant in question 'touches and concerns the land demised' (or 'has reference to the subject matter of the lease' – which means the same thing). There is much learning on the proper interpretation of those expressions, but, broadly, a covenant 'touches and concerns' if, in essence, it is a covenant of a kind which is given and received in the capacity of landlord and tenant as such, as opposed to a covenant which is merely collateral or personal to either party.

It follows that, for as long as Una remains the tenant (and so has privity of estate) she can insist that the landlord observe all the landlord's covenants which 'touch and concern' the land. She can sue for the breach of any such covenant committed whilst she remains tenant; she cannot sue for a breach committed before she became tenant, nor for a breach committed after she ceases to be tenant. By parity of reasoning, for as long as she remains tenant, Una must observe all the covenants given by Tessa which 'touch and concern' the land. Una is not directly liable for any breach of covenant committed before she acquired the lease, but, from a practical point of view, she may have to remedy a prior breach if the landlord has a subsisting right to forfeit the lease. She is not liable for any breach committed after she ceases to be tenant.

Consider next the position of the original lessee (Tessa). She cannot sue the landlord for a breach of covenant committed after the date of her assignment to Una, but it has been held that she may sue for a breach of covenant committed *before* the assignment, even though she does not commence proceedings until *after* the assignment.

More important, however, is the question of the continuing *liability* of the original lessee under an old (pre-1996) tenancy. As with the original lessor, so with the original lessee: the common law holds that Tessa cannot rid herself of her contractual obligation to observe and perform her covenants. Moreover, because she covenants 'for herself and her successors in title', she effectively promises that she will comply for as long as she is tenant, and she *guarantees that all her successors in title* will comply until the end of the lease. It follows that, unless the lease expressly provides otherwise, Tessa may be made liable, notwithstanding the assignment, for any breach of covenant subsequently committed by Una or Val or any later tenant.

There are two crumbs of comfort for Tessa. First, if the landlord wishes to sue Tessa for a successor's failure to pay *rent* or some other *fixed sum of money*, then the LT(C)A 1995 says that the landlord must give her notice (in prescribed form) of his intent within six months of the default; and if Tessa does have to pay out, she is entitled to claim an 'overriding lease' as explained above. Secondly, under the LPA, every assignee of an old tenancy impliedly covenants with his assignor that the assignee will indemnify the assignor against any liability for breaches of covenant occurring after the assignment. In consequence, if Tessa is sued for any default of a successor, Tessa can seek an indemnity from her immediate assignee (on that indemnity covenant) or perhaps from the covenant breaker (in quasi-contract).

(ii)   Reversion

Suppose, finally, Len assigns his reversion to Mike. Where the reversion of an 'old' tenancy is assigned, the position is governed partly by the common law and partly by the LPA.

Consider first the position of the assignee (Mike). There is privity of estate between Mike and the current tenant. As long as Mike remains landlord, he is bound by those covenants given by Len which 'touch and concern the land demised' as explained above. He is not liable for breaches committed before he became landlord. He is not liable for breaches committed after he ceases to be landlord.

As for his rights to sue, he can enforce those covenants given by Tessa which 'touch and concern'. Obviously, he can sue for any breaches committed whilst he is landlord. He cannot sue for any breaches committed afterwards. It might be thought that, on principle, Mike should not be able to sue for a tenant's breach committed *before* Mike became landlord, but here the LPA comes into play. The LPA says that, upon assignment of the reversion, the landlord's rights – his right to the rent and to the benefit of those covenants which touch and concern the land demised – 'shall go' with the reversion. It has been held that the words 'shall go' are strong words and mean that the *whole* of the benefit passes from the assignor to the assignee, so that, upon assignment of the reversion, the assignee acquires the exclusive right to enforce the lease *and the assignor loses it*. Thus if Len assigns the reversion to Mike, then, unless otherwise agreed, Mike alone may sue the current tenant – even in respect of a breach of covenant committed before Mike took his assignment of the reversion.

Lastly, consider the case of the original lessor (Len). It follows from what has just been said that Len loses any right to enforce the tenant's covenants as soon as he assigns the reversion to Mike. He does not, however, lose his duty to observe the landlord's covenants. As explained above, at common law the original lessor is unable to rid himself of the contractual obligations imposed upon him by the lease. In effect, unless the lease otherwise provides, Len remains liable, throughout the term of the lease, as guarantor for the performance of those landlord's covenants which 'touch and concern'.

(9)   REMEDIES

(a)   Action for breach of covenant

If either party fails to abide by the lease, the other may sue for *breach of covenant*, seeking damages, an injunction, or specific performance as appropriate.

(b)   Distress for rent

The landlord may also *distrain* or *levy distress* for non-payment of rent. In common parlance, he sends in the bailiffs to seize and sell the goods and chattels of the tenant in order to pay off the arrears of rent plus costs. This is the modern manifestation of a remedy which goes back to feudal times. The rules are detailed and intricate, but some goods and chattels are exempt from distress – for example, the tools of a man's trade.

(c)   Forfeiture

In the event of a serious default by the tenant, the landlord may contemplate *forfeiture* of the lease, bringing the term of years to a premature end.

(i)   Right to forfeit

The first question is whether the tenant is in breach of *condition* or merely in breach of *covenant*. There is an implied right to forfeit for breach of condition; but a landlord may forfeit for breach of covenant only if there is an express forfeiture clause in the lease (as there almost invariably is). In concept, a condition is imposed unilaterally by the grantor as an inherent part of the grant; a covenant is a promise on the part of the tenant. The payment of rent is commonly both a condition and a covenant; other obligations on the part of the tenant are often covenants only.

If there is a right to forfeit, then the procedure differs, depending on whether forfeiture is for non-payment of rent or for some other cause.

(ii)   Non-payment of rent

In the case of *non-payment of rent*, the landlord must, in theory, make a 'formal demand' for rent, unless excused from so doing. A formal demand involves attending at the property and calling for the rent at such an hour as will enable the tenant to count out his money before sunset. Needless to say, leases always excuse the landlord from making a formal demand. In any event, if the rent is more than six months in arrears, statute may excuse a formal demand.

Having made his demand, or being excused therefrom, the landlord may proceed to repossess the property and thereby forfeit the lease. If he is sure that the property is unoccupied, the landlord may simply re-enter; otherwise, it is safer to seek the formal authority of a court order for possession. In the case of *dwellings*, it is a criminal offence to evict a tenant without a court order; and, whether the property is a dwelling or not, it is a criminal offence to *force* entry when there is someone inside.

The landlord's right to forfeit for non-payment of rent is treated merely as a security for the sums due. If, therefore, the tenant pays off his arrears with costs, the court will not order possession against him. Moreover, the tenant may be able to get his lease back even after the landlord has re-entered (with or without a court order). The court has jurisdiction to grant him *relief against forfeiture*, thereby restoring the tenant to his lease. It is, however, a discretion, and the court will not normally grant relief unless the tenant applies within six months of the repossession, and it may decline relief even within six months.

(iii)　Other grounds

Where the landlord seeks to forfeit for breach of some covenant *other than* rent, then he must follow a different procedure. He must first serve a 'section 146 notice' – that is, a notice under s 146 of the LPA. This does three things. It specifies the breach complained of; it requires the tenant to remedy the breach (if it is capable of remedy), and it demands compensation. The last item is optional: the landlord can forgo compensation if he wishes. As to the second item, requiring that the tenant remedy his breach, some covenants are regarded as remediable (repair, decoration and so on); others are regarded as incapable of remedy. For example, it is said that a covenant against subletting is broken once and for all by granting an underlease; the breach cannot be repaired, even by buying the surrender of the underlease. The landlord does not have to insist on the impossible by requiring the tenant to remedy an irremediable breach.

The notice served, the landlord must allow the tenant a reasonable time within which to comply. Usually, three months is considered reasonable. Even if the breach is irremediable, the tenant is entitled to a week or two to consider his position and seek legal advice. Thereafter, the landlord may proceed to repossess and forfeit the lease, although, for the reasons explained above, he may prefer to seek a court order for possession.

Here again, the tenant may apply for *relief against forfeiture*. It is in the discretion of the court whether to grant relief, and if so, on what terms. A subtenant or mortgagee of the tenant may also apply for relief, because if the lease is forfeited then all rights granted out of it also disappear.

(iv)　Waiver

The right to forfeit may be *waived* and so be lost. There are two elements. First, the landlord must be aware of the conduct of the tenant which renders the lease liable to forfeiture. Second, the landlord must, despite that knowledge, do some act which unequivocally demonstrates that he considers that the lease is still on foot. In other words, he cannot have it both ways. He cannot say he wants to forfeit but behave as though he does not.

Demanding or accepting rent is a typical act of waiver. Rent service is a characteristic of tenure, so that demanding or accepting the rent implies that the lease is still in existence. It is, however, a question of fact whether the landlord has waived. Accepting rent for a period down to the time of the breach complained of is not inconsistent with an assertion that the lease is thereafter forfeit; accepting rent for a period after the breach is dangerous, but apparently not inevitably fatal.

A landlord who waives his right to forfeit does not thereby waive all his rights. He can still claim damages, or an injunction for breach of covenant, or as the case may be.

(10)   TERMINATION

A lease or tenancy may terminate in a variety of ways. In normal circumstances, a fixed term will simply *expire* at the end of the term, and no notice or other action is required to bring about its end. Periodic tenancies continue until terminated by *due notice*. In either case, statute may give some security of tenure. The Housing Acts have already been mentioned, which give some protection to periodic tenants of rented dwellings. Under other legislation, a business tenant may have a right to renew his lease. Other Acts protect agricultural tenants. And a tenant of a dwelling let on a long lease may have the right to buy the freehold or renew his lease for another 50 years.

Leases and tenancies may come to a premature end. *Forfeiture* has been mentioned above. The tenant may, with the landlord's consent, *surrender* his tenancy. Or, conversely, he may buy in the landlord's reversion and so effect a *merger* of the two estates. Less commonly, an assignee, especially a trustee in bankruptcy, may destroy the lease by *disclaiming* it. If circumstances change dramatically, there may be a *frustration* of the lease. There is some authority to the effect that if one party commits a fundamental breach of contract, then the other party may treat himself as thereby discharged from further performance of his obligations under the lease. Lastly, there is an obscure provision which allows a rent-free lease of 300 years or more to be *enlarged* into a fee simple if it still has 200 years to run.

12 Trusts of Land

A trust arises when the equitable ownership of property is separated from its legal ownership. In the typical case, a trust arises because Equity's view differs from that of the Law: according to the Law, ownership is vested in one person or group of people; according to Equity, it is vested in another or others. The legal owner (the trustee) is compelled by Equity to treat the property as if it belonged to the equitable owners (the beneficiaries). The relationship between the two is described as a trust: the legal owner is said to hold the property on trust for the beneficiaries; the beneficiaries are said to own equitable (or beneficial) interests under the trust.

Not all trusts, however, conform to that pattern. It is possible to have a trust for (usually charitable) *purposes*, but that strays beyond the limits of this book. More pertinently, it may happen that a trust arises even though Equity and the Law are agreed upon the ownership. For example, as explained in the next chapter, statute imposes a trust in all cases of co-ownership of land. In consequence, when two people jointly buy a piece of land with their own money, Equity and the Law agree that they are joint owners, but there is, nevertheless, a trust: they hold as trustees upon trust for themselves. On the other hand, when the entire legal ownership and the entire equitable ownership are vested in just *one* person then, as a general rule, there is no trust: the owner is described as the (sole) legal and beneficial owner. Similarly, when the entire beneficial interest under an existing trust is or becomes vested in a person who is or becomes the sole trustee of the property, the trust thereupon comes to an end: the property has become vested in a sole legal and beneficial owner.

The trust is an extremely useful and versatile tool. Its main advantage is that the division of ownership leads to a division of functions: the *management* of the property is segregated from its *use and enjoyment*. The trustees, as legal owners, manage the property; the beneficiaries, as equitable owners, enjoy its benefits. A trust may therefore be established for persons who cannot look after their own affairs (mental patients, minors, persons as yet unborn). More commonly, a trust is established simply because it is more convenient to segregate management from enjoyment. Where beneficiaries are inexperienced in property management and in the ways of the business world, it may be desirable to entrust the management of the property to experienced trustees; where the beneficiaries are numerous (large families, clubs) it becomes a practical necessity. And, as indicated earlier, statute sometimes uses the device of a trust to solve technical conveyancing problems.

Trusts of *land* are subject to special rules. A trust of land is trust of property which is *or includes* land.

(1)   OVERVIEW

The 1925 legislation simplified the law relating to trusts of land; the Trusts of Land and Appointment of Trustees Act (ToLATA) 1996 simplified the law still further. Any trust of land established after 1996 is a *trust of land* within the meaning of ToLATA and is governed by the unified scheme established by that Act. Most trusts of land established before 1997 have also been brought within ToLATA's unified scheme, but not all. Before 1997, a trust of land might be one of three varieties: a *strict settlement* (within the Settled Land Act 1925 (SLA)), a *trust for sale* (within the LPA), or a *bare trust*. Pre-1997 *strict settlements* continue to be governed by the SLA (unless and until they are converted); all other trusts of land are now *trusts of land* within ToLATA.

The *strict settlement* was originally designed for wealthy landowners with dynastic intent. It was an appropriate apparatus for the ancestral homes of the aristocracy, and for others who would imitate them. A 'settlement' here means a series of trusts: there is a settlement where several persons are entitled to the same property *in succession*, that is, one after another. Settlements range from the highly elaborate to the very simple. 'To Adam for life' creates a settlement, because, if nothing more is said, it implies 'remainder to me', thus creating a succession of interests.

A settlement is called a *strict* settlement if its operation is governed by the SLA. Before 1997, strict settlement was the default status, in the sense that every settlement of land (that is, every trust creating a succession of interests in land) was necessarily a strict settlement *unless* the settlement was expressly or by statute made a *trust for sale*. That meant that it was easy to create a strict settlement by accident. Should an ignorant settlor or his negligent adviser omit the vital reference to a trust for sale (or a duty to sell, which means the same thing), then he created a strict settlement.

The central feature of a strict settlement is that the legal ownership of the land, and with it the powers of management, are vested, not in the trustees of the settlement, but in the principal beneficiary – usually the tenant for life in possession. However, the mechanisms of the strict settlement are complex, cumbersome, inflexible and expensive to administer – and the dynastic aims of the strict settlement could (and can) be achieved as well or better by other means. By 1996, it was the case that very few strict settlements were being created, and most of those that were created were created by accident. The decision was taken, therefore, to abolish the strict settlement, in the sense that no new strict settlement may be created after 1996. But strict settlements created before 1997 continue to exist and continue to be governed by the SLA.

Moreover, *resettlements* of settled land may continue indefinitely to exist as strict settlements under the SLA. For reasons too lengthy to explain here, land held on the traditional, dynastic strict settlement is normally resettled once a generation. That is to say, the trustees and the relevant beneficiaries get together and rewrite the trusts upon which the land is held to take account of changed circumstances and of the needs of the next generation. Such a resettlement, derived from an existing strict settlement, may itself be a strict settlement governed by the SLA – if, but only if, the instrument of resettlement so provides. Otherwise, the resettlement will take effect as a simple trust of land under ToLATA's unified scheme.

Before 1997, most trusts of land were *trusts for sale*, and were governed by the LPA. A trust for sale might be expressly created by a settlor by deed or will; a trust for sale might, in certain circumstances, be implied by statute. A trust for sale is simply a trust which imposes upon the trustees a *duty* to sell the land. In most cases, however, the duty to sell is not quite what it seems. In most cases, it is not intended that the trustees should sell immediately. On the contrary, it is usually intended that the trustees should retain the land for a considerable period of time and perhaps indefinitely. The duty to sell is therefore something of a conveyancer's fiction, and in most cases the duty is merely a duty *ultimately* to sell the property. A trust for sale gives the legal title and consequent powers of management to the *trustees* (and there will usually be two or more trustees in a trust for sale).

By 1997, the trust for sale had largely supplanted the strict settlement as a means of settling land. It was comparatively simple, straightforward, adaptable and cheap to administer. But the trust for sale had a much wider application than the settlement of successive interests in land. In particular, a trust for sale (express or statutory) invariably existed in all cases of co-ownership, and statute imposed a trust for sale upon the property of a person dying intestate (without having made a will).

ToLATA now implies a *trust of land* in those cases where previously *statute* would have implied a trust for sale. The main difference between the two is that a trust of land involves a *power* to sell the land instead of a *duty* to sell it. But a settlor may, if he wishes, still create an *express* trust for sale: he may expressly impose upon the trustees of land a duty to sell. And express trusts for sale created before 1997 now operate as trusts of land with a duty to sell superimposed. However, ToLATA gives the trustees a power to postpone the sale for as long as they wish.

The third kind of trust which might exist before 1997 was a *bare trust*. A bare trust, in this context, is a trust where a sole trustee holds on trust for a sole, adult beneficiary. A bare trust was not caught by the SLA (because there was no *succession* of interests). A bare trust did not involve a statutory trust for sale (because there was no *co*-ownership, in the sense that neither the legal title nor the equitable title was vested in two or more people). A bare trust is, however, a trust of land as defined in ToLATA and so is subject to ToLATA's unified regime. (For the sake of completeness it might be added that, where a sole trustee holds for a sole beneficiary who is a *minor*, then that used to involve a strict settlement under the SLA, but it now creates a trust of land under ToLATA.)

(2)   TRUSTS OF LAND

(a)   Creation

Every trust of property which is or includes land is a trust of land as defined, save for any surviving pre-1997 strict settlements and one or two other minor exceptions. The trust may be expressly created, or it may be implied or imposed by law. It is expressly enacted that a 'trust of land' includes a trust for sale and a bare trust.

(b)   Structure

The legal title to the land is vested in the trustees. They hold as joint tenants (see Chapter 13), and, save for charity land, there may be no more than four trustees of land. If more than four are nominated, then only the first four take the legal title. A sole trustee may *hold* land on trust, but two or more trustees may be necessary if the land is to be sold or otherwise dealt with, for a purchaser will normally need to pay his money to two or more trustees (or a sole trust corporation) if he is to overreach the equitable interests arising under the trust.

With the legal title go powers of management. Trustees of land are, by ToLATA, given 'all the powers of an absolute owner'. They may sell, mortgage, charge, lease or otherwise dispose of or deal with the land. They may buy other land, whether as an investment, or as a residence for one of their beneficiaries, or otherwise. However, in the case of an *express* trust of land, the trustees' powers may be restricted by the terms of the trust instrument, and in any trust of land the trustees may be to some extent inhibited in the exercise of their powers by the rights of the beneficiaries (see below, p 146).

Trustees of land may delegate their powers of management to any adult beneficiary or beneficiaries who is or are entitled to an equitable interest in possession under the trust. The trustees may, in that way, delegate all their powers, including their power of sale. But, should the trust land be sold, then a purchaser needs to pay his money to the 'proper' trustees (being at least two in number or a trust corporation) and not to their delegate or delegates. Such an arrangement is, in the result, not unlike an old-fashioned strict settlement.

The equitable interests under a trust of land may be of any variety allowed by the law. There may be one sole beneficiary, absolutely entitled, or several concurrent beneficiaries, or several successive beneficiaries, or a combination of concurrent and successive beneficiaries. The trustees and beneficiaries may be the same people, or different people, or some of the same people. In short, there is compete flexibility within the limits of the law.

(c)   Documentation

An express trust of land may be constituted by one document or two. If two are used, then one will vest the legal title and record the 'public' information needed by a potential purchaser – including the identity of the land, the identity of the trustees, and any restrictions on their powers. The other will record the 'private' information and, in particular, it will set out the trusts upon which the land is held. If only one document is used, then, obviously, it must contain both the 'public' and 'private' elements. The point is that, if one document is used, then that document becomes part of the paper title to the land and must be handed on to a subsequent purchaser or to the Land Registry as the case may be. That in turn means that the 'private' information is revealed to those who have no business to know it, and, more significantly, the trustees lose possession of the document which clothes them with their authority.

Sometimes, those apparent disadvantages are of no consequence. In the common case of a joint purchase of land, the trust applies to that one piece of land only; it is a simple trust whereby the trustees hold on trust for themselves beneficially, and the trust is intended to subsist only for the duration of the ownership of that piece of land. In such circumstances, there is no significant disadvantage in using a single document, and a single document is almost always used. The vendor transfers the legal title to the joint purchasers by deed, and they in that same deed declare that they hold on trust for themselves as joint tenants or tenants in common as the case may be. Where, however, the trust is wider or more complex, then two separate documents will normally be used.

Where the land is registered land, the trustees will be registered as joint proprietors. Save in one case, appropriate restrictions will be entered in the proprietorship register – typically, a restriction to the effect that a sole surviving proprietor is unable to give a valid receipt for any purchase money (unless the proprietor is a trust corporation). That indicates to a prospective purchaser that he needs to pay his money to two trustees (or a trust corporation) if he is to overreach the equities arising under the trust. The exceptional case, where no such restriction is entered on the register, is the case where the trustees hold on trust for themselves as joint tenants in Equity. In this instance (see Chapter 13), the survivor becomes sole legal *and beneficial* owner, the trust terminates, the survivor *can* deal with the property as his own, and so he *can* give a valid receipt.

(d)   Rights of the beneficiaries

In a statutory (as opposed to an express) trust of land, the trustees are expected to *consult* any adult beneficiaries who are entitled to an equitable interest in possession under the trust. The trustees are also expected to *give effect to the wishes* of those beneficiaries or to the wishes of the majority (by value) of them – so far as is consistent with the general interest of the trust. That qualification means that the trustees can, for example, decline to give effect to the wishes of a tenant for life if his proposals would unfairly prejudice a remainderman.

If the trust is an express trust of land, then those duties are implied in the case of a trust coming into operation after 1996, unless the trust instrument expressly excludes them; they are not implied into a trust coming into operation before 1997, unless the settlor by deed directs that they should be implied.

A beneficiary under the trust may sometimes be entitled to demand that the trustees allow him actually to occupy the trust land. There are several conditions: the beneficiary must be entitled to an interest in possession under the trust, the land must be suitable for him, and *either* the purposes of the trust must include making the land available for occupation by a beneficiary *or* the trust land must be available for his occupation. If two or more beneficiaries are so entitled, then the trustees may choose between them and they may impose conditions upon any beneficiary allowed into occupation. For example, the occupier(s) might be required to pay the outgoings of the property, or keep it in good repair and state of decoration, or pay a 'rent' for the benefit of non-occupying beneficiaries.

(e)   The decision to sell

Trustees of land, as such, have all the powers of an absolute owner. They therefore have at least a *power* to sell the land. In the case of an express trust of land, their power of sale may be made subject to any restrictions lawfully imposed by the terms of the trust. On the other hand, an express trust of land may also take the form of a trust for sale. That is, the terms of the trust may impose upon the trustees a positive *duty* to sell the land. A duty to sell may be imposed with or without conditions or restrictions. But, whatever the trust itself says, statute gives the trustees a power to postpone the sale indefinitely.

As long as the trustees are unanimous, therefore, there is no practical difference between a power to sell and a duty to sell: the trustees may sell if they all agree to sell; they may delay the sale if they all agree to delay. If, however, the trustees disagree amongst themselves, then the difference between a power of sale and a duty of sale may be important. It is a basic rule of trusts law that trustees are obliged to discharge their duties. It is also a basic rule that the trustees must be unanimous in the exercise of any power given to them. In concept, therefore, if the trust is merely a trust of land (with a power of sale), then there can be no sale unless and until the trustees unanimously agree to sell; if the trust is a trust for sale (duty to sell, with a power of postponement), there must be a sale unless there is unanimous agreement to postpone.

Matters may not, however, be as straightforward as that. In the first place, the trustees may have to take account of the wishes of the beneficiaries, as explained above, and that may tip the balance one way or the other. In the second place, any serious disagreement is likely to result in an application to the court for directions, and the court will make such order as it considers just in the light of all the circumstances – and the existence or otherwise of a duty to sell is but one consideration to take into account.

(f)   Consent to sale

In an express trust of land, the settlor may, if he wishes, impose a restriction that the trustees shall not sell the land (or, for that matter, otherwise deal with it) without the prior consent of a specified person or persons. A testator might, for example, leave his house to trustees on trust for his wife, but add that it shall not be sold unless she consents. She can then insist on retaining her home for as long as she wants, whatever the trustees may think.

This feature may be adapted as a device to inhibit sale and so tie up the land for a considerable time. The settlor may insist that, in order to sell, the trustees must obtain the consent of some person who he calculates is unlikely to consent.

The settlor may specify that the trustees obtain the consent of any number of persons, and the trustees act in breach of trust if they fail to obtain all the specified consents. The court, however, has power to dispense with any requisite consent, on the application of any interested party. And, in any event, a *purchaser* for money or money's worth need only see that a maximum of *two* consents are obtained. He will get a good title if any two of the settlor's nominees consent, notwithstanding that there are other nominees who do not consent.

(g)   Overreaching

A purchaser for money or money's worth is able to take free of the equities arising under the trust of land by virtue of the doctrine of overreaching. The legal title is vested in *all* the trustees as joint tenants (see Chapter 13). Therefore, the purchaser must take his conveyance or transfer from *all* the trustees. Similarly, he will normally pay the purchase money over to all the trustees, unless the trust deed otherwise provides. But, whatever the trust deed says, he must pay his money to at least *two* trustees, or to a trust corporation; otherwise he does not overreach the equities.

It follows that, as a general rule, a *sole* trustee cannot sell the land free of the equities. There are several points to add. First, as mentioned earlier, a sole trustee can *hold* land on trust; the need for two or more trustees arises only when there is some *dealing* with the land involving the receipt of capital moneys. Second, and obviously, if the sole trustee is a trust corporation, then it can both hold and validly deal with the land.

Third, although a sole *trustee* (not being a trust corporation) cannot deal with land, a sole *personal representative* can. So, where a trust of land arises under a will or on an intestacy, a sole personal representative can validly sell the land in the course of administration (for example, to pay the deceased's debts), but once administration is complete and the title is transferred to trustees of land, then two trustees are required to sell. But how does the purchaser know whether and when administration is complete? He does not and cannot know. In practice, the purchaser has to assume that the administration is continuing unless and until there is a document (an assent in writing) whereby the personal representative hands the land over to the trustees. That is so even in the common case where by his will a testator appoints Tom and Tess to be his 'executors and trustees' and declares a trust of his estate. If Tom or Tess dies, the survivor can validly sell as sole personal representative, but not as sole trustee; but the purchaser must assume that the survivor is still acting as a personal representative unless and until there is a written assent from the survivor as personal representative to himself or herself as trustee.

Fourth, the property may be vested in a sole owner who used to be a trustee of land but who has now ceased to be a trustee because the trust has come to an end. That occurs where trustees previously held the land on trust for themselves as joint tenants in Equity. In those circumstances, the last survivor becomes sole legal and beneficial owner, and the trust terminates. There are technical problems in the case of unregistered land, because the purchaser is not entitled to 'go behind the curtain' of the trust and investigate the equities; therefore, he can never be sure that the only surviving legal owner is also the only surviving equitable owner. However, statute says he can normally take at face value a statement in the deed of transfer that the survivor is such. The problem does not arise in the case of registered land. The purchaser simply inspects the register to discover whether there is any restriction on the powers of disposition of the registered proprietor.

Fifth, it may happen that there is a trust of land which is undiscovered and undiscoverable by the purchaser. A sole vendor may appear to be solely and beneficially entitled, when in reality he holds on trust. The typical case is that of a family home, apparently bought by one partner alone, but in reality paid for by both. The problem and the possible solutions are explored more fully in Chapter 13, but two general propositions can usefully be made here. First, in these circumstances, a purchaser from a sole trustee of land clearly cannot *overreach* the equities; but second, precisely because he is unaware of any trust, the purchaser may claim to *take free* of the equities on general principle – on the grounds that he is a BFP (remembering, however, that a purchaser is expected to make inquiries of any person in actual occupation of the land).

(3)   STRICT SETTLEMENTS

Strict settlements created before 1997 continue to be governed by the old scheme of the SLA, unless and until the settlement is turned into a trust of land upon resettlement, as explained earlier. The SLA's scheme is, briefly, as follows.

(a)   Settled land

As soon as *land* was held in trust for persons by way of *succession*, there was a strict settlement within the SLA *unless* a trust for sale was declared by the settlor or imposed by statute. The element of succession might be express or implied. The following were all examples of settled land: 'to Adam for life, remainder to Beth', 'to Colin for life', 'to Dawn in tail', 'to Ed until he marries', 'to Fran when she graduates'.

There was some tricky detail. A declaration of trust for a minor might create a strict settlement, even without any element of succession. An attempt to convey a legal estate to a minor might create a strict settlement. Imposing 'family charges' upon the land, such as an annuity for grandmama, might create a strict settlement. But it is not worth pursuing those points here.

(b)   Tenant for life

The 'tenant for life' is the person who, under the SLA, is supposed to have the legal title and powers of management. He occupies a dual role. He wears two hats. In his 'official' capacity he acquires and holds the legal estate on trust to give effect to the terms of the settlement. In that capacity, he owes a trustee's fiduciary duty towards the beneficiaries to manage the property in the best interests of all and to act impartially as between them.

In that official capacity, he can sell, lease, mortgage and otherwise deal with the settled land. The tenant for life is therefore a *trustee of the land*, but, confusingly, that does *not* make him a *trustee of the settlement*. Trustee of the settlement is something entirely different (see below).

Wearing his other hat, the tenant for life has his own beneficial interest under the trust. He may deal with that beneficial interest independently of the legal title, and he can, of course, do as he pleases with his own.

The SLA prescribes who shall be the tenant for life. Broadly, the tenant for life is the person currently entitled in possession under the settlement, provided he is an adult. If there is no such person, or if the apparent tenant for life is a minor, then the SLA designates certain persons to be the *statutory owners* to hold the legal title and to exercise the powers of management in default of a tenant for life.

(c)   Trustees of the settlement

'Trustees of the settlement' is a misleading title. The trustees of the settlement are not trustees at all in the ordinary sense of the word. They are not invested with the legal title to the settled land on trust for the beneficiaries. 'Trustees of the *settlement*' are not, as such, trustees of the settled *land*. The nature of their office is that of *guardians* of the settlement as a whole. They are there to keep an eye on the tenant for life, and to make sure that he duly exercises his powers of management. He must give them notice before exercising some of his powers, and get their consent before exercising others, but the management decisions are his, not theirs.

However, if and when the tenant for life decides to sell the settled land, then although the purchaser takes his *title* from the tenant for life, he pays the *purchase moneys* to the trustees of the settlement. At that point, they become true trustees to the extent that they hold the capital money on the trusts of the settlement. They have appropriate powers of investment, but they must exercise those powers according to any directions given by the tenant for life. In other words, he still makes the management decisions, if he wants to.

The SLA prescribes who shall be trustees of the settlement. There is a statutory pecking order. Usually, the trustees of the settlement are the persons expressly nominated as such.

(d)   Documentation

In principle, a strict settlement should be constituted by two documents. One is a 'public' document, a *vesting deed*, which tells the outside world (specifically, a prospective purchaser, lessee or mortgagee) all it needs to know and all it is entitled to know about the settlement. The postman will check to see that a parcel is properly wrapped and stamped and addressed, but what the parcel contains is none of his business. In the same way, a prospective purchaser of settled land needs to be able check the identity of the *land* (which he is buying), the identity of the *tenant for life* (from whom he gets his title) and the identity of the *trustees of the settlement* (to whom he must pay his money). Those three essential items of information are therefore set out in the vesting deed, and the purchaser is entitled and bound to take the statements at face value. The vesting deed also, as its name implies, actually vests the legal title in the tenant for life. In consequence, it becomes part of the paper title to the land. In the case of unregistered land, it is handed over to the purchaser on completion along with all the other title deeds and documents. In the case of registered land, the contents of the vesting deed are translated onto the Land Certificate, the tenant for life is entered as the registered proprietor, and appropriate restriction is entered to alert the purchaser to the fact that the land is settled land, and the purchase then proceeds according to the usual registered land procedures.

So much for the 'public' face of the settlement. But, just as the postman has no business opening a parcel to inspect the contents, so in the case of a settlement, the contents of a settlement, the *trusts* on which the land is held, are no business of the purchaser. That is 'private' information. It should remain 'behind the curtain'. It is therefore set out in a separate document, called a *trust instrument*. The trusts declared continue in effect despite the sale of the land. They continue to apply to the capital moneys produced by the sale, and they apply to any other land bought with that money. The trust instrument is therefore a 'private' document which 'belongs' to the settlement as a whole. It is not part of the title of any particular piece of land. It is not handed over to a purchaser on completion. It does not have to be lodged with the Land Registry.

Sometimes, strict settlements were created by a single document (often by a will). The SLA dubbed a single-document settlement an *imperfect settlement*, treated the one existing document as the trust instrument, and laid down procedures for perfecting the imperfect settlement by creating the missing second document, the vesting deed.

Once established, a strict settlement must, in principle, be operated according to the statutory scheme, and, in particular, the legal title must be vested in, and must be conveyed by, the tenant for life. The SLA declares that any purported disposition by anybody else is ineffective (s 13 – 'the paralysing section'). But there are exceptions. For example, a BFP takes a good title if he buys without notice of the settlement. And, where the settlement is created by will, the deceased's personal representatives (or even his *sole* personal representative) can deal with the land in the ordinary course of winding up the deceased's estate, for the personal representatives' right to deal with the land in the course of administration (for example, to sell the land to pay off the deceased's debts) takes priority over any claim by or under the settlement. And there are a couple of other exceptions to the paralysing provisions.

(e)   Death of tenant for life

The death of the tenant for life may bring the settlement to an end. If the settlement was 'to Adam for life, remainder to Beth', then, after Adam's death, the land no longer stands limited in trust for persons *in succession*. It stands limited in trust for Beth absolutely. Therefore, the settlement comes to an end on Adam's death. The property thereupon vests in Adam's *ordinary* personal representatives, and they take on trust to vest it in Beth absolutely.

If, on the other hand, the settlement was 'to Adam for life, remainder to Beth for life, remainder to Colin absolutely', then there would still be an element of succession (Beth for life, remainder to Colin) even after Adam's death, and so the land would continue to be settled land. In that event, the SLA decrees that, upon Adam's death, the settled land shall vest in Adam's *special* personal representatives. Adam thus has two sets of personal representatives. His ordinary personal representatives obtain a grant of probate or letters of administration *excluding* settled land, and they deal with Adam's own property. His special personal representatives obtain a grant of probate or letters of administration *limited to* the settled land, and they take the settled land upon trust to vest the legal title in the next tenant for life, Beth. The special personal representatives are the trustees of the settlement, in disguise.

(f)   Overreaching

The doctrine of overreaching applies to settled land to enable a purchaser for value to take free of the equitable interests arising under the settlement. As mentioned earlier, it is the tenant for life who transfers the legal title to the purchaser, but, in order to overreach the equities, the purchaser must pay his purchase moneys to the trustees of the settlement. There must be at least two trustees (unless the sole trustee is a trust corporation), and the money must be paid to (or by the direction of) *all* of them.

13 Co-ownership

Co-ownership imports that two or more people own the same estate *concurrently*. The principles of law to be applied to co-ownership are found in the LPA. The rules can appear quite complex, but they were even more complex before 1926. The aim of the 1925 legislation was, as always, to simplify the rules so as to simplify the task of the purchaser's solicitor. The particular mischief in the case of co-ownership was that the purchase of co-owned land might involve many different vendors with many different titles. The LPA ensures that today, save in exceptional cases, the purchaser will have to investigate just *one* title held by not more than *four* vendors.

(1) KINDS OF CO-OWNERSHIP

There are two kinds of co-ownership: *joint tenancy* and *tenancy in common*. Other kinds were (with minor savings) abolished in 1925.

(a) Joint tenancy

The nature of joint tenancy is that it is a *collective* ownership. There is *one* ownership, a *unity* of ownership, but that ownership is vested in a group of persons collectively:

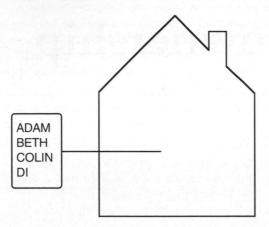

Adam, Beth, Colin and Di cannot claim any *individual* ownership, but each can say: 'I am a member of that exclusive group which owns number 3 Rectory Gardens.' The group can collectively dispose of the joint property, and sometimes an individual can act on behalf of the group, but the individual joint tenant has nothing which he can truly describe as 'mine'; it is all 'ours'.

This concept of collective or group ownership leads to the central characteristic of joint tenancy: the *right of survivorship* or *ius accrescendi*. Because Adam, for example, has no *separate* ownership, he has, as long as he remains a joint tenant, nothing which he can separately dispose of. In particular, as long as he remains a joint tenant, he has nothing which he can leave in his will. When Adam dies, the group shrinks, but that is all. The ownership is still vested in the group, but the group now consists of three instead of four. And when Beth dies, the group shrinks to two. And when Colin dies, the group shrinks to one, namely Di. And then there is no longer a group, there is no longer any *co*-ownership: Di has become sole and exclusive owner and can do with the property as she pleases. Joint tenancy is therefore the conveyancer's equivalent of Russian roulette: it is a gamble in which the survivor takes all.

Those rules are entirely appropriate in some situations. It is, for example, often the case that a husband and wife will want to hold the matrimonial home on a joint tenancy, so that the survivor automatically succeeds to the entirety. In other cases, it might be highly inappropriate, and a joint tenant might feel extremely uncomfortable at the prospect of having to gamble on survival. In that event, he may be able to *convert* his joint tenancy into a tenancy in common and thereby acquire a separate share as explained below. The technical expression for the process of conversion is *severance*. But the proposition remains true that *as long as he remains a joint tenant* the co-owner has no individual ownership; ownership is vested in the group of which he is a member.

The unity of ownership in a joint tenancy is said in fact to consist of *four* unities: the unities of possession, interest, time and title. All the joint tenants are entitled to *possession* of the property and none has the right to exclude any other member of the group. All joint tenants must have the same *estate or interest* in the property; it is not possible to vest the property in Adam in fee simple and in Beth for 99 years as joint tenants. All joint tenants must claim by virtue of the same *title* deed; I cannot by one deed vest a joint interest in Colin and by another deed vest a joint interest in Di, even if the two deeds are executed contemporaneously. In theory, the interests of the joint tenants should all vest at the same moment of *time*, but that rule is not inflexible.

(b)   Tenancy in common

Tenancy in common, by contrast, is an *individual* ownership. The property is owned by several people in such a way that each has a definite *share*:

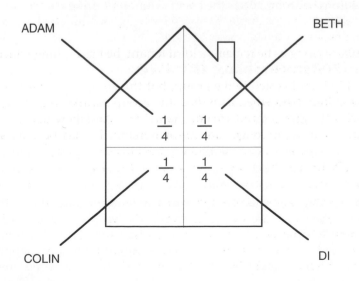

Adam has his quarter, and he may deal with it as he pleases, and he may deal with it without reference to the other co-owners. He may transfer his share *inter vivos*. He may divide it up into smaller shares. If he dies, then there can be no right of survivorship as in a joint tenancy, because Adam's quarter share is his own *separate* property. It devolves under his will, if he made one; otherwise, it passes to his statutory next of kin, or, in default, to the Crown as *bona vacantia*. A tenancy in common is therefore suitable for those who want the security of knowing exactly where they stand.

The shares do not have to be equal shares, although equality is to be assumed in the absence of any contrary indication. It might be that Adam begins with a half; Beth, a quarter; Colin, a sixth; Di, a twelfth. Adam could then leave his half to his four children; Beth could transfer her quarter to trustees on trust for her husband for life, remainder to their children; Colin could give his sixth to the University of Birmingham; and Di might die intestate, so that her twelfth is divided up amongst her numerous next of kin.

Tenancy in common is sometimes called *undivided shares* to emphasise that, although Adam's share is a separate share, it is nevertheless not a *partitioned* share. It is not the case that Adam owns the front bedroom, and Beth, the back. Rather, Adam owns one quarter of each and every part of the house – a quarter of each brick, a quarter of each blade of grass, a quarter of each atom of property. It is always open to co-owners – joint tenants as well as tenants in common – to agree to partition their property if they wish, but that destroys the *co*-ownership and results in each individual exclusively owning his separate parcel: Adam owns exclusively (say) the front bedroom; Beth, the back; Colin, the sitting room; and Di, the kitchen/diner.

(c) Distinguishing the two

Given the drastically different rights of joint tenants and tenants in common, it is obviously vital to be able to distinguish between them. It follows from what has been said above that if the *four unities* are not present, the parties cannot be joint tenants and so they must be tenants in common. But take a typical case where a document vests property in trustees on trust 'for Adam, Beth, Colin and Di'. The four unities are, or could be, present. Is it a joint tenancy or a tenancy in common?

The rule of thumb is this:

In cases of co-ownership, *presume* a *joint* tenancy, *unless*:

- *either* there are 'words of severance';
- *or* it is one of Equity's three special cases.

Words of severance are words which indicate an intention that the tenants shall have *separate* shares – 'in equal shares', 'equally', 'divide between', 'amongst', 'respectively' and so on. Words of severance result in a tenancy in common.

There are, however, three special cases where Equity *presumes* a tenancy in common, even if there are no words of severance. They are:

- where the co-owners are *business partners*, because the right of survivorship is inappropriate in business dealings (*ius accrescendi inter mercatores locum non habet*, which ought to be translated as: 'You'll never survive in the rat race!');
- where the co-owned property is a mortgage and the co-owners are the *lenders on mortgage*, because the assumption is that each lender expects to be paid back what he lent;
- where there is a *purchase in unequal shares*. In Equity, there is a presumption that if you pay a proportion of the purchase price of a piece of property, you expect to receive the same proportion of the ownership (on a 'resulting trust'). So, if Adam pays half and Beth, Colin and Di each pay one sixth, then Equity presumes that Adam gets a half interest and the other three one sixth each. But that means that their ownership cannot be joint and must be in common. Note the trap for the unwary: purchase in *equal* shares is *not* one of Equity's three special cases, and so, in the absence of words of severance, it results in a *joint* tenancy.

(d) Severance

For reasons explained below, at Law, a joint tenancy *cannot* be severed and converted into a tenancy in common. But severance is possible in Equity. Severance is a *unilateral* act. The would-be tenant in common does not have to elicit the agreement of his fellows. The severer acquires a separate and individual share in the property, and so becomes a tenant in common. The size of his share depends upon the number of joint tenants at the date of severance. If he is one of four joint tenants, he becomes a tenant in common as to one quarter, and so on. But severance does not affect the rights of the other members of the group *inter se*. They remain joint tenants of what is left of the property.

So, if Adam severs, he and 'the group' are tenants in common as to one quarter and three quarters respectively. 'The group' consists of Beth, Colin and Di, and they hold their three quarters as joint tenants:

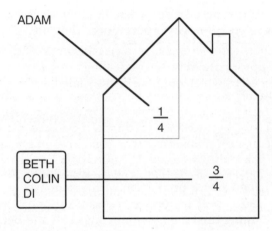

In consequence, if Beth dies, the right of survivorship operates within the group, but only within the group. Adam's share remains one quarter. He elected to sever the joint tenancy. He is no longer a member of the group. He is no longer vulnerable to the right of survivorship. By the same token, he can no longer benefit from the right of survivorship. 'The group' still owns three-quarters, but, Beth having died, the group now consists only of Colin and Di.

The simple and straightforward way of effecting a severance is to serve a formal notice in writing on the other co-owners. Yet, any acting by one joint tenant which implies that he is claiming a separate and individual share is likely to be treated as an act of severance. Thus, a purported alienation of his interest by one joint tenant works a severance. So does a contract to alienate. Severance may also be effected by mutual agreement or understanding between the co-owners.

So, to return to a point made earlier: one joint tenant cannot alienate his *joint* interest; but an attempt to do so causes (in Equity) a severance of his interest, which then becomes a tenancy in common, giving him a share which he can validly alienate. Suppose Adam, Beth, Colin and Di begin as joint tenants, and Adam purports to sell his interest to Pip. Pip does not become a joint tenant, but he does acquire a quarter share as tenant in common. The other three quarters is owned by 'the group' as joint tenants, the group consisting of Beth, Colin and Di.

(2) CO-OWNERSHIP AT LAW

As far as the Law is concerned, co-owners are always *joint tenants*. They cannot be anything else. The *legal* tenancy in common was abolished in 1925. It follows that a *legal* joint tenancy is an *unseverable* joint tenancy – it cannot be converted into a *legal* tenancy in common because there is no such thing. One consequence of insisting that legal co-owners are joint tenants is that the *legal title is always a unity*. The purchaser has just one title to investigate. Another consequence is that the legal title can be dealt with only by the *group as a whole*. A purported disposition by one, or several, or even a majority is incompetent as far as the Law is concerned (although such an act may have significance in Equity – see below, p 163). The legal ownership is vested in 'the group' and only 'the group' can dispose of it effectively.

Furthermore, as far as the Law is concerned, there can never be more than *four* legal joint tenants of land (save in the case of charity). Statute so provides. An attempt to vest the legal title in more than four has the effect of vesting the legal title in the first four named. The others get nothing at Law (but they do get something in Equity – see below, p 162). That simplifies the purchaser's task still further: one title, and not more than four holders of that one title.

(3) TRUST OF LAND

As soon as there is co-ownership of land, whether at Law or in Equity, there will be a trust of land. Frequently, co-ownership is created behind an *express* trust of land. If not, then statute will *impose* a trust of land.

Sometimes, statute does so explicitly; sometimes, statute needs 'interpretation', but it is a fair working rule to say that co-ownership always involves a trust of land. The legal owners are therefore necessarily *trustees* as well as being necessarily joint tenants. Their beneficiaries – the equitable owners – are *all* the intended co-owners, without restriction in number. And, in Equity, the co-owners can be *either* joint tenants *or* tenants in common. Which they are depends upon the application of the rules explained above. And, should it turn out that they are joint tenants, then, in Equity, the joint tenancy is still a *severable* joint tenancy.

The final strut in the structure of the law of co-ownership is to make the trust of land an *overreaching* trust. As long as the purchaser pays his money to all the trustees, being at least two in number or a trust corporation, he acquires the legal title free from the claims of the equitable owners. The equitable claims of the co-owners are taken out of the land and transferred into the purchase money paid to the trustees.

In short, all the complexities of co-ownership can continue to apply, but they are shunted into Equity, the curtain of a trust is drawn across them, and the purchaser is forbidden to look behind the curtain. He does not know, and is not entitled to know, what goes on behind the curtain. He takes things at face value.

(4) EXAMPLES

Take the following as an example of how all these rules meld together. Suppose land is transferred 'to Adam, Beth, Colin, Di and Ed in equal shares'. First, consider the position at Law. There can be no more than four legal owners, so Adam, Beth, Colin and Di take the legal title. Ed is excluded. Legal owners must be joint tenants, so Adam, Beth, Colin and Di take as joint tenants at Law, despite the express words 'in equal shares', which are words of severance importing a tenancy in common. Because there is co-ownership, there is a trust of land, and Adam, Beth, Colin and Di take their legal title as trustees upon trust for … Then consider the position in Equity. The equitable title is vested in Adam, Beth, Colin, Di and Ed – all five. Are they joint tenants or tenants in common? Here, there are words of severance – 'in equal shares' – therefore, they are tenants in common in Equity.

Thus, a complete statement of the title is that Adam, Beth, Colin and Di take the legal title as joint tenants holding as trustees upon trust for Adam, Beth, Colin, Di and Ed as tenants in common in Equity.

Suppose Adam then transfers his entire interest to Pip. Begin again with the Law. At Law, Adam's action has no effect whatsoever. The *legal* joint tenancy is an unseverable joint tenancy. The legal title may be dealt with only by the group as a whole. Adam is incompetent to deal with it alone. Therefore, the legal title remains vested in Adam, Beth, Colin and Di. They continue to hold as joint tenants upon trust. The beneficial interests have, however, changed. Adam was a tenant in common in Equity and his transfer to Pip was perfectly valid in Equity. So, the trustees now hold on trust for Pip, Beth, Colin, Di and Ed as tenants in common in equal shares.

Suppose Beth then dies, by her will leaving all her property to be divided between her two children. At Law, one of the four joint tenants has died. The right of survivorship applies, and the will is of no consequence. The *legal* title is still vested in 'the group', but the group has shrunk to three: Adam, Colin and Di. Those three joint tenants now hold as trustees upon trust for ... In Equity, Beth, as a tenant in common, was perfectly entitled to bequeath her share to her two children, and 'divide between' are words of severance importing a tenancy in common. Beth's children therefore take Beth's share as tenants in common and not as joint tenants. Therefore, the legal title is held on trust for Pip, Beth's children, Colin, Di and Ed as tenants in common: Pip, Colin, Di and Ed are entitled to one fifth each; Beth's children, to one tenth each.

Suppose, finally, the trustees decide to sell. The purchaser will take his title from, and pay the purchase moneys to, Adam, Colin and Di. Because there are two or more trustees, the purchase overreaches the equities. The purchaser takes a clean legal title, and Adam, Colin and Di now hold the purchase moneys on trust for Pip, Beth's children, Colin, Di and Ed in the shares aforesaid.

Observe that Adam does not lose his status as legal owner and trustee merely because he parts with all his beneficial interest. That would be inconsistent with the idea of an *unseverable* joint tenancy at Law. (He could, if he wished, *surrender* his legal ownership to the other joint tenants; but he would have to do so expressly.) Observe that, when Beth dies, so reducing the number of legal joint tenants to three, Ed, as the fourth survivor of the five named in the original transfer, does not automatically step into her shoes as legal owner and trustee. That would be inconsistent with the proposition that joint tenancy requires *unity of title*. (The three surviving trustees could jointly *appoint* Ed (or Pip or anyone else) to be a fourth trustee with them; but they are not obliged to do so.) Observe, finally, that the purchaser of the legal estate must take his title from Adam, Colin and Di. Colin and Di, although two in number and a majority of the trustees, have no power to deal separately with the legal title. The legal ownership is vested in the group of joint tenants as a whole and must be dealt with by the group as a whole.

(5)   REGISTRATION

Where co-ownership exists in *unregistered* land, there is no question of registering the equitable interest of any co-owner as a land charge or otherwise. Registration of incumbrances is appropriate for those kinds of interest which are to *bind* the purchaser, whereas a purchaser of co-owned land obviously expects to take *free* of the rights of the equitable owners. In general, the rights of the equitable owners are sufficiently protected by the existence of trustees. As soon as he sees that the legal title is or was vested in several persons, the purchaser realises that there is or was a trust of land, and he therefore has *notice* of the equitable interests. Unless it can be sufficiently demonstrated to him that the trust has come to an end (for example, by union of legal and equitable titles in a sole survivor), the purchaser will insist on paying his purchase moneys to two or more trustees; he will *overreach* and so take free of the equities; the rights of the equitable owners are transferred to the purchase moneys, and the equitable owners are protected by the continuing trust.

There is one apparent exception to the proposition that a beneficial ownership in unregistered land is not registrable as a land charge, but it is not a true exception.   The case is that of the Class F land charge – spouse's rights of occupation. There is a potential problem where the legal title is and always has been vested in a sole owner, but where, for some reason, there is co-ownership in Equity. That can happen, for example, if the legal title to a matrimonial home is vested in the husband alone, when the house has in fact been paid for by both spouses. The purchaser cannot *overreach* the wife's equitable interest if he buys from the husband alone, because overreaching requires two trustees. On the other hand, in this case the title deeds give no indication of any trust at all, so that, if he does not get notice from any other source, the purchaser can take free of the wife's interest on the basis that he is a BFP. The wife then has rights against her husband. But suppose he absconds with the purchase money and another woman. The wife is homeless and penniless. The law seeks to prevent the potential injustice by insisting that a *spouse* (but not any other cohabitee or co-owner) has certain statutory 'rights of occupation', and by allowing that spouse to register those rights of occupation as a land charge, Class F. Notice, however, that the spouse does not strictly register his or her *equitable interest*. It is the statutory rights of occupation which are registrable as a land charge, and a spouse has those whether the spouse has an equitable interest or not.

Where co-ownership exists in *registered* land, then the rights of the equitable owners are minor interests which should be protected by an appropriate entry in the register. Where there are two or more registered proprietors, the appropriate entry is a *restriction* on their powers. Save in one case, the registrar will automatically enter a restriction to the effect that the survivor of registered proprietors cannot give a valid receipt for the purchase moneys. The purchaser is thereby alerted to the existence of a continuing trust of land, and to the need to ensure that there are at least two transferors/trustees if the equities are to be overreached. The exceptional case is where the registered proprietors hold on trust exclusively for themselves as *joint tenants* in Equity. The right of survivorship operates both at Law and in Equity, so that the last survivor becomes sole legal and beneficial owner. He *can*, therefore, give a valid receipt for capital money, no restriction is necessary in the proprietorship register, and none is entered.

Problems can arise, especially where the legal title is vested in a sole proprietor without any restriction on the face of the register, but where Equity sees a co-ownership. The equitable owner is vulnerable to the purchaser for value. Protection may be obtained in some circumstances by entering a *caution* against dealings, which at least entitles the cautioner to some warning of the need to take positive action in the event that the proprietor decides to sell. That procedure is appropriate, for example, if the vulnerable beneficiary is a spouse who has statutory rights of occupation of the matrimonial home. Otherwise, if the vulnerable beneficiary remains *in actual occupation* of the registered land, then his rights can take effect as *overriding interests*.

14 Mortgages

(1)   TERMINOLOGY

For most people, buying a house is the most expensive purchase they ever make, and few are able to fund the entire purchase from their own pockets. Most people have to go to a building society or to a bank or to an insurance company and get a mortgage. Everybody knows that. And 'everybody' is wrong. The borrower does not *get* a mortgage *from* the financial institution. He *gives* a mortgage *to* it. What he *gets* is a loan of money – a mortgage loan or a mortgage advance, if you will; but the mortgage itself is the *security* he gives for repayment of that loan.

This is not just a silly point made in a silly way. It has a serious purpose. The borrower is the mortgag*or*; the lender is the mortgag*ee*. When you first come to mortgages it is easy to become confused over the terminology. You instinctively expect to find the mortgag*or* giving and the mortgag*ee* getting, and yet it is the mortgagee who is giving the money and the mortgagor who is getting it. Switch the focus to the *security* for the loan, and everything falls into place: the mortgagor (borrower) gives the security; the mortgagee (lender) gets it.

In fact, strictly speaking, the borrower in a typical case does not even give a *mortgage* to the building society or other financial institution. Instead, he gives it a *legal charge*, which has the same effect as a mortgage but which is, conceptually, a different and less complicated beast.

(2)   KINDS OF SECURITY

A security for the repayment of a loan, perhaps it goes without saying, is something belonging to the borrower which he deposits with the lender until such time as the loan is repaid. The function of the security is twofold. In the first place, it provides an incentive for the borrower to repay: he has to repay if he is to *redeem* (literally, buy back) that which he has given as security. Second, if he fails to repay, the lender has something to sell; and that is especially important if the borrower becomes bankrupt. Since a bankrupt's liabilities exceed his assets, the ordinary unsecured creditors will probably recover only a proportion of their respective debts. But the secured creditor is better placed. He can realise his security and repay, or at least reduce, the loan out of the proceeds. If the security is worth more than the outstanding loan (plus interest and costs), he pays himself in full and hands over the balance to the trustee in bankruptcy to swell the fund available for the unsecured creditors. If the security proves insufficient, he may pay himself out of the security, as far as it goes, and then join the queue of ordinary unsecured creditors for the balance.

(a)   Pawn, pledge and lien

The simplest form of security is the *pawn* or *pledge*. The borrower physically deposits some item with the lender as security for repayment of the loan. The borrower gives *possession* of the item, but retains *ownership* of it. For obvious reasons, this is not a very practicable form of security in relation to land.

A *lien* also involves having *possession* of an item as security, but in a lien the debtor gives possession for some other purpose, and the creditor then *retains* possession as security. If you take your car in for repair, the garage has a lien on it until you pay the garage bill; a hotelier has a lien on your luggage until you pay your hotel bill; your solicitor has a lien on your title deeds until you pay your conveyancing bill.

(b)   Mortgage

By contrast, in a *mortgage*, the borrower gives *ownership* as security, but he retains *possession*. Ownership is transferred subject to a proviso for reconveyance on redemption. It is possible to mortgage any kind of property, real or personal. Insurance policies are regularly mortgaged along with a house and land in an endowment mortgage, and mortgages of shares or other choses in action may be encountered. Mortgages of choses in possession are less common, but perfectly possible. A mortgage of choses in possession takes one into the realm of *bills of sale*, which is a fairly recondite area of law; and, if the problem is that a person wants a chattel he cannot afford, then hire purchase probably provides a simpler solution than chattel mortgage.

Mortgages of property other than land are not considered further in this book, although it may be said that the fundamental principles of mortgage are the same, whatever the nature of the property involved.

(c)   Charge

Another form of security is the *charge*. In a charge, the borrower *retains* both ownership and possession. He merely creates an incumbrance on his title; he gives the lender the right to take the property charged, in the event that the loan is not repaid in the agreed manner.

It is sometimes necessary to distinguish charges from mortgages, but more often the word 'mortgage' is used as a compendious word to describe both.

(3)   MORTGAGES OF LAND

As for mortgages of land, the most common form of 'mortgage' – especially in domestic conveyancing – is in fact a simple *legal charge*, but, for ease of understanding, it is better to begin at the beginning. The point might conveniently be made here that, whatever the kind of mortgage, the mortgagee (or the first mortgagee, where there is a succession of mortgages) normally expects to retain custody of the mortgagor's title deeds and documents until the loan is repaid. The purpose is to prevent the mortgagor dealing with his land without the knowledge of the mortgagee.

(a)   Legal mortgage of freeholds

Begin with the case of *unregistered land*, and begin with the largest estate, the legal fee simple absolute in possession. Suppose Martin wants to mortgage his freehold house to a building society. The lender will usually want a *legal* mortgage as opposed to an equitable mortgage, because a legal mortgage gives him greater security. It has already been said that a mortgage involves the transfer of *ownership* as security. One might therefore expect to find Martin transferring his legal fee simple to the building society subject to a proviso for retransfer on redemption. That is not, however, what happens. It used to. But the LPA now prohibits the transfer of the mortgagor's estate by way of security. Instead, it insists that the freeholder may grant no more than a *long lease* – conventionally 3,000 years – to the mortgagee. Martin therefore still gives legal *ownership* to the building society, but *an* ownership, a limited ownership, instead of *his* ownership. The 3,000 year term is a legal estate, a term of years absolute. It is rent-free. It is subject to a 'proviso for cesser on redemption', which, translated, means that the lease is a determinable lease which is automatically determined if and when the borrower repays the loan.

The idea was to make the Law on mortgages conform more closely to Equity's interpretation of the situation. Even if Martin's house is mortgaged to the building society, the common perception is that it is really still Martin's house, not the building society's. Equity agrees. Equity has always looked to the substance of the transaction, and has treated the mortgagor as the owner of the property, and the mortgage merely as a security for repayment of the loan. But, for as long as it was the practice to convey the legal fee simple to the mortgagee by way of security, the Law apparently regarded the house as belonging to the mortgagee until redemption and reconveyance. However, as a result of the LPA, the legal fee simple absolute remains with the borrower, and the lender gets 'only' a 3,000 year lease. This sort of full mortgage is accordingly sometimes called a *mortgage by demise* ('mortgage by lease'), to distinguish it from the *legal charge* described later.

A moment or two's reflection will show that, even though Martin now remains the legal owner of his house, nevertheless his *legal* ownership is a pretty nominal affair; at Law he still gives *substantially* the whole ownership to the building society. His legal freehold may be of superior *quality* compared to the lender's legal leasehold in legal theory; but, in practical terms, his estate is of vastly inferior *quantity*. True, Martin's fee simple will last for ever – but it is a fee simple which (in form) will not fall into possession for the next 3,000 years and which will bring in no rent in the meantime. The building society, on the other hand, has (in form) a lease which entitles it to rent-free possession for the next 3,000 years – something which is far more valuable than Martin's remote fee simple. (It should be said at once that Martin's position in Equity is very different, but that is another story which must wait awhile.)

The question might be raised, how can it be true to say that the building society (mortgagee) is entitled to immediate possession of Martin's house, when in reality it is Martin who will take possession and live there – indeed, that was the whole point of the arrangement? The answer is that, in Law, Martin becomes *subtenant* or *licensee* of the building society, depending on the terms of the mortgage deed. The cake thus has three tiers. Martin sits on the top as estate owner in fee simple; he grants away a 3,000 year lease to the building society; it grants possession back to him by way of subtenancy or licence for as long as he observes the agreed mortgage terms.

A legal mortgage by demise, because it grants a legal estate in land, must be effected by deed.

(b)   Legal mortgage of leaseholds

Similar principles apply if Martin owns a leasehold house. Suppose he has a 99 year lease. It used to be the case that he would assign the whole of the residue of the 99 year term. Now, as a result of the LPA, he must grant no more than an *underlease* to the building society for the residue of his 99 years *less at least one day*. (By conveyancing convention, the underlease is usually granted for 99 years less *10* days, so as to leave room for second or subsequent mortgages.) The building society is theoretically entitled to possession by virtue of its underlease, but in practice, it regrants possession to Martin by way of subtenancy or licence.

(c)   Legal charge

The mortgage by demise is cumbersome and old-fashioned. Modern mortgages are much more likely to take the form of a *legal charge*, or, as the LPA describes it, 'a charge by deed expressed to be by way of legal mortgage'. That adequately sums up the requirements: the charge must be imposed by deed, and the deed must actually state that the borrower thereby 'charges *by way of legal mortgage*' the relevant property. If the deed does not include the italicised words (or words to like effect), then it creates only an equitable charge, not a legal charge.

Both freeholds and leaseholds can be made the subject of a legal charge.

On the face of it, a legal chargee might look less secure than a legal mortgagee by demise. Unlike the mortgagee by demise, the legal chargee acquires no estate in the land. He acquires simply a right or interest in the mortgagor's land, albeit a *legal* interest. However, any deficiency is purely theoretical, for the LPA specifically enacts that the legal chargee shall be entitled to all the same protection, powers and remedies as if he were a mortgagee by demise. For that reason, 'mortgage' should be taken to mean 'mortgage or charge', unless the context shows that the special meaning is intended.

(d)   Equitable mortgages and charges

It is possible to create mortgages and charges in Equity as well as at Law. If the borrower only has an equitable interest (say, a life interest), then, obviously, he can give only an equitable mortgage. (Incidentally, he will still assign the *whole* of his equitable interest to the mortgagee, subject to a proviso for reassignment on redemption). If the borrower has a legal estate, then he may give either a legal or an equitable mortgage. There can be advantages in the latter. Equitable mortgages may involve less fuss, less formality and lower costs (especially in the case of registered land, where there may be a saving of Land Registry fees). Equitable mortgages are, for example, often used to secure short-term indebtedness, such as a bank overdraft. Equitable mortgages do not have to be made by deed; signed writing is sufficient, although in practice a deed is often used. And if what is intended to be a legal mortgage fails for want of formality, then the defective legal mortgage may be good in Equity (under the doctrine of *Walsh v Lonsdale* – see above, p 124).

One distinct kind of informal equitable mortgage is a *mortgage by deposit of title deeds*. If the borrower leaves his title deeds with the lender as a security for repayment of a loan, then, in days gone by that used, in Equity, of itself to constitute a mortgage. However, these days, for reasons too complicated to explain here, a deposit of title deeds needs to be accompanied by a written memorandum of deposit, recording the essential details of the arrangement and signed by borrower and lender.

It might be interjected, although this is not directly relevant to mortgages of land, that Equity also recognises a *floating charge*, where the security is a changing mass of items – such as the stock in trade of a business – as opposed to the particular items comprised in the mass. For example, if a grocer in Grantham gave a fixed charge on his stock, then every can of beans would need a letter of release from the mortgagee before it could be sold, and any new stock would be free of the fixed charge. But a floating charge casts its shadow over the whole of the grocer's stock as it exists from time to time; items sold pass out into the sunshine of freedom, new items fall under the cloud. The borrower is free to deal with the stock, unhindered by the floating charge, as long as he behaves in accordance with the agreed terms. Should he infringe the agreed terms (typically, by becoming insolvent or attempting in some way to defraud the lender), then the floating charge is said to 'crystallise': the cloud descends and becomes a fixed charge on those items which are then under its shadow.

The disadvantages of an equitable mortgage are that the remedies of the mortgagee may be more limited, but some of the disadvantages can be avoided by careful conveyancing. An equitable mortgagee is also vulnerable to the BFP, but he can protect himself by insisting on possession of the title deeds where possible and by registration where necessary.

(e)   Variations on the theme

For the sake of completeness, it might be mentioned that it is possible to have *successive* mortgages of the same property, each one taking effect *subject to* prior mortgages. Martin gives a *first mortgage* on his house to the building society to raise enough money to buy it. He gives a *second mortgage* to the bank to raise the money to extend it. He gives a *third mortgage* to Shark (Loans) Ltd when he needs to borrow yet more cash. If Martin becomes insolvent, the building society can realise its security by selling Martin's house free of the second and third mortgages, because its mortgage was prior to theirs. If the building society stays its hand, the bank can sell, but only subject to the building society's first mortgage. In consequence, either the bank has to find a purchaser who is prepared to take on the building society mortgage, or, more likely, the bank has to pay off the building society and step up to the position of first mortgagee, selling free of Shark's interest.

Second and subsequent mortgages may be legal or equitable, but they should be registered in either case. If the mortgaged land is unregistered land, then a second or subsequent *legal* mortgage will almost invariably be a 'puisne mortgage' and so registrable as a land charge, Class C(i); a second or subsequent *equitable* mortgage will almost invariably be a 'general equitable charge' and so registrable as a land charge, Class C(iii). If the mortgaged land is registered land, then all charges need to be registered or be protected by some entry on the register.

Sometimes one encounters a *submortgage*. A submortgage is a mortgage of a mortgage. Martin mortgages his land by demise to Shark Ltd. Shark itself wants to raise some cash. It owns a 3,000 year lease of Martin's house (subject to his right to redeem) and so it can mortgage that lease to Angler as security for a loan from Angler to Shark. Angler is, however, at some risk. If Martin repays his loan to Shark, Shark's lease is automatically determined and Angler's security vanishes.

(f)   Registered land

In principle, everything which has been said above applies as well to registered land as to unregistered land. In the case of registered land, however, there are some additional points to note. A *legal* mortgage of registered land must be created by deed, but it may be in any form. It may be a mortgage by demise or it may be a legal charge (but in the case of registered land, it is technically not necessary that a legal charge be *expressed* to by way of legal mortgage). In either case the mortgage constitutes a *registered charge* within the scheme of land registration. The Land Registry will withdraw the mortgagor's Land Certificate, and instead issue a Charge Certificate to the mortgagee (or to each of the mortgagees in the event that there are successive registered charges). A Charge Certificate is, in effect, a Land Certificate with a copy of the mortgage deed bound in it.

It is possible to create an equitable mortgage of registered land. In particular, it is specifically enacted that a registered proprietor may create a lien on registered land by depositing his Land Certificate with the lender. But the deposit needs to be recorded in a written memorandum, signed by both parties. In any event, an equitable mortgage or charge can never be a registered charge. It can only be a minor interest, and a minor interest needs to be protected by some entry on the register – either a notice or a caution.

(4)   REDEMPTION

The mortgage document may be blatantly misleading in what it says about repayment. It will often be the case that the borrower has negotiated a loan to be repaid over a lengthy period of time – 10, 20, 25 years. It is quite possible that the mortgage deed will include a promise that he will repay the whole sum, with interest, in six months' time or even less. The explanation lies in history.

(a)   Legal date of redemption

It used to be the case that the borrower transferred his entire legal estate to the lender as security. He had the right to *redeem*, or buy back, his estate on the date specified in the mortgage deed as the date for repayment. That date was, and is, called the *legal date of redemption*. If he missed his chance, then at Law he lost his estate for good. It was as simple as that. Equity intervened. It was unconscionable that a person could lose his inheritance just by being a day or two late. As long as the mortgagor paid up (with interest and costs) within a reasonable time, Equity would order the mortgagee to reconvey the estate – even though the legal date of redemption had passed. To that extent, the legal date for redemption became only a nominal target for the mortgagor.

On the other hand, until the legal date of redemption had passed, it could not be said that the mortgagor was in default; no matter how unlikely it was that repayment would be forthcoming, no matter how much the property might deteriorate in the meantime, the mortgagee could not realise his security until the legal date of redemption had come and gone. There was always the chance that the borrower would turn up with his cash on the day and redeem his estate. The longer the legal date of redemption, the greater the potential prejudice from the point of view of the lender.

As long as the legal date of redemption remained a meaningful date, it had to be set far enough in the future to give the borrower a realistic opportunity of repaying. However, when Equity began to say that the borrower was not prejudiced by the passing of the legal date of redemption, then it ceased to matter, from his point of view, whether the legal date of redemption was long or short. But, for the reasons given, from the lender's point of view it was a case of the shorter the better, and so, by convention, the legal date for repayment became six months from the date of the loan.

Thus, the function of the legal date of redemption stated in the mortgage deed is not what it appears to be. In a routine case it is not, and is not intended to be, the actual date for repayment. Its real function is to mark the date after which the mortgagee can exercise his remedies in the event that the mortgagor fails to abide by the terms of their agreement.

Although mortgages will certainly still be found which stipulate a legal date of redemption six months ahead, a modern bank or building society mortgage may well stipulate a date just a month ahead or make the legal date of redemption the date on which the first monthly payment falls due. Sometimes, such a mortgage contains a covenant by the borrower to repay the loan by monthly instalments, followed by another clause which provides that, if any monthly payment shall be in arrears for a certain number of days, then the whole of the loan shall fall due for repayment. In that case, the legal date of redemption is not defined in advance; it does not occur unless and until triggered by some default on the part of the borrower.

(b)　Equity of redemption

The *equity of redemption* is the label given to the borrower's reversionary interest in the mortgaged property, or, by derivation, the value of that interest. In the latter sense, if Martin mortgages a £90,000 house to the building society to secure a loan of £60,000, he is said to have an equity of £30,000. But to call the borrower's interest an *equity* of redemption is misleading. In a mortgage of freehold property, the borrower's 'equity' of redemption is in fact the *legal* fee simple absolute in possession, but subject to the mortgage; in a mortgage of leasehold property, it is the *legal* term of years, but subject to the mortgage.

The explanation for the apparent paradox lies, as might be expected, in history. It has been said more than once that a legal mortgage used to take the form of a transfer of the whole of the mortgagor's interest. In the eyes of the Law, therefore, the property belonged to the *mortgagee*, subject only to the mortgagor's right to redeem. Equity took entirely the opposite view. In Equity, the property remained the *mortgagor's*, subject, however, to the mortgagee's right to take it from him in the event that he failed to repay. Equity treated the mortgage as a mere incumbrance on the mortgagor's title, and allowed the mortgagor to deal with 'his' property, subject to that incumbrance. In those days, the borrower's 'ownership' existed only in Equity and the label *equity of redemption* was coined for it. In 1925, the law was amended, as described above, so that nowadays, even the Law regards the property as belonging ultimately to the mortgagor, subject to the outstanding mortgage. The label *equity* of redemption is therefore no longer strictly accurate, but it is hallowed by tradition and ingrained in conveyancing language.

(5) MUTUAL RIGHTS AND OBLIGATIONS

The rights and obligations of the parties are defined initially by the mortgage deed. A traditional mortgage deed is quite a lengthy document, containing a covenant by the borrower to repay, a formal charge (or demise) of the property as security for that promise, and a goodly number of 'the usual mortgage clauses' and other clauses special to the particular transaction. A modern bank or building society mortgage may be terse. It often contains just two clauses: first, a statement that the mortgage incorporates the society's standard terms – which are set out in a booklet which has already been given to the borrower – and second, a clause formally charging the property as security for repayment.

(a) Usual mortgage clauses

The usual mortgage clauses, whether set out in the deed or incorporated by reference, are designed primarily to preserve the value of the security. The borrower is obliged to keep the property in repair, to insure it, not to make structural alterations without the mortgagee's consent, to observe Town and Country Planning regulations, to observe any restrictive or other covenants affecting the property. There may be other clauses whereby the lender promises, for example, that he will not call in the loan prematurely unless the borrower defaults on the agreement, or he may covenant to make re-advances (lend back to the borrower what he has already repaid) or make further advances (lend him more still).

Four points are worth special mention: leasing, 'clogs on the equity', restraint of trade and consumer credit.

(b) Power of leasing

Put shortly, the point is that the borrower is not in practice allowed to grant any lease or tenancy without first obtaining the lender's consent.

Put at greater length, the point is this. At common law, the borrower and the lender each has the capacity to grant a tenancy, but neither has the power to grant a tenancy binding on the other. The borrower, as owner of the legal fee simple or legal term of years, can create a tenancy, but he can do so only subject to the existing rights of the lender, so that the lender, having a prior claim, can always evict the borrower's tenant. On the other hand, the lender is entitled to possession of the mortgaged property and he too can grant leases, but he may do so only subject to the borrower's right to redeem, so that on redemption the borrower can evict the lender's tenant. The LPA resolves the problem by enacting that, unless the mortgage deed stipulates to the contrary, a tenancy granted by whichever of them is in possession shall be binding on the other. Predictably, mortgage deeds invariably deprive the borrower of any power to grant tenancies without the consent of the lender.

(c)   Clogs on the equity

It is axiomatic that there must be 'no clogs on the equity'. This may look like double Dutch, but it means that there must be no clutter or impediment on the equity of redemption. In the eyes of Equity, the property truly belongs to the borrower, and the purpose of the mortgage is to provide security for repayment of the loan and nothing more; therefore, in principle, the borrower ought to be able to get his property back by paying off the loan, and he ought to be able to get it back in its original condition. The perceived mischief is that, in negotiating for a mortgage loan, the borrower is often negotiating from a position of economic inferiority. The lender may drive a hard bargain, but that has to be accepted as good business. The lender may, however, seek to take *unfair* advantage of the situation, and if his conduct can be castigated as unconscionable, then Equity will intervene on behalf of the oppressed borrower and deny the lender his ill-gotten gains. Two potential clogs are particularly important: an attempt to make the mortgage irredeemable, and an attempt to secure some collateral advantage.

(i)   Irredeemability

Equity holds that, in principle, a mortgage cannot be made irredeemable: 'Once a mortgage, always a mortgage.' At Law, a mortgage used to be irredeemable once the legal date of redemption had passed. Equity, having intervened to remedy that injustice, will not now allow its remedial action to be subverted by clever conveyancing. An express provision that the mortgage shall be irredeemable is void and unenforceable in Equity (save that, by statute, *limited companies* may lawfully create irredeemable debentures). A provision which has the effect of making the mortgage *substantially* irredeemable is also void, as where the borrower promises not to redeem a mortgage on leasehold property until a month or two before his lease expires.

The doctrine is then extended to render void any *undue postponement* of redemption, but the emphasis is on 'undue'. The parties may have good reason for agreeing a long term loan, and early repayment might put the lender at a serious disadvantage. On the one hand, the borrower should not be allowed lightly to avoid his solemn obligations; on the other, he must be protected from unconscionable oppression. It is a question to be decided in all the circumstances on which side of the line the particular case falls, but the bargaining power (or lack of it) of the respective parties is especially significant.

(ii)   Collateral advantages

Particularly in the case of a mortgage of business premises, the lender may negotiate for some side advantage – a pub landlord may be tied to selling only the lender's beer, or the owner of a petrol filling station may be tied to a particular brand of petrol (an arrangement which is sometimes referred to as a solus tie). Equity divides these collateral advantages into three classes, and again the proper categorisation is a question to be decided in all the circumstances of the particular case. First, the collateral advantage may be condemned as unconscionable and oppressive if it is imposed in a morally reprehensible manner; it is then altogether void and unenforceable. Second, the collateral advantage may be considered fair and enforceable for as long as the mortgage lasts, and many solus ties fall into this category; collateral advantages of this class cease to be enforceable upon redemption, for the doctrine of 'no clogs' means that the borrower is entitled to have his property back in its original condition. Third, and exceptionally, the collateral advantage may survive redemption of the mortgage: if the collateral advantage is part of a larger commercial deal done between two parties who are well able to look after their own interests, then Equity is not concerned to intervene. Equity intervenes to protect the vulnerable from oppression; it does not assist the strong to avoid a fair bargain.

(d) Restraint of trade

'Clogs' is a doctrine of Equity, but the Law will also strike out mortgage clauses if it considers them illegal. One doctrine which is particularly relevant is the doctrine of *restraint of trade*. An obligation is illegal, and so void and unenforceable at Law, if it is an unreasonable restraint of trade. The reasonableness or otherwise is to be judged both from the point of view of the parties and from the point of view of the public interest. So a solus tie which escapes Equity's net because it is fair as between the parties may nevertheless be trapped by the Law if it is considered unreasonable in the public interest.

(e) Consumer credit

Mortgage arrangements may also be struck down under the Consumer Credit Act 1974. The Act aims to protect *individuals* (but not companies) against so called 'loan sharks'. Amongst other things it is enacted that, if a loan (whether secured or not) constitutes an *extortionate credit bargain*, then the court may re-open the transaction and 'do justice between the parties'. An extortionate bargain is defined as one which is grossly exorbitant or which otherwise grossly contravenes ordinary principles of fair dealing.

(6) REALISING THE SECURITY

Suppose the borrower defaults. What can the lender do? He can obviously sue in contract on the borrower's covenant to repay, but he is unlikely to do that unless the security proves deficient. The whole point of taking security in the first place was to avoid the need to chase the borrower in the event of default. If the lender wishes to enforce his security, he has four principal remedies: he can *take possession* of the mortgaged property; he can *appoint a receiver* of it; he can *sell* it, or he can *foreclose* on the mortgage.

(a) Sale

The lender's most important remedy is his statutory power of sale under the LPA. The lender is empowered to sell and convey the whole of the *borrower's* estate, subject to any incumbrances which existed at the date of the mortgage, but free of any incumbrances created by the borrower thereafter. The statutory power is implied in every mortgage *by deed*. (Even an equitable mortgagee has a statutory power of sale if his mortgage is by deed; there are some technical difficulties in the case of a sale by an equitable mortgagee, but they can be avoided by careful draftsmanship.)

The statutory power of sale *arises* as soon as the legal date of redemption has passed. To say that the power *arises* means that, as between the lender and the outside world, the lender can give the purchaser a good title which overreaches the rights of the borrower. Observe that the lender does not have to demonstrate that the borrower is in default in any way. The purchaser is concerned to see that the mortgage is by deed and that the legal date of redemption has passed, but that is all. He cannot be expected to investigate the state of account as between the lender and the borrower. It is none of his business. Observe also that the lender does not have to seek the court's permission to sell. That is the main point of the statutory power of sale: it is exercisable out of court. (But the lender may need to go to court to get vacant *possession* of the property – see below, p 183.)

Although the statutory power of sale *arises* as soon as the legal date of redemption has passed, a further condition must be satisfied before it is properly *exercisable*. To ask whether the power is *exercisable* is to ask whether, as between the borrower and the lender, the latter may lawfully sell. The further condition to be satisfied before the power becomes *exercisable* is one of the following:

- that the lender has given the borrower three months' notice to repay the loan, and he has not repaid; or
- that some interest payment is two months overdue; or
- that the borrower has broken some other term of the agreement – he has failed to insure or repair, or he has taken in tenants, or whatever it may be.

A premature sale is a breach of contract, and the borrower can seek an injunction to restrain a premature sale; but it may be repeated that a *purchaser* is not concerned to see that the power is properly *exercisable*; he need only ascertain that it has *arisen*.

The statutory power of sale is not the only power of sale. The court may order a sale in various circumstances. But the statutory power is of far greater importance.

(b)   Foreclosure

Foreclosure was once memorably defined by a student as 'chopping off his whatsit', by which she meant, of course, chopping off the borrower's equity of redemption. Foreclosure is an order of the court which declares that the mortgaged property belongs to the mortgagee, free of any claims on the part of the borrower.

It has been explained how Equity pays little attention to the legal date of redemption and says that the borrower has an equitable right to redeem even after the legal date has passed. His equitable right to redeem lasts for as long as is reasonable in all the circumstances. But how long is reasonable? The lender must ask the court, and an action for foreclosure is the means whereby he may ask. An order for foreclosure is, in effect, a ruling that the equitable right to redeem has finally expired.

Foreclosure is not a very common remedy. From the lender's point of view, it is a 'messy' remedy, compared to the statutory power of sale. He must go to court, which will involve additional expense and delay. If he makes out his case, he obtains no more than a foreclosure order *nisi*, giving the borrower another six months in which to pay. The lender must then return to court (more expense and delay) for his foreclosure order absolute. And even then he is not entirely home and dry. There is always the possibility that the borrower will ask the court to re-open the foreclosure and restore the property to the borrower.

(c)   Receivership

The lender has a statutory right to appoint a receiver, if the mortgage is by deed and the statutory power of sale has become *exercisable*. He may choose to appoint a receiver rather than sell if the property is income-producing (say, if it is let to tenants or if it is a business) and if his main concern is to recover arrears of interest as opposed to capital. The receiver, as his title implies, receives the income from the mortgaged property, and thereout he defrays his own costs and commission, pays any rates, rent, insurance premiums and other outgoings, pays off the arrears of mortgage interest, and hands the balance (if any) to the borrower unless the lender directs that the balance go towards discharging the capital sum outstanding on the mortgage.

(d)   Possession

In theory, a mortgagee might want to take possession in order to claim the income of the land, but if that is what he wants he is more likely to appoint a receiver. In practice, these days, a mortgagee is likely to seek possession only as a preliminary to the exercise of his statutory power of sale.

A legal mortgagee by demise has a right to take possession by virtue of the legal estate vested in him, and, by statute, a legal chargee has the same rights as a mortgagee by demise. An equitable mortgagee, by definition, has no legal right to possession, but he may in some circumstances ask the court for an order for possession.

The mortgagee's right to possession is, however, limited by statute in the case of *residential* property. In an action for possession of mortgaged property which is or includes a dwellinghouse, the court has a discretion to postpone an order for possession if appears likely that the borrower will be able to pay off any arrears, or remedy any other default, within a reasonable time. Strictly, a legal mortgagee can demand possession without beginning court proceedings (and if he does so, the statutory restriction has no application), but mortgagees are generally unwilling to risk evicting a residential occupier without the protection of a court order.

15 Easements

(1) EASEMENTS AND PROFITS

An easement is the right of one landowner to use the land of another without actually taking possession of it. Examples are more useful than a definition. The most common easements include a right of way – a right to cross another's land, perhaps on foot, perhaps in a vehicle – and wayleave – a right to bring electricity or other cables over or under his land. An easement of drainage gives the right to run sewers or soil pipes under neighbouring land, and there are various rights of water – for example, a right to bring water through pipes under a neighbour's land. An easement of support entitles the owner of a semi-detached or terraced house, or an upstairs flat or office, to have his building supported by the adjoining buildings. Rights of light prevent a person from building on his own land if that would make his neighbour's house too dark.

A *profit à prendre* (or 'profit' for short) is in many ways similar to an easement but is a larger right. It entitles a person to go onto another's land *and diminish it* by taking something away with him. There may, for instance, be a right of *pasture*, allowing one's horses or cattle to graze on another's land, or rights of hunting ('venery'), shooting, and fishing ('piscary'), or rights to take peat or turf ('turbary') or sand, gravel, or minerals.

In general, the discussion will be confined to easements. Conceptually, the main differences between an easement and a profit are first, that an easement allows you to *use*, a profit allows you to *use and diminish*; and second, that the benefit of an easement must attach to a piece of land, whereas the benefit of a profit may attach to land, but it may also belong to a person independently of any ownership of land. In the latter case, the profit is said to exist 'in gross'. So, supposing as owner of number 3 Rectory Gardens, I want to give my neighbour the right to take a short cut across my land. I cannot grant an *easement* of way to my neighbour personally;

I must grant an easement of way to the owner of number 2 Rectory Gardens. As long as my present neighbour lives there, she enjoys the benefit of the easement; when she leaves, the easement remains for the next owner of number 2. But the owner of a trout lake could grant a right of fishing (a profit) *either* to the owner for the time being of some neighbouring land *or* to some angling club which owns no land at all.

Another practical difference between easements and profits is that easements can be acquired by prescription – by long user for 20 or 40 years, as explained later. Profits can also be acquired by prescription, but by longer user: it takes 30 or 60 years to prescribe a profit.

Following is a schematic outline of easements. There are three main questions to consider: Is the right claimed *capable* of being an easement? If so, was it validly *created*? If so, is it still *enforceable*?

(2)   IS THE RIGHT CAPABLE OF BEING AN EASEMENT?

The law recognises a variety of easements, and the list is not closed. New rights may be, and from time to time are, admitted to the category of easements. The question may therefore arise whether some right asserted by the claimant should be recognised as a novel easement. Alternatively, it may be contended that, although the right claimed – say, a right of way – could in theory be an easement, nevertheless, in this particular instance it is not an easement which attaches to the land but a mere *personal* right (or 'licence'). The test is a fourfold test.

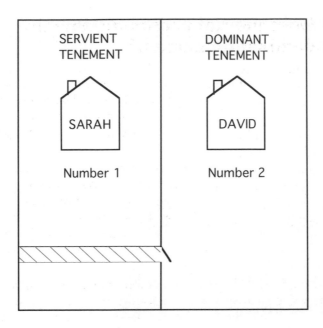

(a) Are there dominant and servient tenements?

The point has already been made that an easement is a right which exists as a burden on one piece of land for the benefit of another piece of land. The land which enjoys the benefit is called the *dominant tenement* and the land which carries the burden is called the *servient tenement*. If there is no dominant tenement, there is no easement. A right of way granted to a person who is not a landowner may therefore be a mere permission ('bare licence') or a contractual right ('contractual licence'), but it is not an easement.

(b)   Does the right accommodate the dominant tenement?

To 'accommodate' the dominant tenement means to benefit the dominant tenement. The right must benefit the land itself, in the sense of making the dominant land more advantageous for each succeeding occupier, as opposed to being for the benefit of the person who just happens to be the current occupier.

That has several implications. For example, the dominant tenement must be close enough to the servient tenement to be capable of benefiting. It need not be adjoining, but it must be adjacent. How adjacent is a question of fact. For example, land down a side turning could be accommodated by a right to have a direction sign in a field next to the main road two miles away; but that same land might not be accommodated by a right of way across the corner of that same field.

Less obviously, a distinction is sometimes drawn between benefiting the land and benefiting a business conducted on the land. Typically, a business has no *necessary* connection with the land, and businesses frequently relocate. To that extent, a right for the benefit of a business on the land is not for the permanent benefit of the land itself. However, sometimes, the courts have been prepared to stretch a point where the business was long established or where the nature of the business is, in a sense, special to the land – for example, where the business is that of a public house.

(c)   Are the dominant and servient tenements in different ownership or occupation?

An easement is a right against another. It follows that, if the dominant and servient tenements are owned and occupied by the same person, there can be no easement; for a person cannot have a right against himself. Consider the diagram set out above. Assume David, the dominant owner, has an easement of way to walk along the hatched path over number 1, owned by Sarah, the servient owner. Suppose David then buys number 1 from Sarah with vacant possession. Thereafter, he can stroll at will anywhere on number 1. He needs no easement. Indeed he has no easement, for the rule is that if dominant and servient tenements come into the ownership and occupation of one and the same person, then all easements which existed beforehand are destroyed, and are not, as such, revived on subsequent separation of the two plots. The expression 'quasi-easement' is sometimes used to describe something which is potentially an easement, but which is prevented from being an easement because of common ownership and occupation.

It is only common ownership *and* possession which destroys the possibility of an easement. If, in the above example, David takes a tenancy of number 1 (common occupation, diverse ownership), his easement of way is suspended but not destroyed. If David buys number 1 from Sarah on the basis that she shall remain in possession as his tenant (common ownership, diverse occupation), the easement continues; for a tenant is entitled to *exclusive* possession of the land, and David's ownership of number 1 gives him no right to walk across the path while the lease subsists; he must rely on the easement which attaches to number 2.

(d)   Does the right lie in grant?

To ask if the right 'lies in grant' is an obscure way of asking if the right is a recognised or recognisable property right. A grant is a deed, and the theory is that all easements are or could have been created by deed. That has several implications – there must be a capable grantor and a capable grantee – but the most important is that the right itself must be one which is capable of being created or conveyed by deed as a *property* interest, as opposed to being a mere personal or contractual right. The argument is in danger of becoming circular; if the right is an easement, it can be created by deed; if the right can be created by deed, then it is capable of being an easement.

In truth, there is a policy decision lurking in the undergrowth here. If the right claimed is one of the recognised categories of easement, then clearly it does 'lie in grant'. Faced with a novel claim, the judge has a choice. He may say the right is too fanciful to be an easement; therefore it cannot be *granted* as a property right, but only contracted for as a personal right: it does not 'lie in grant'. Alternatively, he may decide that, all things considered, this novel claim is of such a kind that it should be admitted to the family of easements.

So, in comparatively modern times, the right to use a neighbour's lavatory has been recognised as an easement (!), and so has the right to park a car in a car park. But there are some well known 'non-easements'. I can have an easement of light which will prevent my neighbour building

189

in such a way as to darken my house, but I cannot have an easement of view and thereby claim that he must not obstruct my panoramic prospect of the Clent Hills. I can have an easement of support for my buildings which will prevent my neighbour from demolishing his adjoining buildings so as to render mine structurally unsafe, but I cannot have an easement of protection against the weather so as to prevent him leaving my walls safe, but exposed to wind and rain. Preservation of view and protection against the weather can, perhaps, be achieved by other means, but not by the law of easements. In a similar vein, I can have an easement to store things on my neighbour's property; but an easement, of its nature, gives no right to possession, so if my right of storage is so large as to amount in substance to a claim to possession of his land, then my right may be a lease, or it may be a licence, but it cannot be an easement.

(3) HAS THE EASEMENT BEEN DULY CREATED?

If the right claimed is demonstrably capable of being an easement, the next question is whether it has in fact been duly granted. Leaving aside such special cases as easements created by statute, easements are, as mentioned above, theoretically created by deed. Sometimes, however, the deed is imaginary. There are three routes: express grant, implied grant, presumed grant.

(a) Express grant or reservation

An easement may be created by express words in a transfer of registered land or in a conveyance of unregistered land or by a separate deed of grant. It is then a question of construing the words used and applying them. Any ambiguities are construed against the grantor; that is to say, in cases of doubt the right granted is interpreted widely rather than narrowly.

There is said to be a *reservation* of an easement when one person transfers part of his land to another, but keeps back an easement for the benefit of his retained land. Suppose, in the example of David and Sarah given above, that David originally owned both number 1 and number 2; he then agrees to sell number 1 to Sarah, but wants to keep a right of way over the hatched path; he can transfer number 1 to Sarah *reserving* an easement of way for number 2. The theory is that he grants the whole of number 1 to her, and she then *re-grants* the easement back to him. That theory gives rise to a technical difficulty with regard to ambiguities. Given that ambiguities should be construed against the grantor, who, here, is the grantor? – David, because the deed is in reality his deed? Or Sarah, because she is in theory the grantor of the easement? Current authorities controversially hold that Sarah is the grantor.

(b) Implied grant

Easements may be implied in four ways. In each case, there is an actual deed which is silent as respects the right claimed. The question is whether the right can be read into the deed.

(i) Necessity

An easement may be impliedly granted or impliedly reserved if the dominant land would be unusable without it. There is said to be an easement of necessity in such a case. The simplest example is land-locked land. Suppose Simon owns a large piece of land abutting a public highway. He transfers part of it to Diana, but the deed mentions no right of way:

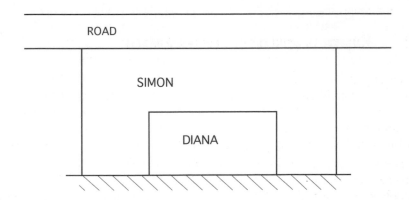

Here, Diana gets an implied easement of necessity – a right of way from her land to the road – because otherwise she cannot use her land at all. There is an analogy here with contract law, where terms may be implied into a contract if it is necessary to do so in order to give business efficacy to the contract. The inference is that Simon and Diana must have intended an easement of way; the transaction does not make commercial sense without it.

The doctrine of easement of necessity is, however, a narrow one. The easement must be *necessary*. If the shaded area is land which already belongs to Diana, then she can gain access to her newly acquired land without crossing Simon's land, and there is no easement of necessity. Moreover, the easement must be *absolutely* necessary; it is irrelevant that Diana cannot use the land as she intended; the question is whether she can use it at all. If the shaded area is a public highway, with a road at the bottom of a 30 foot cutting, Diana gets no easement of necessity over Simon's land; for she *can* get to and from her land via the shaded road – access is difficult, but not impossible.

Furthermore, the inference that the parties must have intended an easement can be rebutted by an explicit indication in the deed itself that they did not. Why Diana should want an inaccessible piece of land is her affair, but if that is what she wants, so be it.

(ii)   Intended easements

The grant or reservation of an easement may be inferred to give effect to the common intention of the parties. This is wider than an easement of necessity. Here the question is whether an easement is necessary in order that the land may be used *in the manner intended*. But it is not enough for the dominant owner to show that he needs an easement for what *he* wants to do. He must go on to show that the servient owner knew and intended that he should be able to do it. A simple example would be mutual easements of support for a pair of semi-detached houses.

There is some sort of analogy here with the 'officious bystander' test in contract law, whereunder a term may be implied into a contract on the basis that it is something which is so obvious that it goes without saying.

(iii)   Wheeldon v Burrows *easements*

Where a landowner grants away part of his land, the grantee may acquire easements over the grantor's retained land under the rule in *Wheeldon v Burrows* (1879) 12 Ch D 31. The rule says that, in these circumstances, the grant is deemed to include all those easements which:

- are continuous and apparent; and

- are necessary for the reasonable enjoyment of the part transferred; and

- have been and are at the time of the transfer used and enjoyed for the benefit of the part transferred.

Strictly, the 'easements' within the rule are 'quasi-easements' – advantages or 'rights' which, *if* the dominant and servient tenements were in different ownerships, *would be* easements; they do not actually become easements until the moment of transfer, when the ownerships become separated.

The rule in *Wheeldon v Burrows* is part of a larger principle that a grantor may not derogate from his grant. A grantor cannot, for example, transfer a house and land, and then deny the transferee a continued water supply through existing pipes under the grantor's land simply because no easement was expressly mentioned in the deed of grant. The deed itself may expressly deny any such easement; otherwise, an easement to continue to use the water pipes will be implied.

The rule is based on the assumption that a sensible purchaser will inspect the property before he buys it, and that he is entitled to expect a transfer of the property 'as seen', unless the vendor disabuses him. Hence, the rule is principally concerned with those easements (quasi-easements) which are *continuous and apparent*. 'Apparent' means visible, which seems absurd, since an easement is, by definition, a *right*, and a right is necessarily invisible. What, however, is meant is that there must be some *physical feature* which would indicate (to the aforesaid reasonable purchaser) that an easement exists – a path indicates a possible right of way; a manhole cover, a possible easement of drainage, and so on. Similarly, the requirement that the easement should be 'continuous' does not mean that the easement itself must be used non-stop, but that the physical feature which indicates its existence should be (more or less) permanent: is there something which would alert the purchaser, no matter what time of day or year he makes his inspection? So the requirement that the easement should be continuous and apparent is to be understood as meaning that some *physical manifestation* of the easement must be *continuously apparent* on the property.

The second requirement, that the easement must be necessary for the reasonable enjoyment of the part transferred, is in the nature of an exception. The transferee does not necessarily acquire all continuous and apparent easements, but only those which are reasonably to be inferred in the circumstances. Take, by way of illustration, the example given above of the vendor who transfers a house and land and then seeks to deny the continued use of water pipes under his retained land. He might have good cause. He might, in anticipation of the sale, have laid on a new water supply to the house through pipes wholly beneath the part transferred. It would not then be reasonable for the purchaser to insist on a continued supply route through the old pipes.

Finally, the right claimed must have been used for the benefit of the part transferred down to the time of transfer. The transferee cannot claim to resurrect a use which has been abandoned; nor can he claim to begin a use which was planned but never implemented; nor can he appropriate for his land a use which properly belongs to some other land – he cannot, for example, claim under *Wheeldon v Burrows* to tap into water pipes which *cross* the part transferred *en route* to a house beyond.

(iv)   Section 62

Finally, where a grantor grants part of his land to a grantee *who is already in possession*, then certain easements may be implied into the grant by virtue of s 62 of the LPA. The main function of s 62 is to ensure that a conveyance of land carries with it all ancillary rights. To that end, it recites a long list of items which, without express mention, are deemed to be included in a conveyance of land (and 'conveyance' here includes a lease, mortgage, etc). Among other things, s 62 says that a conveyance impliedly includes all liberties, privileges, easements, rights and advantages attaching to the land at the time of conveyance. It thus ensures that the conveyance carries all *existing* easements in, over or under land of a third party.

It has, however, been held that, where a grantor transfers part of his land, then s 62 has the effect of *converting* into easements any lesser liberties, privileges, rights and advantages presently enjoyed by the part conveyed over the part retained. One limitation is that such lesser rights must be *capable* of being easements – so that a personal permission to cross land (a mere licence) may become a property right (an easement), but the benefit of a covenant not to obstruct the view from the land cannot become an easement of view, because the law knows no such easement.

Another important limitation is that the statutory conversion can take effect only in favour of a grantee who is already in possession. This is sometimes referred to as a requirement of 'diversity of occupation'. The argument is that the section operates on all 'liberties, privileges, easements, [and] rights' whatsoever, but each of those words implies that one person is *already* at the date of the conveyance *allowing*, or is obliged to allow, another person to do something. In the present context, where a grantor is transferring part of his land, it implies that the transferee of part is already in possession, so that he *already has* some 'liberty, privilege, or right' against the grantor, which upon conveyance is converted into an easement. The final word in the list contained in s 62 is 'advantages': a conveyance is also deemed to include all 'advantages' appertaining to the land conveyed. In isolation, 'advantages' would *not* import the need for diversity of occupation; but as a matter of statutory interpretation it is to be dismissed as being *eiusdem generis* with (of the same nature as) the other, adversarial words.

From a practical point of view, the most likely situation in which s 62 can operate to convert a lesser right into an easement is upon renewal of a lease. A lessor grants a lease. Subsequently, he informally allows the lessee some additional right (licence) – say he allows the lessee to take a short cut across the lessor's adjoining land. He then renews the lease. Since a lease is a 'conveyance' for the purpose of s 62, the new lease is deemed to include an easement of way across the short cut.

Another situation in which the principle might be applied is where a purchaser of part of a piece of land is let into possession before completion: he enters a contract to buy (or lease) the part; unusually, he is allowed to take possession before the transfer (or lease) is completed; he is technically a licensee; he is permitted to use a short cut across the remainder of the land; the transfer (or lease) is then executed, and by virtue of s 62 he acquires an easement to continue to use the short cut. In practice, however, that situation is unlikely to arise; in such circumstances, the contract will normally contain a clause excluding the effect of s 62.

Finally, it should perhaps be emphasised that the statutory conversion of lesser rights into easements can take place only as against the grantor of the land. A conveyance of land from Sarah to David cannot affect the rights and obligations of some third party. If, before the conveyance, David has a licence to cross Tom's land, then after the conveyance, he still has only a licence to cross Tom's land. A conveyance by Sarah cannot increase the burden on Tom.

(c)   Presumed grant or prescription

The law tends to assume that long use is lawful use. If a person can show that for 20 years or more he and his predecessors in title have been behaving as if an easement existed, then it will usually be the case that there is indeed an easement. There are, however, three or four routes to prescription. The common law first invented the fiction that long user was evidence that a proper grant had been made at some time before 1189 (the significance of the date is explained below, p 197). If that theory proved inadequate, it was prepared to invent the fiction that there must have been a 'modern' (that is, post-1189!) deed of grant which had somehow been lost. Statute – the Prescription Act 1832 – then complicated matters further. It enacted a new and different basis of prescription to sit alongside the common law method, but it also tinkered with the common law rules. A systematic way through the maze is as follows.

(i)   Statutory prescription

If the claimant can show that he has actually exercised the right he claims for a period of 40 years without interruption, then his claim to the easement is absolute and indefeasible unless the user was by express written consent. There is much tricky detail here, too much to investigate in a book of this sort. But, briefly, the *quality* of the user must be 'as of right'; the claimant must behave as though he had a right to do what he is doing. Moreover, user must be by or on behalf of a fee simple owner against a fee simple owner. In principle, the quality of user must be, in the traditional phrase, *nec vi, nec clam, nec precario* – not by force, nor by stealth, nor by permission. Violent user – smashing down fences and suchlike – does not count. Secret user – creeping down a footpath only when the servient owner is away – does not count. And user by permission is the opposite of user by right, but this is one of the many snags in the law of prescription. The Act says the 40 year prescription can be defeated by *written* permission, the implication being that *oral* permission does not defeat the 40 year claim. But how does that square with the idea that the quality of user must be 'as of right' and not by permission? The answer seems to be that oral permission *which is periodically renewed* renders the user permissive, and not as of right, and therefore defeats the claim; but if there has been 40 years' user *since* the last or only permission, then the strong wording of the Act must prevail: written permission defeats the claim; oral permission does not.

The 40 years in question are, however, a specific 40 years: the 40 years 'next before the action'. Litigation is necessary to crystallise the statutory claim – either the dominant owner sues to assert his right or the servient owner sues to deny it. The date of the commencement of legal proceedings is the critical date. The 40 years must be the 40 years ending on the eve of that date.

The 40 years' user must be 'without interruption', as defined. Interruption is taken to mean some obstruction or hostile act which prevents the dominant owner from continuing to exercise his claim; but, for statutory purposes, the obstruction does not become an 'interruption' unless the dominant owner *submits* to it for at least a year. Blocking a claimed right of way is not an 'interruption' if the dominant owner continually unblocks it.

(ii)   Common law plus Act

The basis of the traditional, common law claim is that user began before 1189. The significance of the date is that it is 'the date of legal memory'. If something has been going on since 'time immemorial', then, in law, it has been going on since 1189, and its rightfulness cannot now be challenged. The reason for the quaint rule is this. Every legal system has some scheme for limitation of actions, some principle whereby stale claims are ruled out of time and out of court. Today, the Limitation Acts fix a set number of years within which legal action must be started. In the early law, however, the Limitation Acts, such as they were, enacted that the litigation slate should wiped entirely clean as at some specific date. The last such Act was the Statute of Westminster 1275, which provided that no action should be brought on any matter arising before the commencement of the reign of King Richard I in 1189.

To return to easements, it is obviously more than a little difficult for a dominant owner to prove that he and his predecessors in title have been exercising a right since 1189, and the law is not so much of an ass as to expect him to do so. If he can show user for 20 years or so, then that is enough to raise a *presumption* that the right was first exercised before 1189 and that user has continued ever since, so that its lawfulness cannot now be contested. The generosity of the common law may not, however, avail the dominant owner much. The presumption of user since 1189 is rebuttable, and in many cases the servient owner can easily rebut the presumption by demonstrating that the user must have begun in 'modern' times – that is, at some time since 1189 – so destroying the basis of the common law fiction. An easement of light claimed for a suburban semi can hardly have existed in 1189 if the house was not built until the 1930s.

It is at this point that the Prescription Act 1832 may become relevant. If the dominant owner cannot establish full statutory prescription, as explained above, he may, nevertheless, be able to take advantage of the tinkerings made by the Act with the common law scheme of things. If he can show not just any 20 year period of user, but the 20 year period *specified by the Act*, then that will do two things. First, it will be enough at common law to raise the presumption of user since 1189; second, the statute will rob the servient owner of his most potent defence – he is not allowed to defeat the easement by showing that user *actually* began at some time since 1189. Everybody knows the suburban semi was built in the 1930s, but, by statute, that ceases to be an objection. The servient owner can, however, still defeat the easement on other grounds – if, for example, he can demonstrate that the user was permissive and not as of right.

The nature of the user required by the Act in order to achieve this dual effect is the same as that required for the 40 year period, namely user *as of right* and *without interruption* for the period of 20 years *next before the action*. There are, however, some differences in the method of calculation of the two periods, and, most importantly, the effect of *oral permission* differs in the two cases. As explained above, oral permission given *before* the 40 year period does *not* render the user permissive for the purposes of prescription; but oral permission given before the 20 year period can render the whole user permissive and therefore non-prescriptive. Where user began as permissive user, it is a question of fact whether it continued as permissive user, or whether the dominant owner started to act as of right.

(iii)   *Common law* simpliciter

If the dominant owner cannot take advantage of the Prescription Act 1832 at all, he is thrown back on the common law. It may be that he can show that he and his predecessors in title have been exercising the right claimed for as long as anyone can remember, but he may, nevertheless, be unable to prove user throughout the specific period required by the Act, or he may have suffered a statutory 'interruption' at some point in that period.

The common law claim and its limitations have already been explained: if the dominant owner can show user as of right 'within living memory' (as long as anyone can now remember) or for 20 years or more (even if not the statutory 20 years), then that will raise the presumption of user since 1189, and so put the onus on the servient owner to defeat the claim by rebutting the presumption. He may do that in several ways, but in particular, he may defeat the presumption by showing that user actually began at some point since 1189.

(iv)   Lost modern grant

If all else fails – and this claim may be pleaded only as a last resort – then the dominant owner may be able to rely on the doctrine of lost modern grant. If he can show user as of right within living memory or for 20 years or more, and if the presumption of user since 1189 is rebutted, then the common law will proceed on the fiction that the user must stem from a lawful grant made at some time since 1189 (hence 'modern'), but that the relevant deed has been lost. So far will the common law go in order to uphold a user which remains uncontested for a long period of time. The doctrine is pure fiction. Nobody believes there really was a grant. The fiction cannot be defeated by evidence that no grant was in fact made. It can, however, be defeated by evidence that the alleged grant would have been a legal impossibility – say, because there was no capable grantor or no capable grantee.

(4)   IS THE EASEMENT LEGAL OR EQUITABLE?

Given that the dominant owner has established an easement against the servient owner, the question arises whether the easement is binding on successors in title of the servient owner. That depends principally upon whether the easement is a *legal* easement or an *equitable* easement. If it is legal, then in principle it will bind successors because, in principle, legal rights bind all the world. If it is equitable, then it is vulnerable, and may need to be registered.

An easement may be legal if:

• it is granted by deed (actual or presumed); and
• it is either perpetual (equivalent to a fee simple absolute in possession) or for a fixed period of time (equivalent to a term of years absolute).

An informal easement is necessarily equitable, even if perpetual or for a fixed period; an easement which is neither perpetual nor for a fixed period is necessarily equitable, even if formally granted.

If the servient tenement is registered land, then the burden of any express easements will usually be noted on the title. A *legal* easement which is not noted on the register is, nevertheless, an *overriding interest*, so that it will bind successors in title. The LRA appears to say that an *equitable* easement is *not* an overriding interest, but is a minor interest which should be protected by entry on the register. Accordingly, if it is not registered, a purchaser for value should take free. There is, however, authority to the effect that an unregistered equitable easement *is* an overriding interest, binding on the purchaser, if the easement is openly used and enjoyed at the time when the servient tenement is transferred.

Where the servient tenement is unregistered land, then the position is more straightforward. A legal easement binds the world; an equitable easement should be registered as a land charge, Class D(iii), otherwise it will not bind a purchaser for value. It has, however, been held that not all easements which exist in Equity are 'equitable easements' within the meaning of the Land Charges Act 1972. For example, an easement arising from an estoppel may be binding in Equity without, it is said, being an 'equitable easement' which requires registration. That sort of easement may bind a purchaser with notice despite non-registration.

16 Covenants

Covenants can be confusing. The main cause for confusion is that covenants in relation to land operate on four different levels, and so it is important to get the storey right.

(1) DEFINITIONS

In common parlance, 'covenant' means nothing more than a solemn promise. In law, and especially in property law, it has a stricter meaning: a covenant is a promise *in a deed*. The significance is, of course, that putting a promise in a deed makes it *ipso facto* enforceable at Law, whether or not consideration is given for the promise. Equity, by contrast, 'looks to the substance and not to the form'. In consequence, if the person to whom the promise is made (the covenan*tee*) gave actual consideration for the promise, then he may enforce it against the promisor (covenan*tor*) *either* at Law (typically by an action for damages for breach of contract) *or*, other things being equal, in Equity (typically, by injunction or by an order for specific performance). If, however, the covenantee gave no real consideration for the promise, then he may sue at Law, because the Law regards the formality of a deed as itself sufficient to create a unilateral contract; but he has no claim in Equity, because Equity regards a covenant unsupported by actual consideration (a *voluntary covenant*) as a mere, unenforceable promise.

Perhaps the *benefit* of the covenant and the *burden* of the covenant should also be mentioned. The benefit simply means the *right* to have the promise performed; the burden is the *duty* or *obligation* of performing the promise. So if Pippa covenants with Victor that she will not use her land otherwise than as a single private dwellinghouse, then Victor is said to have the benefit of the covenant and Pippa has the burden of it.

(2) FOUR DIMENSIONS

Covenants can operate in four different dimensions. To illustrate, take the following example. Victor owns numbers 2 and 3 Rectory Gardens. He sells number 2 to Pippa, and she covenants with him that she will maintain the boundary fence and will not to use number 2 otherwise than as a single private dwellinghouse. Subsequently, Victor sells number 3 to Walter, and Pippa sells number 2 to Quentin. The fence has now fallen down, and Quentin proposes to turn number 2 into a fish shop.

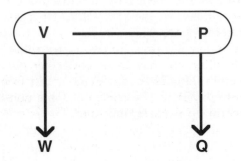

(a)   Contract

In the first place, a covenant is a contract. Putting a promise in a deed makes the promise a contract at Law and, if actual consideration is given, then there is also a contract in Equity. In principle, a covenant is enforceable in the same manner and to the same extent as any other contract. There is privity of contract between the original parties, and the proposition is that where there is privity of contract, all covenants bind. But, as a general rule, contracts are enforceable *only* by and against the parties to the contract. Contracts neither bind nor benefit third parties. So in the above example, Pippa's covenants constitute a contract between her *and Victor*, but only between her and Victor. Walter cannot sue on it. Quentin cannot be sued on it.

There is, however, more to the contract than meets the eye. Statute implies terms on either side. When Pippa covenants, then, by virtue of s 79 of the LPA, she is deemed to covenant 'on behalf of herself and her successors in title'. That does not mean that Pippa's successor in title, Quentin, is bound by Pippa's promise. He cannot be. He is not party to the contract. What it means is that Pippa is deemed to guarantee the good behaviour of future owners. Her promise is in two parts. First, she expressly promises, 'I will do this and that'. Second, by virtue of the LPA she impliedly adds, 'And I promise that all future owners will continue to observe these covenants'. The consequence of that is that *Quentin's* acts and omissions put *Pippa* into breach of contract.

This guarantee element is often made express. The covenant will typically be phrased as a covenant 'by the covenantor for herself and her successors in title'. Otherwise, the LPA will imply a guarantee, unless the deed expresses a contrary intention. In view of that, when Pippa sells to Quentin, she should demand from him a covenant that he will indemnify her against any liability she may incur under her guarantee. (Likewise, when he sells, Quentin should demand an indemnity from *his* purchaser, in case Quentin has to pay Pippa by reason of some non-observance of the covenants by Quentin's purchaser, and so on.)

Similarly, on the other side of the contract, the covenant is actually made with Victor, but s 78 of the LPA implies that it is made with Victor 'and his successors in title'. Now s 78 is a complex provision, and what is said now will be qualified to some extent by what is said later, but in principle, the importation of a reference to successors in title does not, *of itself*, give Victor's successor in title, Walter, any right to sue on the contract. How could it? Walter is not himself a party to the contract; nor can the contract be construed as conferring a benefit on him directly, for the simple reason that he was unidentifiable at the date when the contract was made. No, what the section means is that the benefit of the covenant which is given to Quentin is deemed to be a *transmissible* benefit, a benefit which is not *personal* to Quentin. Pippa is, in effect, promising Quentin on the understanding that, if he wants to, he can pass the benefit of her promises on to future owners of number 3.

As before, the reference to successors is often made express: 'the Purchaser for herself and her successors in title hereby covenants with the Vendor and his successors in title …' Otherwise, the LPA implies such a reference, although Pippa could avoid the implication by inserting appropriate words to make clear the intent that the promises were to be enforceable by Quentin and Quentin alone.

Those principles are, however, qualified in the case of *leasehold* property. A lease is both a contract between the parties and a grant of an interest in land. There is privity of contract between the original lessor and the original lessee, but, as explained in Chapter 11, statute severely limits the contractual rights and liabilities of either after he has assigned his interest in the land.

(b)   The benefit as personal property

A covenant, then, is basically a contract. But there is more to it than that. The *benefit* (but *not* the burden) of a contract, and therefore the benefit of a covenant, may be regarded as an item of *personal property* – a chose in action – and, as such, the benefit of a covenant may be transferred to another. The benefit of a contract is not transmissible if the contract is *personal* to the promisee – and the benefit may be impliedly personal (as, obviously, in the case of a contract of marriage) or else it may be expressly made so. But covenants concerning land are, by their nature, typically transmissible, and, as explained above, s 78 of the LPA confirms that they are impliedly transmissible.

At Law, a chose in action may be assigned to another by signed writing complying with s 136 of the LPA. Equity is more flexible, looking, as usual, to the intent and not to the form, so that, for example, even a contract to assign may, in some circumstances, be treated as a valid assignment in Equity.

So, when Pippa covenanted with Victor 'and his successors in title', she gave him liberty to transfer the benefit to another. It might therefore be the case that, when Victor sold number 3 Rectory Gardens to Walter, he contemporaneously assigned to him the benefit of Pippa's covenants. If so, it is Walter, not Victor, who now has the right to sue Pippa for breach of her guarantee.

(c)   The benefit as land

Moving on to the next level, it is possible, and indeed likely, that the *benefit* of Pippa's covenants has become part of the land, part of number 3 Rectory Gardens, so that the benefit will pass automatically with the land. The benefit is said to 'run with the land'. Here, however, Law and Equity take different approaches.

As far as the Law is concerned, the benefit of a covenant will run with the land if the covenant 'touches and concerns the land' of the covenantee and is intended to run with it. The idea is that a sensible distinction can be drawn between, on the one hand, a covenant which benefits the land as such, in the sense that it benefits every successive owner of the land by making the land more valuable or more pleasant or more convenient, and, on the other, a covenant which is intended to benefit the covenantee personally, but not any future owners of the land. So Pippa's covenant to maintain the boundary fence will be of benefit to anyone and everyone who lives at number 3. That covenant touches and concerns Victor's land. Similarly Pippa's promise to use number 2 for residential purposes only will also benefit every successive owner of number 3. It, too, touches and concerns Victor's land. On the other hand, if Pippa were to covenant to transfer another piece of land to Victor, or to lend him some money, or to carry out some work for his company, or not to set up in business in the village in competition with his corner shop, then the benefit would *not* touch and concern number 3. In those cases, Pippa covenants with Victor personally; the covenants are of no relevance to his ownership or occupation of number 3. Consequently, the benefit of those covenants does *not* run with the land to Victor's successors in title to number 3.

The Law is thus quite liberal in its attitude to the passing of the benefit of a covenant. The benefit runs with the land at Law if the covenant touches and concerns the land and is intended to run with it. (Until 1925, it seems that, strictly, the benefit ran with the covenantee's *estate* rather than with his *land* – but that learning is now obsolete.) However, what it gives with the right hand, the Law all but takes away with the left hand. In the eyes of the Law, although the *benefit* of a covenant can pass quite freely, the *burden* of a covenant *never* passes, save in the case of landlord and tenant. To put the point another way, the Law allows the benefit to pass so as to enable successors of the covenantee (Victor's successors) to sue the *original* covenantor (Pippa), but no one else.

So, returning to the original example, Pippa's covenants to fence and to use for residential purposes both 'touch and concern' number 3. It is to be inferred that they were intended to run with it (s 78). Therefore, the benefit of them runs at Law so as to enable Walter (the current legal owner of number 3) to sue Pippa (the original covenantor). Pippa is no longer in possession of number 2, but Walter can still sue her on the guarantee part of her covenant, as explained above. She has promised that she will behave in a certain way, and she has promised that her successors in title will also conform. Quentin's misbehaviour therefore puts Pippa into breach of covenant, and makes her liable to Walter.

Equity's attitude to the running of the benefit of a covenant is more complicated. Equity follows the Law as far as it goes; but Equity then goes further. As explained below, Equity will, in certain conditions, allow a covenant to be enforced directly against a *successor in title* to the original covenantor (Pippa's successors). That represents a dramatic extension of liability, and so, in order to keep the potential liability within reasonable bounds, Equity insists that, if the benefit of the covenant is to run *automatically* to the covenantee's (Victor's) successors so as to enable them *directly* to sue the covenantor's (Pippa's) successors, then the bounds of liability should be prescribed with some particularity. Equity considers that, if this extended liability is to operate, then the benefit of the covenant should be specifically attached to the covenantee's land, so that it is obvious to all concerned precisely *which* land is to benefit from the covenant.

If Victor sells number 2 to Pippa, and retains only number 3, then it is pretty clear that the benefit of Pippa's covenants is intended to run with number 3. But suppose Victor also owns number 4. Is the benefit to run with number 3, or number 4, or both? In principle, Equity insists that it should be clear from the terms of the covenant – expressly or impliedly – exactly what land is to carry the benefit of the covenant. This process of attaching the benefit of a covenant to the land is called *annexation.*

Skilled conveyancers draw their covenants with some care, identifying precisely which land is to be benefited, and *expressly* annexing the benefit of the covenant to that land. One method of expressly annexing the benefit of a covenant is, so to speak, to anchor the benefit directly into the land itself: the covenantor covenants 'to the intent that this covenant shall enure for the benefit of number 3 Rectory Gardens ...', or some such formula. Another method is to 'earth' the covenant through the covenantee, by making it clear that the covenant is made with him in his capacity as owner of the relevant land: the covenantor covenants with 'the covenantee and his successors in title, owners or occupiers for the time being of number 3 Rectory Gardens ...'.

This traditional process of express annexation is still the safest, and therefore the best – if only because it reduces the likelihood of dispute. Equity is, however, flexible, and, in the absence of express words, Equity may *infer* annexation, if it is clear from the document as a whole exactly which land is to be benefited. Suppose, for example, Pippa simply covenants with Victor without expressly stipulating that the benefit is to be attached to number 3, but the document includes a plan, showing number 3 with the legend, 'Land retained by the Vendor'. In such circumstances, Equity may say that there is an *implied* annexation.

There is a special kind of implied annexation, called a *scheme of development*. That is explained later.

Implied annexation is a contentious issue. Leaving aside the special case of schemes of development, some traditionalists always doubted the validity of anything short of express annexation. The Court of Appeal, has, however, ruled that s 78 of the LPA impliedly works a *statutory* annexation, at least if the land to be benefited can be identified by *intrinsic* evidence – that is, by clear inference drawn from within the four corners of the document itself (*Federated Homes Ltd v Mill Lodge Properties Ltd* [1980] 1 WLR 594; [1980] 1 All ER 371, CA). Controversially, the court also entertained, but found it unnecessary finally to decide upon, an alternative view that s 78 works a statutory annexation if the land to be benefited can be identified by *extrinsic* evidence – that is, evidence from outside the document itself of the conditions and circumstances in which the document was made. However, that is a highly dubious proposition, for the issue whether the claimant has the benefit of the covenant may not arise until many years after the covenant is created; the original parties may have died or disappeared, and who can then prove what truly were the circumstances in which the covenant was agreed, and what truly was the intention of the original parties?

However, in a simple case like that of Pippa and Victor, it must now be accepted that, if the benefit of Pippa's covenants was not expressly annexed to number 3 Rectory Gardens, then it was impliedly annexed thereto by s 78.

In consequence, the benefit has now run to Walter, not only at Law so as to enable him to sue Pippa (the original covenantor), but also in Equity so as to raise the possibility of suing Quentin (successor to the original covenantor) directly – *if* other conditions are also satisfied, as explained below, p 209.

(For the sake of completeness, it should be said that, if for some reason the benefit of a transmissible covenant does *not* run automatically with the land, it may nevertheless be *assigned* separately to the transferee of the land as a chose in action, as explained above.)

(d)   The covenant as a land obligation

The *burden* of a covenant is never *assignable* as such, whether at Law or in Equity. And, as a general rule, the burden never *runs* with the land at Law either. There is, however, one major exception to that proposition: the burden may run at Law in the case of *leasehold* land. Moreover, in Equity, given certain conditions, the burden of a covenant may run with land, even freehold land, under the doctrine of *restrictive covenants.*

(i) Privity of estate

At Law – and Equity follows the Law – the benefit and the burden of leasehold covenants (that is to say, covenants contained in a lease) run with the lease and run with reversion respectively, so that the covenants may be enforced by the current landlord against the current tenant, and by the current tenant against the current landlord. This is the doctrine of *privity of estate*. To say that there is privity of estate is another way of saying that the parties are landlord and tenant.

If there is privity of estate, then, in the case of a lease granted after 1995, all landlord and tenant covenants bind. Landlord and tenant covenants are all the covenants, conditions and obligations, whether contained in the lease or in any collateral agreement, which bind the landlord or the tenant respectively, but not any covenant expressed to be personal to either.

In the case of a lease granted before 1996, the position is similar, but not quite the same. Where there is privity of estate under a pre-1996 lease, then all those covenants bind which 'touch and concern the land demised' (or those which 'have reference to the subject matter of the lease' – the meaning is the same). A covenant 'touches and concerns the land demised' if, broadly, it is one of that class of covenants which are *characteristically* landlord and tenant covenants – covenants which are in principle relevant for every succeeding landlord and every succeeding tenant of the property, whoever they may be. Other covenants may be regarded as collateral, or personal to the particular parties. It is, so to speak, a coincidence that the covenantor and covenantee just happen to be landlord and tenant. In that event, the covenants do not run under the doctrine of privity of estate, and, if the covenants are to be binding, some other basis must be found for enforcement.

There is no infallible test for determining whether a covenant 'touches and concerns the land demised' or not. It is something which has to be decided on the facts of the case and in the light of precedent, but two particular instances are worth mentioning. It is held that a covenant which gives the tenant an *option to renew* the lease *does* touch and concern the land demised and so *does* run with the lease. On the other hand, a covenant which gives the tenant an *option to purchase* the reversion does *not* touch and concern the land demised and so does *not* run with the lease, but has to be expressly assigned to the new tenant.

Note in particular that, where there is privity of estate, *all* landlord and tenant covenants (or, as the case may be, *all* covenants which touch and concern) will bind, whether the covenants are 'positive' (requiring the expenditure of money) or 'negative' (obliging the covenantor to refrain from acting in a specified manner). So, all the usual leasehold covenants will automatically run with the lease and reversion respectively – covenants by the tenant to pay the rent, to repair, to redecorate, to insure and so on, and also the covenant by the landlord for quiet enjoyment.

(ii)   The doctrine of restrictive covenants in Equity

Equity takes a broader view of covenants than does the Law. In certain conditions, Equity regards a covenant as creating an *incumbrance* on the covenantor's land, a land obligation akin to an easement, so that the burden of the covenant attaches to one piece of land and can be enforced against the current owner of that land for the benefit of some adjoining or adjacent piece of land. This is known as the doctrine of restrictive covenants, or as the rule in *Tulk v Moxhay* (1848) 2 Ph 774, after the case which invented the doctrine. By this doctrine, Equity was able to develop a sort of private planning law, long before the Town and Country Planning Acts were introduced.

There are two main conditions to be satisfied if the covenant is to be one to which doctrine applies. In the first place, it must be intended to benefit one piece of land and to burden another piece of land – but ss 78 and 79 of the LPA will imply that intention in the absence of some contrary indication. In the second place, the covenant must be *restrictive* in nature. It may impose a negative duty on the owner of the burdened land to refrain from acting as he otherwise might act; it may not impose a positive duty on him to act in a certain way, and, in particular, it may not oblige him to spend money.

So, to return to the example given above, of Victor and Pippa: her covenant to maintain the fence is a *positive* covenant, and the burden of it is not capable of running under the doctrine of *Tulk v Moxhay*. Even if the covenant were expressed in negative form, 'not to let the fence fall into disrepair', it would still be positive in substance and so outside the doctrine. The user covenant is, however, negative in substance and so is of a type to which the doctrine may apply – whether the covenant is expressed in negative form, 'not to use otherwise than as a single private dwellinghouse', or in positive form, 'to use only as a single private dwellinghouse'.

Given that the covenant is of the right type – negative in nature and intended to benefit and burden land – so that the burden is *capable* of running with the covenantor's land, it is then necessary to inquire whether the benefit *has in fact* reached the claimant and whether the burden *has in fact* reached the defendant.

The claimant can demonstrate that he has the benefit in one of three ways. First, he may be the *original covenantee*. Second, the benefit of the covenant may have been *assigned* to him, as explained above, along with the land which is benefited thereby. Third, it may be that the benefit was *annexed* to the covenantee's land, expressly or impliedly, in which case the claimant will automatically acquire the benefit of the covenant along with the land.

As for the question whether the defendant has the burden of the covenant, the first question is whether he now owns the land, or part of the land, which was intended to be encumbered with the covenant. The covenant needs to be construed to see whether and what land was intended to bear the burden. Often, the servient land will be defined expressly, 'to the intent that these covenants shall bind *the land hereby transferred* into whosesoever hands the same may come …'. If not, the identity of the servient land can usually be inferred without much difficulty.

The next question is whether, when he took the land, the defendant took subject to the burden of the covenant or free from it. The doctrine of restrictive covenants is an equitable doctrine. The burden of the covenant runs only in Equity. The claimant's right to sue a *successor* to the original covenantor is only an equitable right. And equitable rights are, in principle, vulnerable to the BFP. The question is, therefore, whether the purchaser took with notice of the covenant; but notice in this context usually – but not always – means registration:

- If the land affected is *registered land*, then the burden of a restrictive covenant ranks as a minor interest, and as such it should be noted on the charges register of the relevant title. If there is no notice in the charges register, then a transferee for value of the registered title takes free of the covenant. (Observe that entering a notice of a covenant on the register does not guarantee that the covenant is *enforceable*; notice is what it claims to be, merely a warning that the land might be encumbered.)

- If the burdened land still has an *unregistered* title, then the date of the restrictive covenant may be critical – that is, the date upon which the covenant was first *created*. If the covenant was made before 1926, then the doctrine of BFP still applies. If the covenant was made after 1925, then, unless the covenant was contained in a lease, the burden of the covenant ranks as a *land charge*, Class D(ii), and as such it should be registered in the Land Charges Register. Registration fixes the purchaser with notice, whether he searches the register or not; if the covenant is not registered, then a purchaser for value takes free of it, even if he knew of its existence.

* Covenants contained in leases are *not registrable* as land charges. As between the landlord and his tenant, the covenant may well run with the lease and with the reversion and be binding by virtue of privity of estate, as explained above. In any event on a sale of the lease or of the reversion, a sensible assignee will inspect the lease and see what covenants it contains. But there can be snags. One snag arises where the *tenant* enters a restrictive covenant and then grants a sublease. There is no privity of estate between the superior landlord and the subtenant, and the subtenant has no automatic right to inspect the superior lease. The subtenant is, however, treated as having constructive notice of the contents of the superior lease, because he could and should have contracted for a right to inspect it. Another snag arises where the *landlord* enters a restrictive covenant affecting other land of his in the vicinity – for example, he grants a lease of a public house and covenants that no alcohol shall be sold on any part of his neighbouring land. Here the covenant is not registrable, because it is contained in a lease, and so the question whether a purchaser of any of the other land is bound by the landlord's covenant depends on the doctrine of the BFP.

Assuming the defendant takes subject to the covenant, the claimant can sue him. But the claimant can sue only in Equity. That has several implications. In the first place, equitable remedies are always *discretionary*, so that the claimant will not succeed if the court considers it unjust that he should succeed. He will be denied a remedy if has no genuine interest in enforcing the covenant, or if he delays too long, or if he does not come to Equity with clean hands, and so on.

In the second place, if the claimant succeeds, then he obtains only an equitable remedy. The usual remedy will be an injunction; but if the court feels that that is too severe a penalty, it may award equitable damages instead.

(iii) Schemes of development

One special application of the doctrine of restrictive covenants should be mentioned, and that is *schemes of development* or *building schemes*. The problem and its solution are as follows. Suppose a property owner decides to develop a housing estate. He may get more for his houses if he can set a certain tone for the estate, and so he may decide to impose a scheme of restrictive covenants: nobody is to put more than one house per plot, nobody is to alter the front elevation without his permission, and so on. As long as everybody abides by the scheme, everybody is happy; but if someone breaks rank and breaks a covenant, then that will tend to lower the tone of the estate, and so lower the resale value of all the houses. The doctrine of restrictive covenants may be prayed in aid to prevent a breach; but a routine application of that doctrine can lead to anomalies. It might easily happen that, for technical reasons, earlier purchasers cannot enforce against later purchasers; and the last purchaser of all might be liable to no one but the developer who, having sold all his land, would have no legitimate interest in suing him.

Equity is inclined to take a broad view of the matter. If it is clear that there was a common intention – common, that is, to the developer and all the purchasers – that a reasonably standard set of restrictive conditions should apply to a reasonably well defined neighbourhood, so as to create a sort of local community law, then Equity will deem every plot of land on the estate to be burdened with the scheme for the benefit of every other plot on the estate, whatever the order in which the plots were sold. Because the benefit is deemed annexed to each plot, the benefit will, in Equity, pass automatically to each succeeding purchaser. Because the burden is deemed to attach to each plot, then in principle it will run with the land and bind each succeeding purchaser, but the burden runs only in Equity. Therefore, in most cases, the covenants will need to be *registered* in respect of that plot on the appropriate register; otherwise, a purchaser for value will take free of them.

(3) PIECING THE JIGSAW TOGETHER

It will now be apparent why covenants are so complicated, but the complications of a covenants problem can be reduced if it is approached in a systematic way. The following system is not infallible, but it will deal adequately with most cases. First, you identify your claimant and your defendant. Assume that, in the example set out above, Walter, the current owner of number 3, wants to know what (if any) remedies he has against Quentin, the current owner of number 2. Then you pose the following questions in the following order:

1 Is there privity of contract?

In other words, are the claimant and defendant respectively the original covenantee and the original covenantor? If so, *all covenants bind*, and (unless the parties are original lessor and original lessee) the case is comparatively simple. Here there was privity of contract between Victor and Pippa, but there is none between Walter and Quentin.

2 Is there privity of estate?

In other words, are the claimant and defendant respectively landlord and tenant? If so, *all landlord and tenant covenants* (or, as the case may be, *all covenants which touch and concern the land demised*) will bind, and there may be no need to proceed further. Here, there is no lease, so the proposition has no application.

3 Is the defendant the original covenantor?

If so, the only real question is whether the benefit of the covenant has reached the claimant, for, as against the original covenantor, the *benefit* may pass either at Law or in Equity (or both). The claimant needs to demonstrate that he has the benefit either because it was *assigned* to him as a chose in action or because it has *run* with land which he now owns. Notice in particular that the benefit may pass *as against the original covenantee* whether the covenant is positive or restrictive. On the basis that Pippa's covenants touched and concerned number 3 and, by virtue of s 78 of the LPA, were impliedly intended to run with it, Walter can sue *Pippa* for breach of the guarantee part of both covenants – both the (positive) fencing covenant and the (restrictive) user covenant. He can sue her at Law for damages, but he cannot get an injunction or specific performance because the land is now outside Pippa's control. However, *Quentin* is not the original covenantor, and so the enquiry must proceed further.

4 Is it the sort of covenant that Equity will enforce?

If the claimant has not succeeded under any of the earlier heads, he will need to rely on the doctrine of restrictive covenants. He is trying to prove that the burden has run to a *successor* of the original covenantor; and, aside from landlord and tenant cases, the burden runs only in Equity. Broadly, Equity is interested in enforcing a covenant which (1) was imposed to benefit one piece of land and burden another piece of land, and which (2) was restrictive in nature. It follows that Walter has no hope of enforcing the fencing covenant against Quentin. The user covenant, on the other hand, is the sort of covenant that Equity will enforce.

5   Does the claimant have the benefit?

The claimant may be the *original covenantee* or he may have acquired the benefit by *assignment* or *annexation*. Here, Walter can prove annexation by virtue of s 78 of the LPA.

6   Has the burden run to the defendant?

Quentin is a *bona fide* purchaser of a legal estate. The covenant is a post-1925 covenant. If the burden of the covenant was duly noted on the Land Register, or, as the case may be, registered as a land charge in the Land Charges Register, then Quentin is bound; otherwise, he is not.

Index